This edition published by Barnes & Noble, Inc., by arrangement with Hamlyn.

First published in Great Britain in 1998 by Hamlyn, a division of Octopus Publishing Group Ltd

2005 Barnes & Noble Books

M 10 9 8 7 6 5 4 3 2

ISBN 0-7607-1157-7

Printed and bound in China

Publishing Director
Laura Bamford
Executive Editor
Jane McIntosh
Copy Editor
Jane Royston
Assistant Editor
Nicola Hodgson
Proof-reader
Anne Johnson
Creative Director
Keith Martin
Executive Art Editor
Mark Winwood
Designer
Les Needham
Picture Researcher
Wendy Gay
Production Controller
Bonnie Ashby

'Domestication and the Early Horse Peoples' by Marsha Levine from pp 315–317 of *Oxford Companion to Archaeology*, edited by Brian M. Fagan. Copyright © 1996 by Oxford University Press, Inc. Used by permission of Oxford University Press, Inc.

General Editor: Elizabeth Peplow

Encyclopedia of the
HORSE

Foreword by David Broome CBE

BARNES & NOBLE BOOKS
NEW YORK

Part One:
The Development of the Horse

Part Two:
The Breeds of the World

Contents

Part Three:
Equestrian Sports and Recreation

Part Four:
Physiology, Behavior, and Care

Foreword by David Broome, C.B.E.

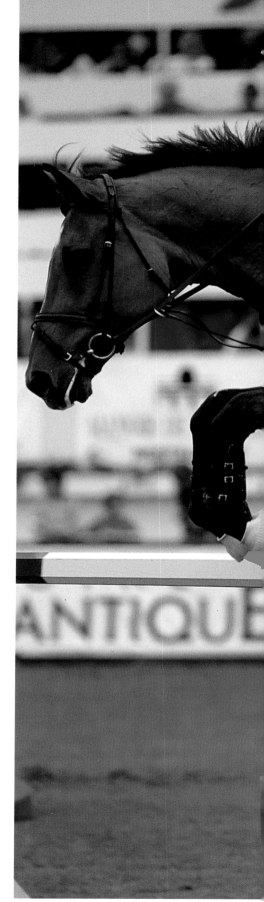

Horses have so much to give us—David Broome and Llanegan at La Baule 1991.

FOR ME, HORSES HAVE BEEN a lifelong fascination. I gave them up just once, when I was five years old. My father used to train Welsh Mountain ponies and he always needed a light jockey. I just got bucked off once too often. I came back after 18 months and have never stopped since.

I have been lucky in that being able to ride has saved me from having to do any other kind of job. I was born the son of a greengrocer, but through horses, I have traveled the world and met so many wonderful people. However, my first press cutting was not encouraging; it was a picture of me, aged nine, at Henllys Show near Newport, England. The caption read: "D. Broome sat back a bit on Ballanlad and caught the rebound, and unfortunately fell off on landing."

My father gave me a useful piece of advice which was "never get mad with a horse, but if you are having a fight with a horse and you are about to give in, always stick it out for another five minutes and you will have a breakthrough"—the number of times I have had to go for hours in order to get to that last five minutes! It's a question of always remembering that a horse is a lot stronger than you, so you won't ever win with strength. You have to use your brain to get inside a horse's head. A lot of people forget that the horse has a brain, and that it is a question of working with him to build the kind of relationship in which you can achieve things together. Being able to do this with an animal as big and as strong as a horse is a wonderful thing.

The better trained the horse, the happier he usually is and the better chance you have of establishing a bond and the kind of relationship in which he is always trying to please you. Probably the best bond I ever had with a horse was with Sportsman. He was so intelligent. We just hit it off, and he always understood exactly what I wanted.

Horses have so much to give us. It is a tribute to them above all that they are such forgiving, noble beasts. They react to the sound of your voice and can be led with a piece of string, and it is our duty that whatever we ask them to do, it has to be achieved with dignity.

David Broome

Introduction by Elizabeth Peplow

THOSE OF US WHO CHOOSE HORSES ahead of golf, sailing, cycling, or tennis as our favorite pastime are the lucky ones. Whatever your connection with horses, whether you ride once in two weeks at your local riding school, enjoy racing on television, are a horse owner, or if horses are your living, you are part of an ongoing relationship that began several million years ago. The idea of sharing a common thread with the ancient horsemen of Mongolia may seem far fetched, but think about it next time you are about to ride. Apart from certain refinements of breeding, the horse is essentially unchanged and shares the same instincts and impulses as his brothers on the steppe.

As a rider, once on horseback, you can forget mobile phones and faxes. You are bereft of all modern means of communication and your tools are much the same as those ancient warriors. As David Broome says, communication with a horse is dependent on the meeting of minds and at its most successful, it is a complex art based on immense resources of intuition, persuasion, and sympathy.

To gain a little knowledge of horses is to discover how much you will never know. This book is aimed at all those who have embarked on that journey.

Elizabeth Peplow

Horses have bewitched
mankind for centuries—
these, painted c.15,000 B.C.,
will dance forever in the
caves of Lascaux,
Dordogne, France.

Part One:
The **Development** of the **Horse**

THE PRE-DOMESTIC HORSE

right: Wild Mustangs, Nevada, United States. The Mustang is descended from Spanish horses introduced to America by the conquistadors in the sixteenth century.

NTIL THE END OF the eighteenth century, two races of the wild horse, *Equus ferus,* existed in Europe and Asia: the Tarpan in eastern Europe and the Russian steppes, and the Mongolian wild horse, or Przewalski's horse, in Mongolia (see also page 82). These two races were the relics of vast populations of wild equines that inhabited virtually the whole of Europe, Asia, and North America at the close of the last Ice Age, 12,000 years ago. It is possible that some foals were tamed by humans, but at this time horses were much more frequently eaten than they were ridden. From 9,000 years ago the wild horse became increasingly rare; its remains are seldom found on archaeological sites in Europe, while in North America all equines became totally extinct.

From around 6,000 years ago, remains of horses begin to appear in cultural contexts that indicate domestication. The most authentic of these come from Neolithic sites in central Asia, such as Dereivka on the river Dneiper, where subfossil remains reveal a pattern of specialized human exploitation of the horse. Stallions were probably killed for their meat, mares could have been milked, and both sexes may have been used as draft animals. Until recently, archaeologists generally believed that there was no evidence for horse riding until the much later period of approximately 1000 B.C. However, it is known that at least some of the Dereivka horses were driven or ridden with bridles and bits: abnormal wear was found on the premolar teeth of buried skulls, and six perforated tines of red-deer antlers—which probably served as bridle cheek pieces—were also discovered.

It has been suggested that domestication of the horse occurred at this time because it enabled the expanding human populations to move away from the river valleys (which were becoming deforested and overhunted)

above: The Caspian pony, thought to be an an ancestor of the Arabian and a handful of allied breeds found mainly in Persia, is the second oldest equine breed in existence after Przewalski's horse.

and into the steppes, where the wild horses provided a new resource. It must be emphasized, however, that there are very few hard facts to substantiate the "where and when" of early horse domestication, although new evidence is accumulating all the time from the dating of and osteological (skeleton and bone) study of excavated material.

By 2000 B.C., while the wild horse continued to be pushed into its eastern refuges by loss of habitat, climate change, and human hunting, the domestic horse had begun to spread rapidly around the whole of the Old World. Most of this newly domesticated stock was probably derived from the core area north of the Caspian Sea, but it is not inconceivable that some local domestication occurred with individuals taken from the dwindling wild-horse herds found in several parts of Europe.

Since ancient times, there have been different forms of domestic horse. There are small, stocky ponies in the cold north, heavy horses in middle Europe, and slender-legged Arabians in the hot, southern regions—yet biological, molecular, and pictorial evidence indicates that all domestic horses of the past and present are descended from the single ancestral species, *Equus ferus*. (The division of domestic horses into the so-called "cold-blooded" and "warm-blooded" types is a reflection of the species' adaptation to different climatic regions—these terms have no scientific validity. All horses have the same body temperature, and all the different breeds are able to mate and to produce fertile offspring.)

Despite the great variation of coat color found in domestic horses, there is a sporadic occurrence of a longitudinal dark band along the ridge of the back, together with stripes on the shoulders and forelegs, on horses of different breeds from countries as far apart as Britain and China. These stripes occur most frequently in dun-colored ponies, and—like the mealy muzzle of the Exmoor pony (see page 83)—probably represent a reversion to the wild type. On this basis, Charles Darwin believed that all domestic horses were descended from "a single, dun-colored, more or less striped, primitive stock, to which our horses still occasionally revert." It is a conclusion against which there can be little argument today.

above & left: Przewalski's horse, also known as the Asiatic Wild Horse, is the only "primitive" horse to survive in its original form. Some herds have been bred in captivity and reintroduced to their natural habitat in Mongolia.

DOMESTICATION AND THE EARLY HORSE PEOPLES

THE IMPACT OF the earliest domestication of the horse on human society must have been as profound as that of the invention of the steam engine, and yet we know very little about when, where, or how it happened. The increased mobility provided by the horse would have enabled people to move further, as well as faster, and to take more with them than ever before. They could exploit larger and more diverse landscapes, maintain larger families, and increase the range of their trade contacts. They could move into previously uninhabitable regions such as the Eurasian steppe. And since a man on foot is no match for a man on horseback, the military implications of horse domestication would have been revolutionary. John C. Ewers has shown how profoundly the introduction of the horse into North America changed Blackfoot culture. We should expect no less of its early domestication in central Eurasia. And yet, until recently, very little attention has been paid to this problem.

It is important to note, first of all, that wild horses, particularly as foals, can be captured and tamed and, as such, ridden, harnessed, slaughtered, and even eaten without being domesticated. Aboriginal peoples throughout the world are known to tame all kinds of wild animals to keep as pets. There is no reason to think that this would not have been the case at least from the time of the earliest anatomically modern *Homo sapiens*. And when the need arose, taming would probably have been the first step toward domestication.

Though customarily defined as the controlled breeding of plants or animals by humans, the real distinctiveness of domestication lies in the fact that it involves ownership and thus results in a completely different level of human commitment from hunting. Taming also involves ownership, but its social and economic implications would have been, at most, superficial and localized, and would have disappeared with the death of the animals involved, while the repercussions of domestication would have spread throughout the whole society. What this means is that we are not simply trying to identify horse riding, traction, milking, and meat eating in the archaeological record, but rather, we are looking for evidence of horse breeding, which is, as such, archaeologically invisible. It may be approached indirectly, however, through an investigation of population structure, archaeological context, and other characteristics of the data.

Paleolithic horse exploitation

We have no convincing evidence that horses had either been tamed or domesticated during the Paleolithic. Paul Bahn has put forward iconographic and anatomical arguments propounding such a theory, but they are not supported by the available data. On the one hand, the evidence of cave art is inescapably ambiguous. On the other hand, the tooth wear anomalies Bahn has described as arising from cribbing or from rubbing against the strap could more easily be explained by bark biting, abnormal occlusion, or accidental chipping. Moreover, the stratigraphic integrity of sites excavated around the turn of the century is not reliable.

This does not prove that horses were never ridden in the Paleolithic, or that they were not domesticated, but it does mean that we have no evidence at all that they were, or even could have been. On the other hand, there is strong evidence, based upon kill-off profiles from a series of relatively recently excavated sites—including Solutré, Feldkirchen-Gönnersdorft, Combe Grenal, and Pech de l'Azé—that throughout the Middle and Upper Paleolithic in western Europe, horses were, in fact, hunted.

Evidence of early horse husbandry

Horses are relatively uncommon in Mesolithic and Neolithic archaeological deposits. It has, therefore, commonly been held that they could not have been domesticated during those periods. On the other hand, relatively large quantities of horse bones and teeth have been recovered from Chalcolothic (or Eneolithic) sites on the central Eurasian steppe. Although other information, such as teeth morphology, population structure, representation of anatomical elements, and taxonomic distinctions based upon measurements are credited as evidence for horse domestication, until recently the real evidence has been that of the increased representation of horse remains at archaeological sites. In fact, until recently, the methodologies employed for interpreting the data have been seriously flawed. This is not meant as a criticism of past scholarship, but rather as

recognition that the analytical techniques of zooarchaeology have progressed quite considerably in recent years.

Dereivka, an Eneolithic habitation site, is central to the problem of horse domestication. It is situated on a tributary of the Dnepr River in the Ukraine and dated between 3380 and 4570 B.C. (Sredni Stog, Phase IIa). Excavated by D.Y. Telegin (Institute of Archaeology, Kiev) between 1960 and 1983, Dereivka has been regarded as the site with the earliest evidence for the domestication of the horse. Moreover, until recently, there was a consensus that horses had been raised there first of all for meat, but also for riding—the evidence being the remains of what have been described as bridle cheek pieces.

The methodological framework used to reach these conclusions was, however, the conventional but unsound one just described. Criteria used as evidence that the horses from Dereivka were domesticated include the following: (1) the absence of old horses, (2) the presence of a high proportion of male skulls, (3) the presence of objects identified as bridle cheek pieces, (4) the results of a morphological analysis comparing the Dereivka horses with other equine material, (5) their association with other domesticates—cattle, sheep, goat, pig, and dog—and (6) the relatively high percentage of horse bones and teeth in the deposit.

right: A fragment of a relief depicting harnessed horses and chariots found in Egypt and dating from 1352–1336 B.C.
left: Horses permeated Egyptian art. This scene, painted on the side of a casket belonging to Tutankhamen, was found in the Valley of the Kings.

above: Greek horsemen. These two young horsemen preparing to join a procession are depicted on the frieze of the Parthenon.

right: Horsemanship revered: this depiction of equine training in India dates back to the seventeenth century.

left: For the Kabardin herdsmen of the Caucasus mountains of Eastern Europe, horses are central to a traditional way of life.

left: Herd instinct. Wild horses roam in groups and do not like to be separated from their peers.

left: There is widespread assumption that horse domestication evolved on the steppe.

In reality, on the basis of archaeological, ethnographical and ethological comparisons, the absence of old individuals is much more likely to indicate hunting than herding. Males would outnumber females if either bachelor groups or stallions protecting their harems were targeted in the hunt. The cheek pieces may not have been cheek pieces at all. The morphological study involved very small and disparate samples and produced contradictory results. The association of horses with other domesticates is not evidence of horse domestication. In any case, they were also associated with the remains of wild animals. In fact, the most important criterion is the relatively high proportion of horse bones and teeth present at the site. This apparent change could also have resulted, however, from an increase in horse hunting by comparison with earlier sites.

M.A. Levine's reassessment of the data related to population structure indicates that the vast majority of the horses from Dereivka had been killed in the hunt. The possibility that horses were being ridden at Dereivka was initially lent support in a paper by D.W. Anthony and D.R. Brown, in which they described bit wear on teeth from a so-called ritual head and hoof burial. However, a recent radiocarbon date for that skull, at around 3000 B.C., shows that it was almost certainly a Bronze Age intrusion. This is confirmed by the work of Y.Y. Rassamakin, which demonstrates that

considerable disturbance had taken place at the site in ancient times. In other words, there is no compelling evidence for horse husbandry at Dereivka.

Anthony and Brown have also claimed to have identified bit wear on a small sample of teeth from Botai, an Eneolithic site, dated to around 3500 B.C., located in northern Kazakhstan. Over 99 percent of the hundreds of thousands of horse bones and teeth excavated at Botai belonged to the horse. Levine's analysis of the population structure of the teeth from part of this site suggests that the vast majority (if not the totality) of the horses from Botai, as at Dereivka, were wild. If both Anthony and Brown are correct, then it is possible that tamed or domesticated horses could have been used to hunt wild ones for their meat.

The spread of horse husbandry

Our understanding of the spread of early horse husbandry is as bedeviled by obsolete methodologies as is the problem of its earliest domestication. Nonetheless, it seems clear that the period bridging the Copper and Bronze ages was characterized by important social and economic changes. These involved increased trade, the development of social ranking, and possible changes in land tenure, which may have been associated with a less egalitarian society. All of these could have arisen in connection with the increasing importance of the domesticated horse.

After the Early Bronze Age, although horses were apparently no longer killed in very large numbers, their wide distribution throughout Europe and their association with high-prestige human burials leaves no doubt as to their importance. Then, during the first half of the second millennium B.C., a series of conquests by charioteers shook the ancient world, bringing social, economic, military, and political change in their wake. They all belonged to aristocratic federations, usually described as feudal in nature, in which horses played a crucial role.

Throughout subsequent millennia, horse-powered polities were able to increase the scope of their conquests to encompass progressively larger geographical areas. During the first millennium B.C., the horse-riding tribes of the two Scythias, European and Asiatic, controlled central Eurasia from the foot of the Carpathians to Mongolia. The horse-dominated military machine reached its apogee during the thirteenth and fourteenth centuries A.D. under the Mongols, whose empire at its greatest extent reached from Hungary to Korea. It was the largest continuous land-based empire in history. The horse was the main instrument of destruction in warfare until well into the Gunpowder Age, that is, until around 1500 A.D., when it was superseded by firearms.

This pattern was echoed in the Americas, where the power conferred by the horse and the terror it inspired played a crucial role in the European conquest. Moreover, the subsequent acquisition of the horse by the indigenous inhabitants of the New World transformed their own societies in ways that remind us of the beginnings of horse husbandry in Eurasia—for example, in the development of the less egalitarian and more hierarchical social structures and in the increased exploitation of previously marginal ecological zones.

New directions

Although progress has been made in the study of the development of horse husbandry, all of the big questions concerning the horse's early domestication and subsequent diffusion still need to be addressed.

It seems that by the period 3500 to 3000 B.C., the horse had either been tamed or domesticated for riding on the Eurasian steppe. No other region has been studied intensively enough for us to know whether such behavior was widespread or had developed earlier elsewhere, or whether it has developed from a single or from many loci. Research is now in progress on the Eurasian steppe and forest-steppe, but further work also needs to be carried out in the adjacent Carpathian and Caucasus regions, the northern Black Sea coast, and possibly further west as well. Both widespread assumptions—that horse domestication must have evolved on the steppe and that it must have arisen out of a settled agricultural community—need to be challenged.

The problem of the evolution of social ranking in Europe has been debated extensively, but without taking the horse into the equation in any serious way. Data must be collected that will help us better to understand the links between the dispersal of horse husbandry and the development of trade, warfare, and the differential distribution of wealth and power.

left: *By the period 4500 to 3400 B.C., the horse had been domesticated for riding in the Ukraine. Research on early horse husbandry is also ongoing in the Caucasus region.*

THE DEVELOPMENT OF CLASSICAL EQUITATION

THE FIRST DEFINITIVE RECORDS of man riding horses date back to 1600 B.C., but it was a Greek cavalry officer called Xenophon, born in Athens in 430 B.C., who provided the first landmark in classical equitation. His two books, *Hippike* and *Hipparchikos*, provide a wealth of information on a system of riding that formed the basis of the classical equestrian art and is still valid today. However, despite his advanced thinking, Xenophon's great disadvantage as a cavalry officer attempting to withstand the enemy's charge was the lack of a saddle, and it was not until this came into use (see page 25) that the course of mounted warfare changed.

The Middle Ages brought the Age of Chivalry, with jousts and tourneys between knights riding Arab or Barb-type horses and wearing chain mail; the tourneys were also the start of an early form of musical ride or carousel. The influence of the mounted knight persisted until 1346 when the bow and arrow decimated French troops at Crécy, forcing the knights to encase themselves and their larger, heavier mounts in cumbersome armor. They became virtual sitting targets, and their end came in 1525 with the Battle of Pavia. However, the chivalrous age did produce a high degree of schooling in the horse—albeit imposed by long curb bits and sharp spurs.

Equitation as an art form

Riding was first recognized as an art form in the Renaissance period. No nobleman's education was considered complete until he had acquired an appreciation of equitation, and elegant Baroque riding halls sprang up all over Europe to house the stately carousels performed by these aristocrats. Xenophon and his works were rediscovered, and High School riding had begun. In a book written in 1559, Count Cesare Fiaschi advocated patience in training—as Xenophon had done—but in practice results were achieved by barbaric methods. Hedgehogs or cats were tied to horses' tails, hot irons and iron bars with hooks were used to force horses to go forward, stirrups often had sharp edges, and severe curb bits and spiked nosebands were also used.

Fiaschi's best-known pupil, Federico Grisone, whose own system of training spread through Europe and whose book *Gli Ordini de Cavalcare* was translated into English on the orders of Queen Elizabeth I, is generally credited as the first Master of the Horse. His successor, Giovanni Baptista Pignatelli, developed his methods further and incorporated some circus training and movements, noting that the high degree of obedience and balance required was achieved by careful training, not by mechanical means. Gradually, classical riding as a whole took on a lighter appearance as severe "aids" were abandoned. Horses of a lighter Spanish build became popular, and studs were set up to breed them—the best known being the Lipica stud now in Slovenia, founded in 1580, which established the Lipizzaner breed.

Pignatelli's pupils went on to continue his teaching throughout Europe in the early seventeenth century. The Chevalier de St. Antoine became First Master of the Horse to James I of England, while Antoine de Pluvinel (1555–1602) taught King Louis XIII in France. A sympathetic trainer, de Pluvinel considered the use of whip or spur "a confession of failure," and laid great stress on patient handling. He refined the aids to make them almost unnoticeable and was the first Master to use pillars to teach horses in the *manège*, requiring pupils to sit on their horses without reins while performing the High School airs.

While de Pluvinel was at work in France, William Cavendish, Duke of Newcastle (1592–1676), who had been trained in the School of Naples, had started a riding school in Belgium. He believed that horses obeyed their riders from fear rather than respect, but he rarely resorted to severe punishment. He was one of the first to realize that horses have a memory, and that this could be exploited—as well as being a disadvantage if a horse was wrongly taught.

Further developments

As the enlightened approach to horsemanship spread across Europe, the way was paved for the Frenchman known as the "Father of Classical Equitation," François Robichon de la Guérinière (1688–1751). His influence changed the course of classical equitation, and his teachings are at the base

left: Severe methods in the training of horses were regarded as a "confession of failure" by the early classical trainers.

of modern schooling methods. It was largely due to his work that two great streams of classical equitation sprang up in Europe: one based on the French Schools of Versailles and Saumur, and the other on the Spanish Riding School of Vienna. His riding school at the Tuileries was founded by Louis XIV and managed by de la Guérinière from 1730. It became famous across Europe, mainly due to the refinements in de la Guérinière's schooling methods and to the quality horses used (mainly English Thoroughbreds). He perfected exercises to cultivate the horse's natural movements and invented the shoulder-in as a suppling exercise; he also designed a modern form of saddle, similar to that used in the Spanish Riding School today.

Meanwhile, in Versailles, de Nestier had become riding master to Louis XV, but at the outbreak of the Revolution, he and other *écuyers* were driven into exile. As military supremacy became increasingly important, the first cavalry school was set up in Saumur and, although it was temporarily closed down through lack of funds, another was established in 1744 at Versailles. Seven years later, a "Military School" was created in Paris; this lasted only 37 years, but left its influence on French equitation in its aim of making the rider's position less formal and stiff, and military equitation "simpler, more natural and bolder."

The war years did little to further equitation in France, but, with the return of Louis XVIII, the School of Versailles was

above: A cavalcade in the Winter Riding School in Vienna.

ever, train Cordier, who later became the first *écuyer en chef* of the School of Saumur when the School for Mounted Troop Instruction was moved there and academic equitation again took over at Versailles. The first of the carousels, for which Saumur is famous, was presented under Cordier in 1828. This was just two years before the School of Versailles closed forever, leaving Saumur to perpetuate the traditions of the French School.

Systematic training

A butcher's son from Versailles called François Baucher (1796–1873) aspired to

re-established. The National School of Equitation, created in 1793 at Versailles, subsequently changed its name to the School for Mounted Troop Instruction, its purpose being to train officers. It did, how-

become *écuyer en chef* at Saumur after the retirement of Cordier's pupil, Novital. Although he never fulfilled this ambition, he founded a School in Le Havre and another in Rouen, and published his *Dictionnaire Raisonné d'Equitation* in 1833. Baucher used a systematic training of the horse to destroy resistance, and his achievements have left their mark—not least by his invention of the flying change of leg at every stride, which was written off by others as "nothing but a cantered amble."

Baucher's contemporary, who succeeded Novital as *écuyer en chef*, was Antoine Cartier, Viscount D'Aure. Rather than teaching pupils on perfectly trained horses, he treated each horse as an individual, although, by opposing resistance with resistance, he led it mechanically into the required movements. The man who brought together the teachings of Baucher and D'Aure was Lt. Alexis François L'Hotte, a pupil of Baucher who later came under D'Aure as a cavalry officer at Saumur. A brilliant horseman, his book *Questions Equestres* was gathered from lessons with both teachers, and expounded his motto of "calm, forward and straight." Taking over as *écuyer en chef* at Saumur, L'Hotte became probably the greatest horseman of the century.

Another versatile horseman was James Fillis, an Englishman who became *écuyer en chef* at the Cavalry School in St. Petersburg. He taught pupils without stirrups so that they gained a deep, flexible seat, placing great importance on balance rather than grip. Fillis practiced some unorthodox movements for the circus ring, such as the reversed pirouette with crossed feet and the canter backwards on three legs; he also introduced jumping—leaning back on the descent, allowing the horse free head movement and keeping his legs in contact throughout to obtain a *bascule*. Fillis was

left: *The Spanish Riding School of Vienna uses exclusively Lipizzaner stallions. The training of these magnificent horses takes several years, with the emphasis on balance and muscular development.*

probably the last great horseman to use this position over fences, as Federico Caprilli (1868–1908), a captain at the Italian Cavalry School at Tor di Quinto, evolved the forward seat and established its use at about the time of Fillis's death in 1900. Caprilli's justification for the forward seat was in accordance with the classical principle of keeping the rider above the horse's center of gravity when crossing country at speed. Cross-country riding today uses a combination of Caprilli's system and the purely classical method.

The Spanish Riding School

During the nineteenth century there were frequent interchanges between Saumur and the Spanish Riding School. Few documents exist concerning the early beginnings of the latter, but the Imperial Court in Vienna had long been concerned with equitation. Spanish horses were introduced in 1562 to found the Court Stud at Kladrub and, three years later, an exercise area was built. Work began on the present School in 1726: it was opened by the Emperor Charles VI in 1735 and festivals, balls, and exhibitions were held there in addition to the daily training sessions of the horses. Carousels were also popular, with the most spectacular—to which all the kings of Europe were invited—held in 1814. After 1894, the School was devoted solely to the training of horse and rider in *Haute Ecole*, and entrance to the School was restricted to officers and aristocrats. Although the French Revolution and the Napoleonic Wars put an end to the classical art in most European countries, in Vienna the School continued to adhere strictly to its principles.

The training of horse and rider at the School—then as now—follows the pattern drawn up in 1898. This stated that the "High Art of Riding" comprises three parts: the first stage, in which the horse is ridden in "as natural a position as possible with free forward movement along straight lines"; "campaign riding," or riding the collected horse at all gaits and in turns and circles in perfect balance; and riding in a more collected position with the haunches deeply bent and performing all the gaits and jumps that comprise the "Airs."

With the collapse of the Austro-Hungarian monarchy in 1918, the Spanish Riding School was taken into state

possession and its future looked uncertain. However, due largely to the fund-raising efforts of the Chief Rider, Moritz Herold, it was saved, and in July 1920 gave its first public performance. Since then, the School has attracted visitors from all over the world to see the highly schooled Lipizzaners performing the classical art of equitation, in what is believed to be the last Baroque riding hall in the world.

*above left: Classical ballet—a horseman of the Cadre Noir (**above right**) encourages his horse to perform the ballotade, in which all four legs are raised off the ground.*

left: Horse and rider perform the levade, in which the hind legs move under the body, taking the weight off the forehand which is lifted off the ground.

THE HISTORY OF WESTERN RIDING

I N THE IBERIAN PENINSULA during the late fifteenth century, there were two distinct styles of horsemanship. In the north, as in western Europe, men rode *a la brida*: straight-legged and with the feet rather forward, in a saddle with a high pommel and cantle. The bit was a severe curb, with a high port and cheek pieces as long as 15 in. (37 cm). The whole was the product of a long-obsolete battle tactic—namely, the lance charge of the armored knight, in which the knight braced himself using the stirrups and cantle to absorb impact, and needed a severe bit to control his horse with one hand. Throughout western Europe and much of the United States, this style of horsemanship prevailed for centuries after its original purpose had disappeared.

By contrast, in the south of the peninsula where the Moorish influence was strong, horsemen rode in the style of the steppes and the desert, described by a contemporary English author as "riding short in the Turkey fashion." The reason for this was that their principal weapons were the bow and the curved scimitar, which could best be used if the rider stood in the stirrups. Young horses were trained by Arabs and Moors with a bitless bridle, which were known to them as a *hakma*, to Spaniards as a *jaquima*, and were familiar to us as the hackamore (see page 165).

The first western horses

When Christopher Columbus crossed the Atlantic in 1492, he took a number of gentlemen adventurers as his mounted escort. Before embarking on such a doubtful enterprise, these men had exchanged their chargers for others that were more expendable, but even these—against American Indians who had never seen horsemen—proved as formidable as tanks would have been to an eighteenth-century army. It is reasonable to suppose that the first horses taken to the mainland—Mexico in 1509—were of far better quality.

From the horses of the conquistadors descended the Mustangs, through animals abandoned by early explorers or through those that strayed from ranches and missions. By the nineteenth century these were roaming over the great plains west of the Mississippi, and proved a good foundation stock. Mustangs had hard feet, sound legs, and were tough and self-reliant. On the dry prairie grass they increased and multiplied, but two or three centuries of hard conditions, with no selective breeding, impaired their size and beauty. By the nineteenth century the typical Mustang tended to be hammer-headed, ewe-necked, roach-backed, cow-hocked, and tied-in below the knee, as revealed in early photographs.

Horses transformed the lifestyle of the plains Indians. As hunters they had always been at a disadvantage in pursuing animals on foot, but when mounted they could kill buffalo by the thousand. The horse also meant nobility in war and wealth: it was

above: *The plains Indians of North America displayed remarkable horsemanship.*
right: *The horse symbolized nobility in war and wealth. This Dakota chief was photographed by Edward Curtis in 1890.*

left: A Blackfoot brave and his pony in Alberta, Canada, in the 1890s.
right: A Cheyenne brave painted by Frederic Remington in 1901.

above: Drifters of the plains—a cowboy and his pony painted by C.M. Russell.

left: Ulysses Simpson Grant (1822–85), commander of the Union forces in the Civil War, with his officers in a nineteenth-century painting by E. Boell.

currency, status symbol, and bride-price in one. In just a few generations the plains tribes—especially the Comanches—became horsemen as complete as the Scythians, Mongols, and Huns. They virtually lived on horseback and, when a war-leader died, his favorite horses were sacrificed to accompany him.

The early cowboys

The first American rancher was a Puritan gentleman named John Pynchon who, in the mid-seventeenth century and with the help of his cowboys, drove a herd of fat cattle from his farm at Springfield down to Boston for shipment to the West Indies. Around Springfield, ranching techniques developed on a small scale, and spread to the "cowpens" in several southern states.

When Americans came to Texas as industrialization opened up lands west of the Mississippi after the Civil War, they found a different tradition of ranching, developed by the wealthy Charros and their Mexican *vaqueros*. The cattle were lean, wild Longhorns. As immigrants flooded into the west after the Civil War, it became apparent that the toughest beef would find a buyer if only it could be brought to market. It was also discovered that the Longhorn could survive winter on the prairie and would put on weight as it was moved over the plains in spring and summer. In 1867, an entrepreneur built a complex of stockyards on the railway at Abilene to which cattle could be driven from Texas before being railed east or west to the consumer—and so began the cattle kingdom. It was finished in the 1880s by over-production, a slump in prices, wire, sheep-farming and successive hard winters—although on the screen and in fiction it has never ended. The cowboys of the 1860s, with the exception of Mexican *vaqueros*, were nearly all Texans: indeed, the two terms were almost synonymous.

The stock saddle used by the cowboys was designed to fit a horse of almost any size; to be comfortable on long rides; and, with its deep seat, to make it easier to sit a difficult horse. A cowboy's saddle was his trademark, and every cowboy took pride in having the best and most elaborate that he could afford.

In-bred instincts

The Mustang seemed to inherit—or to develop very quickly—the essential quality of cow-sense: it simply anticipated what a cow would do next so that, with a rider on its back, it could establish an extraordinary mental ascendancy over the savage Longhorns, which would kill a man on foot. Although no attempt was made to school a horse in the modern sense, it had to be taught its trade—to remain steady under a whirling lariat, and to brace itself against a roped steer. The star of any ranch was the good cutting horse (a horse used to "cut out" a steer from the herd), which only had to be shown the wanted animal and would then do the job itself—even without a bridle.

above: Gradually, the long trail became a thing of the past and cowboys' work centered on the ranch.

Other western riders

Of course, there were plenty of western riders who never worked with cattle—among them the cavalry troopers, Texas Rangers, hunters, trappers, miners, prospectors, homesteaders, and livery-stable keepers. However, they all rode—in western style with western tack—and were part of the tradition. Most famous among them were the Pony Express riders of the early 1860s, described as: "young, skinny, wiry fellows, not over 18, willing to risk death daily." The horses were selected for speed and endurance, and were bought at high prices. The Express averaged 9 miles (15 km) an hour over 25 mile (40 km) stages, with two minutes for changing horses. A rider's round trip of 70–100 miles (110–60 km) was covered twice a week, and at every staging post were the best of oats, bedding, and ostlers. This was very expensive, and eventually the service became priced out of business.

top left: A cowboy's saddle was his trademark and designed to be comfortable on long rides.
top right: A traditional stock saddle.

above: The wild Mustangs. Harnessing the quick-wittedness and determination of animals was an art. The best horse on a ranch could learn to "cut cattle" on its own, even without a bridle.

Changing requirements

With the decline of the cattle kingdom, ranching conditions altered. The long trail was a thing of the past, and a cowboy's work consisted mostly of repairing fence-line breaks. Fewer horses were needed for this, and it became more convenient to have something faster than a pony. More emphasis also began to be placed on pleasure riding, and casual contests between cowboys developed into the highly organized rodeo industry of today (see page 138). Later still, the internal combustion engine put many ranch horses out of business. All this resulted in the gradual phasing out, or breeding up, of the mustang by imported Arabs, Morgans, Quarter Horses, and Thoroughbreds, producing an enormous improvement in their size, speed, and appearance.

Western tack also underwent various changes: the old stock saddle was altered by sloping the horn forward, making the seat less deep, and bringing back the stirrups so as to give the rider a balanced seat over the horse's center of gravity. Milder bits were also found to be perfectly suitable for Western horses.

Western clothing

Western riding clothes are very different from the breeches and narrow boots of flat-saddle riders. Whatever their present purpose, the cowboy's dress and equipment evolved as the most practical and comfortable for the work he had to do. The nineteenth-century cowboy wore a wide-brimmed hat with a flatter crown than that of the modern Stetson. This sheltered him from sun and rain, protected his head and face when he forced his way through thorny scrub, and served as a pillow. A cotton bandanna acted as sweat rag, bandage, water filter, dust mask, and mosquito net. A flannel shirt with cuffs was as warm as a jacket, yet less sweaty and constrictive; in winter a sheepskin coat might be necessary. The trousers were loose, and worn tucked into high-heeled boots which would not slip through the wide stirrups and could be dug into the ground when holding a roped steer. Leather chaps gave a good grip on the saddle, were used as a groundsheet, and protected the legs against friction, thorns, kicks, snake bites, and rain. The spurs had huge rowels; these made a clink that a horse would recognize as its master came to catch it at night.

The lariat was used for roping cattle, for tying between trees to make a corral, for stringing up horse thieves, and any number of other purposes. It was made of rawhide, cotton, or braided horsehair; this last was expensive but was believed by Mexican *vaqueros* to keep off rattlesnakes when put around the bed roll. Cowboys generally wore a gun to dispatch an injured horse or cow, although—contrary to another great tradition—the cost of practice ammunition meant that most were very poor shots.

left: Practicality counts: these modern day cowboys in Nevada favor the same clothing and equipment as their forefathers.

right: Mustangs developed cow-sense—they seemed to know what the cow would do next.

THE HORSE AT WAR

NO DISCOVERY OR INNOVATION has had so profound an effect on warfare as the militarization of the horse, which fundamentally changed the nature of armed conflict—to a greater extent, even, than gunpowder was to do. To understand this, it is necessary to look back no further than the beginning of the twentieth century. Just two months before the end of the First World War—a period that had seen enormous advances in terms of artillery, the gasoline engine, and powered flight—Field Marshal Sir Douglas Haig, Commander-in-Chief of British forces in France, wrote: "The power of an army as a striking weapon depends on its mobility. Mobility is largely dependent on the suitability and fitness of animals for army work."

Before the horse came into use in battle, armies were limited in their striking power to the endurance of the man-at-arms on foot. Only once the horse had been adopted for military purposes could armies truly campaign—that is to say, use mobility to defeat the enemy. Hitherto, they simply fought pitched battles where and when they happened to come across the enemy.

Early involvement

For a millennium or more after its militarization the horse was little more than a means of carrying the fighting man from one battlefield to another, because on the battlefield its rider dismounted for combat. Contemporary art shows such warriors sitting on the point-of-croup of animals no bigger than small ponies—12 h.h. (hands) or so—and, although this position allowed the horses to bear their weight, it was not a position from which they had great control. Some of the earliest true mounted warriors—those who fought *from* the horse—were the Assyrian archers from the region of the River Tigris in what is now Iraq. They sat, without saddles, toward the back of their horses with their legs raised high,

above: The knights of the Middle Ages were portrayed in a colorful and romantic vein. Their horses were their accessories.

above: Renaissance man and horse at war—Simone Martini's portrait of Giovanni da Fogliano in Sienna.

above right: Horses are to the fore in Paulo Uccello's famous Renaissance scene of the Battle of San Romano.

and for stability used short, stiffened reins that were easier to seize quickly. Their favored mount was the type that today would be recognized as the Akhal-Teké, a supremely resilient horse with great endurance, and very possibly the ancestor of the modern Arabian (see page 34).

It was some years before horsemanship as we know it developed, in the fifth century B.C. with the teachings of Xenophon (see page 16). The forward seat made it easier for men to fight from their horses in battle, although they were hampered by what seems an extraordinary fact—they had no stirrups, and rode for 1,000 years at this disadvantage. Xenophon himself rode bareback, maintaining that a man's naked leg gave greater adhesion to his mount's sweating back if the two were in direct contact. In battle, however, the

adhesion was insufficient to withstand the enemy's charge because the rider's seat was fundamentally insecure.

The horse's size was not important: endurance and speed were the prime qualities of the horse, as it had little weight to carry and was not expected to deliver "shock-action" in the charge. For these reasons it was rarely more than 15 h.h., and sometimes as small as 12 h.h. However, an

exception to the general rule of small, light-weight horses used in battle were the cold-bloods ridden by the Goths of what is now northern Germany. These were probably descended from the forest horses of that region, and were large, docile beasts—so docile, in fact, that if their rider was unseated they would stand stock-still until remounted, or until a foot soldier seized the horse's mane to carry him to or from the enemy.

A changing role

As the horse changed the nature of warfare, so the stirrup changed the face of battle. Saddles—which were used initially by a group of Nubian mercenaries from the Nile valley, and were built high at both pommel and cantle—provided a base against which the soldier could brace his back when clos-

ing with bodies of infantry. Stirrups provided further security; they are known to have been in existence in Arabia in around 650 A.D., and possibly much earlier.

Stirrups were slow to be adopted in the West but, once the benefits of a more secure seat were recognized, armor developed rapidly. At first this was little more than chain mail for protection from arrows (the Carolingian cavalry of the Rhineland wore a particularly effective pattern), but the

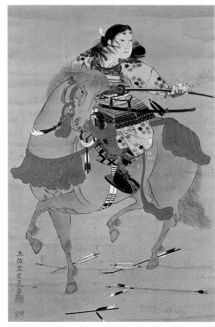

right: *Japanese painting of a warrior on horseback, wiping his sword.*

right: *Lord Cardigan and his horse Ronald lead the Charge of the Light Brigade in 1854.*

striking power of broadswords and lances increased with the use of the stirrup, and heavy plate armor had to be worn. As the weight of armor increased, so did the size of the horses. At the beginning of the sixteenth century, a knight in tournament armor might have worn 132 lbs. (60 kg) or more of plate, as well as carrying a heavy lance and shield; his horse would also have worn plating. The Great War Horses of the Middle Ages, the best of which came from Flemish stock, often stood upwards of 17 h.h. and had plenty of bone. Carrying as they did up to 484 lbs. (220 kg) in weight, it is not hard to see why.

Qualities of the war horse

After the invention of gunpowder, cavalry became less important on the battlefield but remained essential for reconnaissance, communications, raiding, and pursuit. A premium was placed on smaller, handy animals, although there was still a demand for weight-carrying horses—especially for the heavy cavalry which acted as a last resort on the battlefield and as household troops. Some countries, notably Hanover and Prussia, had their own studs to breed particular types of troop horse—the Hanoverian and the Trakehner, for example (see pages 56 and 57)—but, in general, horses for the European armies were bought and sold on the open market. In nineteenth-century India, stud farms were established to supply the increasing demands of the British Army, but a large proportion of remounts (as replacements were known) were imported from New South Wales, Australia. These hardy horses, known as Walers, served in the Middle East during the First World War.

In the United States, the versatile Morgan horse was popular with the Army. The breed was founded by a tough 14.2 h.h. stallion foaled in 1789; thought to have been of Thoroughbred and Arab extraction,

above: *The bravery of the war horse depicted powerfully by Elizabeth Southerden Thomson in her painting "Scotland Forever."*

possibly with some Welsh blood, he was a horse of incredible endurance. After being sold several times, he was bought by the United States Army, which established the Morgan Stud in Vermont.

The British Army experimented with Arabian horses from time to time—most memorably in the abortive attempt to

left: *There were more horses involved in the First World War than at any previous wartime period.*

rescue General Gordon in Khartoum in 1885, when 500 of them crossed the desert in an unprecedented feat of endurance. However, although the breed's hardiness was acknowledged, it was never considered to have the speed and substance for cavalry work. In any event, the Arab's best qualities had been bred into the English Thoroughbred, which by this time served as many an officer's charger, and had sired or foaled many a troop horse.

Twentieth-century war

At the outbreak of war in 1914, the armies of the great powers were equipped with machine guns, quick-firing artillery, radios ,and airplanes. They also had more horses than in any previous war. Although the gasoline engine had been invented some two decades earlier, all artillery and transport was horse-drawn, and there were large numbers of cavalry ready to exploit success and turn defeat into rout. The British Army alone mobilized 140,000 horses in 10 days as the first expeditionary force made ready to sail for France. These carried substantial weight: with rifles, ammunition, feed, spare horseshoes, and other equipment, the cavalry rode heavier—up to 308 lbs. (140 kg)—than at any time since the knights of the Middle Ages.

In France and Belgium, overwhelming firepower and obstacles—such as barbed wire—relegated the cavalry to the wings after the initial period of maneuver, although artillery and transport remained predominantly horse-drawn throughout the War. Only in the Middle East did there seem to be a place for the mounted arm. Here, 20,000 horsemen in General Allenby's Desert Mounted Corps, mounted mainly on Walers, swept through Palestine and pushed the Turks back to their own frontiers.

After the War, all but the most die-hard cavalrymen recognized that the future of mobile warfare lay with the internal combustion engine, and most armies began a systematic—if slow—progress toward full mechanization. However, there were exceptions. For instance, the United States Army initially closed down its tank corps and the cavalry increased its horse numbers due to the Government's determination not to become involved again in war outside its own continent.

When the Second World War broke out in 1939, the German Army still relied heavily on horses for transport, even though it possessed many tanks and had vigorously developed the doctrine of *blitzkrieg* ("lightning") war. In 1945 it still had three mounted divisions on the Eastern Front, and it is estimated that 3,000,000 German horses were used during the War, while the Russian Army—especially the partisans—probably had even greater equine resources.

Since 1945 the horse has virtually disappeared from every army except for ceremonial purposes, although the Indian Army still uses large numbers of horses (and mules) as pack animals for operations in the country's mountainous border regions. However, for almost 3,000 years the horse was, in the words of the great Sanskrit work The *Hitopadesa*: "the strength of the army ... a moving bulwark." The horse at war is now merely a memory, but a cherished and respected one.

above: *The British army mobilized 140,000 horses in ten.days at the start of the First World War.*

THE WORKING HORSE

EVEN TODAY, a century after the invention of the internal combustion engine and two centuries after steam was first harnessed as an energy source, the power of an engine is measured against that of the horse. Perhaps this is unremarkable, however, for until the end of the eighteenth century horsepower was virtually the only motive power available.

The horse's first role was that of pack animal, and in prehistoric times it carried anything from baskets of peat to the carcasses of game. Several thousand years later, trappers in North America were using the same means to take their furs to the trading posts, while Shetland ponies to this day carry peat to the crofts in the Highlands of Scotland.

above: A stopping place on the road in 1868: such watering holes sprang up on new routes throughout Europe and America in the mid-nineteenth century.
above right: Coach travel reached its height in Europe in the eighteenth century.

Horse-drawn vehicles

The yoke came into use in the Bronze Age (from 5000 B.C. in the Middle East, and from 2000 B.C. in Europe), allowing the horse to pull more weight than it could carry, and so began the history of the horse-drawn vehicle. First came the chariot, but its evolution was slow: in Europe it was not until the eleventh century that persons of rank were conveyed in carriages, and even these were crude—little more than painted, unsprung carts. However, with the development of spring suspension in the fifteenth century, regular long-distance travel by coach became possible.

Cities in Europe began to prosper and increase in size from the mid-seventeenth century, and their citizens wished to be conveyed about town as well as beyond it. An example of this was in London, England, when in 1694 King William III gave assent to a bill granting licenses to 700 Hackney carriages; as a result, smaller, handier roadsters became sought after in place of the heavier types of horses used to pull big, lumbering coaches along the country's rutted, pot-holed open roads.

Eighteenth-century advances

It was well into the next century before real advances were made. Roads were greatly improved in Britain through various Acts of Parliament and, after the invention of steel springs, coaches could at last travel at speed, so that the more delicately built coach horse became the norm instead of the Great Horse of Medieval times. Royal Mail coaches made their first appearance in August 1784 on the Bristol to London route, completing the journey—a distance of 119 miles (191 km)—in 17 hours, making an average speed of 7 miles (11 km) per hour. Once the roads had been properly surfaced 30 years later, this speed had increased to 10 miles (16 km) per hour, and there followed the golden age of coaching in Britain. The number of horses servicing the Royal Mail coaches was prodigious. The usual stage for a team was 8–10 miles (13–16 km) and, with provision for rests, accidents, and so on, the mails needed one horse per journey-mile. The "up" and "down" coaches of the Bristol Mail would together have required, therefore, a total of 120 horses.

left: and below: The horse still provides the sole mode of transport for many communities around the globe.

The eighteenth century in Europe was also the age of the canal, and big horses were used to tow heavily laden barges for long distances inland. Horses had also been at work since the fifteenth century hauling coal both above and below ground along "wagonways," especially in central Europe, although at first the rails were wooden rather than metal and so wore down easily.

The nineteenth century

In mid-nineteenth-century America, it was the horse which opened up the West. Covered wagons known as prairie schooners transported settlers across the Rocky Mountains; the Pony Express, using fleet-footed mustangs, relayed messages from Missouri to San Francisco until the invention of the electric telegraph (see page 22); and the stagecoaches of the legendary Wells Fargo Company carried passengers and the United States Mail on both sides of the Rockies.

Urban growth in both the Old and the New World also meant an increase in the number of horses in cities. By the middle of the nineteenth century horses were pulling omnibuses and trams, and in Paris the Postier—a lighter type of Percheron—was bred specifically to haul the city's buses. Horses were also the mainstay of the embryonic emergency services in Britain: London's Metropolitan Police, formed in 1829, soon had a mounted branch; horse-drawn ambulances were appearing in large towns; fire engines raced through the streets behind fast and handy roadsters; and, around the coast, teams of Shire horses launched and recovered lifeboats.

However, railways were spreading rapidly and coaching soon started to fall into decline, especially in Europe and the American East. Horse prices fell, and many breeders gave up the practice although, ironically, heavy draft horses actually increased in number during this period because of the short-haul work created by the railways.

The horse in agriculture

In farmyard and field, there was little change in the traditional role of the horse until the twentieth century. For 1,000 years the horse had pulled the plow (prior to the tenth century, oxen were more usual). Large, docile animals known as coldbloods (from the German *kaltblutigkeit*, meaning calmness) were favored, and breeds such as the Ardennais, Clydesdale, Murakoz, and

left: The role of the horse in agriculture has steadily declined. These Shires are seen haymaking on a farm in Yorkshire, England.

left: In today's pollution-conscious society, the working horse still finds a role.

Percheron—their broad feet allowing greater traction in tillage—worked the fields of Europe. Percherons were taken to the United States as early as 1839.

Perhaps because of the coldblood's calm temperament, it has never been entirely replaced by mechanical alternatives. Some forestry work, for example, is better done by horses, especially on uneven ground; while soil compaction in heavy clay is also less severe when worked by the horse.

In large parts of eastern Europe the horse is as common a sight in front of a plow or agricultural wagon as it ever was, and government regulation often applies to working breeds. In Austria, for instance, all the Haflinger studs are government-owned. Even in as northerly a country as Finland, there are an estimated 150,000 horses working in farms and forests. There were over 500,000 horses in agricultural work in Britain as late as 1939, and today there are still hill-farmers who prefer the horse or pony to the four-by-four vehicle, as well as lowland farmers who can plow heavy clay soils more economically using the horse.

Other contemporary roles

There are now mounted police worldwide, of which perhaps the best-known and distinctive are the Royal Canadian Mounted Police. Everywhere, too, there are ceremonial horses: in London, for instance, members of the Household Cavalry stand sentinel at the Horse Guards, and the King's Troop Royal Horse Artillery fires salutes in Hyde Park on state occasions. Brewers' drays are more economical for deliveries in towns, especially where motor-vehicle access is denied. Horses also attract publicity, and vans in the livery of large department stores promote an image of exclusivity and reliability. Some estimates place London's total working-horse population as high as 5,000 today.

The role of the working horse is still evolving, and it regularly finds new work—or rediscovers old work. The last pit ponies in Britain, from the deep mines, are now in retirement, but even greater numbers are to be found being used as handy hauliers in open-cast mines. In parts of Wales, ponies have never ceased working in the slate quarries, and in mines and quarries throughout the developing world they are still the prime means of haulage. In Australia—and especially in the United States, where rodeos celebrate the continuing work of the cowboy (see also pages 20–3 and 138–141)—the horse is the mainstay of ranching, for the rancher has unsurpassed observation from the saddle, while the horse is handier and less threatening than the jeep in a press of sheep or cattle. The Waler (or Australian Stock Horse,—see page 74) is bred and prized especially for its endurance, while in the United States a greater premium is put on sprinting speed to enable cowhands to cut out steers (i.e., to separate individuals from the herd), making the Quarter-Horse/Mustang cross a popular choice.

In today's pollution-conscious society, the need and search for eco-friendly motive power increases—and this means more than just lead-free gasoline. One local authority in England has recently acquired two Percherons to haul its waste-recycling cart, making as much a statement as a savings measure. It is conceivable, then, that although the horse has been largely surpassed by cheaper and more convenient means of power, the day of the working horse is not yet over—nor even its end in sight. The drudgery of labor has, to be sure, been relieved by machines, but some of the satisfaction of physical work has also disappeared. Perhaps we are now acknowledging that, while the mechanization of every process may be feasible, it is not always desirable.

above: Crowd control is a common task for the working police horse.

right: The best-known mounted police force in the world—the Royal Canadian Mounted Police or "Mounties."

*Diomed, winner of the
1780 Derby with the jockey
Sam Arnoll, in a painting by
Sartorius of the same year.*

Part Two:
The **Breeds** of the **World**

THE INFLUENCE OF THE ARABIAN

THE ARABIAN, to which the horse world owes so much, always evokes strong emotions—both for and against its perceived qualities. Aficionados praise the spirit, courage, stamina, toughness, gentleness, intelligence, and above all the ethereal beauty of the breed; detractors argue that it is temperamental, hot-headed, has poor or peculiar conformation which makes it unsuitable for competition riding, and that it cannot jump well.

The fact remains, however, that the Arabian has exerted a significant influence on hundreds of other breeds throughout the world. What contributed to the mobility of carriage, intelligent response to training, delicate head, and well-set eyes of the Lipizzaner? What gave the Hungarian Shagya, a horse of marked Arab type which was instrumental in the Lipizzaner's development and takes its name from an "original full-blood Arabian" purchased in 1836 from a Bedouin tribe, its renowned speed, courage, and endurance? Where did the English Thoroughbred find its spirit, beauty, and stamina? The Commonwealth of Independent States (CIS) has the greatest number of horse and pony breeds in the world, most of them owing something— and in some cases a very great deal—to the Arabian horse; two notable examples are the Akhal-Teké, a saddle horse of great endurance, and the Orlov Trotter.

Type and conformation

The primary purpose of the Arabian is to be a riding horse, and type and good conformation are both essential hallmarks of the breed. It is the loss of the latter in pursuit of the former, which is caused by injudicious breeding, that has been behind many of the criticisms leveled at the Arab, and it is primarily for this reason that true enthusiasts of the breed throughout the world are lobbying for more responsible breeding policies.

above: Handlers attempt to catch an escaped Arab horse in an eastern landscape painting by John Frederick Herring (1795–1865).

right: The Arab has a distinctive wedge-shaped head with large, low-set eyes, a wide forehead, breadth across the cheeks, which tapers to a fine, small muzzle.

Type comprises those features which distinguish a breed from others. In the Arab, this includes a wedge-shaped head with a wide forehead and breadth across the cheeks, with a slight dish and tapering to a fine, small muzzle; large, low-set eyes; large nostrils, which are capable of great expansion; fairly close-set ears, which are fine and often curve in at the tips; and a head set on the neck at a wide angle with a high carriage. The short, fairly level back, rounded rib cage, and low flank are contributing features, and the high tail carriage is perhaps the most obvious distinguishing characteristic of all.

The essential qualities of Arab conformation include an arched neck which has good length; a long, well-laid-back shoulder with clearly defined withers; a deep and reasonably wide chest; a relatively short and strong back, with a deep body and well-sprung ribs; a good length from point of hip to buttock, with strong, well-muscled thighs; long and well-muscled forearms, with strong and muscular gaskins and short cannon bones; and hard and well-formed feet, with the hind feet being slightly more oval than the forefeet.

Characteristics and qualities

Exaggerated characteristics seen in the breed—such as the extremely dished head (which is not typical of the original desert Arabian), and the excessively horizontal line of back and quarters—are aspects developed purely for the show ring, and which have helped to damage the breed's reputation as a riding animal. The fashion

for the stretched-out showing stance—which often attempts to disguise conformational defects—has not helped, while the fast trot on a long rein used for showing frequently highlights the poor action that can result from breeding for extreme type at the expense of good conformation. At the other end of the scale, the revival of Arabian horse racing has seen loss of type in favor of breeding for speed, particularly in the French blood lines.

Nevertheless, the Arab is unsurpassed as a pleasure-riding horse and in endurance competition, with its quick intelligence and propensity to thrive in a one-to-one relationship with its owner/rider making it a joy to own for both activities. Arabs of good conformation can be trained for dressage as readily as any other breed, although they may lack the solid power of the Warmblood. Contrary to common belief, jumping is also well within their scope, and this, combined with their speed and general agility, has made them successful in cross-country team events.

Origins of the classic Arab blood lines

It is perhaps ironic that the Arab has circumnavigated the world only to return in considerable numbers to its lands of origin, as the Sheikhs of the Persian Gulf today seek out the best of the exported blood lines in a massive cultural revival. The dispersion of the breed began centuries ago. The earliest recorded date of the Arabian's

arrival in India, for example, is about 1290, and in 1350 the Rajput Sultan Allah-ud-Din distributed 500 Arab horses as gifts on his son's marriage. The Moghul rulers, who brought with them the Persian tradition of owning horses of great beauty as well as size, were the first to import Arabian sires with the aim of improving the Indian breeds. Arabians of varying quality and origin continued to be imported regularly from Iran, Iraq, and the Persian Gulf until late into the nineteenth century, and, by gradual infiltration over this vast continent, the Arabian spread its dominance.

The dispersion of the breed to Britain began before the turn of the nineteenth century, when Lady Anne and Sir Wilfred Scawen Blunt (of Crabbet fame) toured the deserts for their ideal horses and exported them from 1878 onward. These included the important mare Rodania and, from the stud of Ali Pasha Sherif in Egypt, the stallions Mahruss II and Mesaoud. Prior to this, Arabian horses—including the Godolphin Arabian (see page 38)—were registered in the *British General Stud Book*, established in 1791 by Weatherbys. Crabbet today describes horses entirely descended from the lines owned by the Blunts.

The Egyptian influence is pervasive, and nowhere more so than in the United States where it is found both in quantity and quality. Modern Egyptian Arabians derived from the herds of Mohammed Ali Pasha

right: The stallion Elijah at Carn Stud, Texas.

right: Throughout the world, the Arab has made its mark, being prized for its intelligence and its ability to thrive in a one-to-one relationship with its owner.

and his grandson Abbas Pasha, as well as 20 horses from Crabbet which were sent to Lady Anne Blunt's Sheikh Obeyd Stud in Egypt. The stallion Nazeer distributed his quality through his three sons. Ibn Halima and Morafic went to the United States, descendants of the latter including the stunning stallion El Shaklan and the lovely mare Imperial Phanilah. President Nasser of Egypt gave the third son, Aswan, to the Tersk Stud in Russia, where he was widely used, especially on racing lines and mares of Polish breeding. Once the Russian Studbook was accepted by the World Arabian Horse Organization (WAHO), Aswan's descendants were in demand for export, and the resulting influence in Europe and the United States has been extensive.

Russian Arabians are noted for their athleticism and superb action, developed between the First and Second World Wars from mainly Polish, French, and Crabbet stock, before the arrival of Aswan. Poland has also had a consistent influence, producing horses of substance and beauty that have been successful both in performance and in showing. The stallion Piechur, winner of the Polish Derby, was also a magnificent show-ring champion, while Grojec, sire of the great British national champion Sky Crusader, also sired numerous British race winners.

In France, the emphasis has been on breeding for the race course, with the charge brought that many French racing Arabs resemble Thoroughbreds more closely than their own breed. Indeed, the quest for speed has often exacted the penalty of a rather plain appearance, although all the old French lines are accepted as pure by WAHO. A partial explanation for this may be that today's top French racing Arabs are descended from just a few ancient mare lines, and that the original desert imports did not possess the refinement of type that is characteristic of the modern breed. The success of the French breeding policy is self-evident from their success on the racetrack and the international demand for their stock—for example, of the family which produced Manganate, Djelfor, Dormane, Pavot al Maury, and Bengali D'Albret.

Throughout the world, the Arabian horse has made its mark. Australia has produced some wonderful specimens, with particularly good limbs and feet and often excelling in endurance work. The Jordanian Royal Stables concentrate on maintaining classic lines of distinctive type for both showing and performance. The Babolna Stud in Hungary is famous for the development of the Shagya Arab, a strong breed originating from a combination of local horses and oriental blood, and carefully line-bred to evolve a specific type of light cavalry horse. Other countries also pursue their own programs.

In the final analysis, breeding is an imprecise art and so the debate of conformation versus type is unlikely to disappear, but the Arab horse should not be judged merely standing on its pedestal, but in the full freedom of movement. Notable members of the breed, including such unforgettable mares as Aliha and FA Protea and, on the male side, El Shaklan, World Champion Aukubra, and the charismatic Qatar champion Kamil Batal, surely prove that the Arabian horse is one of the most versatile.

below: Arab horses on the racetrack. The breed is renowned for its athleticism.

THE THOROUGHBRED

right: *Young Thoroughbreds at stud: the breeding of Thoroughbreds today is a science, but all are believed to be the descendants of just three stallions.*

THE DEVELOPMENT of the Thoroughbred as a breed to race began at the end of the seventeenth century, and is the most successful story in the history of horse breeding. The end result has been not just the creation of the fastest and most valuable horse in the world, but of a breed that has been a major influence on the development of other breeds and types.

While the effect of the breed has been felt worldwide, it was in Britain that the Thoroughbred embarked on its most crucial stage of development. The main type of racehorse in Britain prior to this had been the Galloway pony, a tough breed which stood at little over 13 h.h. However, it was widely known among racehorse breeders that the Arabians, Barbs, and Turk horses of the Middle East were capable of greater speed than the British ponies, and more than 200 of them were imported into the country between 1660 and 1760, most of which were used for breeding purposes.

The three founding stallions

As a result of poor records, there is considerable debate as to whether the Thoroughbred developed entirely from eastern stock, or whether Galloway blood lines were involved. This question is unlikely to be resolved, but sufficient records do exist to prove that of the stallions imported to Britain, three in particular—the Byerley Turk, the Darley Arabian, and the Godolphin Arabian—became highly influential in the development of the Thoroughbred that we see today.

The Byerley Turk was the first of this important trio to be imported into Britain, and legend relates that he carried his owner to escape at the Battle of the Boyne in 1690. Taken to a stud in the north of England, he was used to cover a wide range of mares from Galloway, Spanish, Connemara, Welsh, and, increasingly, oriental stock.

When the next of the three stallions, the Darley Arabian, arrived in Britain from Syria, he was also taken to the north of England where he stood at the Yorkshire stud belonging to Thomas Darley's brother. The third stallion, the Godolphin Arabian, was born in the Yemen and brought to England by the great livestock breeder Edward Coke of Derbyshire, who sold the horse to Lord Godolphin in the 1720s.

The first great racehorse, Flying Childers—a son of the Darley Arabian—

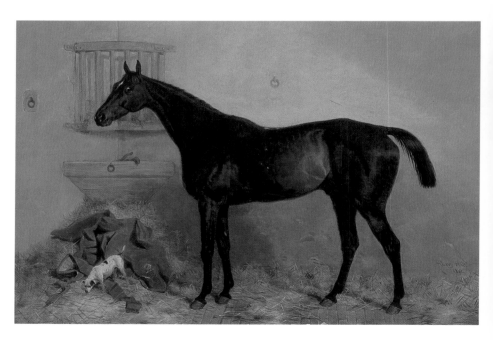

was born in 1715. He was never beaten in a race, and also passed on his talent to his offspring. It was his great-great nephew, Eclipse, who became probably the most famous racehorse of all time. He was born in 1764 and remained unbeaten in every one of his 18 races. He went on to produce the most outstanding stock including over three hundred winners, often unbeaten in the twentieth century,.

above: *The grace and beauty of the Thoroughbred has long captivated artists. This stable scene was painted by Harry Hall.*

right: The Thoroughbred's elegant, refined head is instantly recognizable. This is the legendary racehorse and sire of countless winners, Nijinsky, pictured at Clairborne Stud, United States.

Developments in racing and breeding

Breeders had assiduously kept their pedigrees but, in 1791, *An Introduction to a General Stud Book* was published in England by Weatherbys, with Volume I of *The General Stud Book* appearing in 1808. All the horses included in the book were known as Thoroughbreds and, by this time, were rather different from the pony-sized mature horses which had raced over 4 miles (6.66 km) or more in the first stages of the Thoroughbred's development. Breeders were by now investing heavily in their charges and wanted quicker returns on their money, so races were shortened and the weights carried by the horses—formerly up to 170 lbs. (77 kg)—were reduced to make it possible for younger individuals to compete.

With these changes, speed and early development of the Thoroughbred became the primary considerations. Racehorses no longer had to be as tough, so they were fed well and kept warm to help them to mature more rapidly. This led to finer and taller horses: during the late eighteenth and early nineteenth centuries the height of the average Thoroughbred increased by 6 in. (15 cm) to 16 h.h. By the mid-nineteenth century the size of the breed had peaked, and since then there has been no marked increase in either size or speed.

There is quite a range in conformation of pure-bred Thoroughbreds, from compact, muscular sprinters that are equipped with powerful hindquarters, to the classic distance horses that run over 1–1¾ miles (1,500–2,700 m); and from the angular, long-legged flat racers to the much more robust steeplechasers that must race over fences.

Breeders worldwide have long relied on Thoroughbred imports from Britain for the foundation stock of their racehorses. Diomed, for example—the winner of the inaugural Derby in 1780 (see page 120)—was imported by an American breeder and went on to found a dynasty. Iroquois, one of Diomed's descendants, was sent over to Britain from America for training as a yearling and, two years later, won the 1881 Derby. French breeders also began importing and breeding Thoroughbred horses, and in the 1830s the Thoroughbred was recognized as an official national breed. In 1865 the French-bred Gladiateur was sent to Britain to race, and achieved the rare honor of becoming a triple-crown victor by winning the three classic races: the 2,000 Guineas, the Derby, and the St. Leger.

Other countries around the world—from Japan and the former USSR to Germany and Italy—have also imported the Thoroughbred; as with the Arabian (see page 34), the situation has also come full circle with the Thoroughbred in that, most recently, the Middle East—where the progenitors of the breed were developed—has become a major importer. In the southern hemisphere, Australia, New Zealand, Brazil, Peru, and South Africa are just some of the countries that today run thriving industries based on the breeding and racing of the Thoroughbred.

Competition under saddle

With the exception of the ancient pure-breeds such as the Arabian and Andalusian, and many pony breeds, there is hardly a breed in the world that has not benefited from the injection of Thoroughbred blood to provide class, elegance, refinement, and speed. Today, with the huge growth in popularity of equestrian competitions, the competition or sports horse—used for show-jumping, dressage, eventing, and driving, as well as for leisure—is in great demand. The Thoroughbred has played a key part in the development of such horses, and their cross-breeding with heavyweight farm horses, carriage, and army horses has produced the elegant and athletic animals capable of winning such competitions.

The German Hanoverian is generally recognized as the most successful of the competition-horse breeds, with its representatives having won Olympic gold medals in the three disciplines of dressage, cross-country, and show jumping. Thoroughbreds were used in Hanoverian breeding programs soon after the Celle State Stud was founded in 1735, and today the same stud includes Thoroughbreds among its stallions. The German Holstein is another horse that is equally dependent on the Thoroughbred; 16 Thoroughbreds were imported to upgrade the Holsteiner after the end of the Napoleonic Wars. More recently, Thoroughbreds of the quality of Cottage Son and Lady Killer have been instrumental in turning the Holsteiner into a breed with the ability to win medals in the challenging sport of three-day eventing.

The Selle Français from France, which—together with the Hanoverian—dominates the field of show jumping, and the Dutch Warmblood—which has been particularly successful in dressage, driving, and show jumping—have both been influenced by the introduction of Thoroughbred blood lines, and have developed into major contenders for the top honors in the expanding competition-horse industry following the use of Thoroughbreds to upgrade stock during the 1960s and 1970s.

Harness racing

This form of racing is another important equine industry (see also pages 136–137), and there are a number of different breeds successful at the sport: namely the French Trotter, Orlov Trotter from Russia, and the Standardbred of the United States, all of which have Thoroughbred roots. In France, probably the most influential foundation Thoroughbred sire of the nineteenth century was Heir of Linne. In the United States the foundation sire was Messenger (born in 1780), which traces back to all three foundation sires of the Thoroughbred: the Byerley Turk, the Darley Arabian, and the Godolphin Arabian.

The Trotters from Britain were generally used in the nineteenth century for pulling carriages and there was never much racing, but they still had Thoroughbred blood in their veins. Today, this trotting line is represented by the Hackney pony and horse with their spectacular high-stepping action. Shales, the original Hackney (born in 1755), was a grandson of Flying Childers and a foundation sire for the breed.

below: A contemporary of Nijinsky, the great Mill Reef, bred in the United States and trained in England by Ian Balding, dominated the flat race scene as a three-year-old, winning both the English Derby and at Royal Ascot. His abilities were passed to his offspring, who included two Derby winners.

THE SPANISH HORSE

left: *The proud and noble Spanish horse, the Andalusian, is believed to be the world's most ancient riding horse breed.*

S PANISH HISTORY WAS BORN on the back of the horse and, throughout the country's history, a good horse has been a symbol of wealth, chivalry, and power. The Spanish horse, the Andalusian, is believed to be one of the most ancient riding horses in the world. Although the origins of the breed are not clear, Spanish experts are adamant that it is native to Spain and does not owe a single feature of its make-up to any other breed.

At the time of the Moorish invasion in 711 A.D., the Arabs used the term Andalus to denote almost the whole of the Iberian peninsula. The name gradually came to refer to the southern provinces, and today the province of Andalucia is the undisputed center of horse breeding in Spain.

Breed regulation

By 1492, the Iberian peninsula had built up one of the greatest cavalries in the world. However, it was the Carthusian monks who, during the fifteenth century, first introduced the element of organization into horse breeding, with carefully planned breeding programs at the stud called Hierro del Bocado, which was situated next to the monastery on the Fuente del Suero estate in Jerez. Descendants from these blood lines are still in great demand today, and fetch high prices.

In 1810, what is now one of the most renowned herds in the world was saved from dispersal by José Zapata. Vicente Romero purchased some of the brood mares, with the result that the breed was protected and kept pure; it is now in the hands of the Spanish state. Indeed, the breeding of all Spanish pure-bred horses is strictly controlled by the government, and the *Jefatura de Cria Caballar*, the Spanish stud book, includes registers for pure-bred, part-bred, and Hispano-Arabs. The Hispano-Arab is a cross between an Arab mare and an Andalusian stallion, and was

right: *Courageous, agile, and obedient, the Andalusian is today gaining more respect in the competition arena.*

originally bred for the Spanish Army. The breed was only officially recognized in 1987, and horses have to pass the same grading process as the pure-bred horses.

Far-reaching influence

In 1912, the Spanish Breeders' Association decided that all horses previously described as Andalusian would from then on be known as Spanish. This was due to the mis-interpretation of the term Andalusian, and was implemented largely to appease breeders from areas outside Andalucia, who felt that stud farms within the region were enjoying an unfair advantage.

The Spanish horse has had a far-reaching influence on the horse breeds of the world. In 1580, some of the best horses in

Spain were sent to the newly formed stud at Lipica, now in Slovenia, thereby founding the Lipizzaner breed. The stud's owner, Archduke Charles II, had already founded a riding school in Vienna eight years previously (see page 18). Many other breeds—including those from Germany—carry Spanish blood; while in Portugal, the Alter Real—used by the Portuguese School of Equestrian Art—is believed to have been founded on mares and stallions taken from Andalucia in 1747.

The Spanish horse today

With its courage, agility, and obedience, the Andalusian was ideal for its former use as a cavalry horse, as well as for bullfights. As fiestas became a national way of life,

above: In 1912, the Spanish Breeder's Association decided that all horses previously known as Andalusian would be known as Spanish. This was to appease Spanish breeders from outside the region.

below: Fiestas are a traditional way of life in Spain and the Andalusian is a key player in all the celebrations.

above: The Andalusian is typified by its strong, short-coupled body, active paces, and sheer presence.

celebrating the coming of spring and the autumn harvest, Andalusians pulling carriages and carrying *caballeros* —dressed in the traditional gypsy costume with their *señoritas* riding pillion, perched sideways on the horses' croups—have become a spectacular tradition.

Although considered the perfect type of horse for High School riding, the

Andalusian has always been discriminated against in the competitive arena because of its high-stepping action. However, the breed today has a less pronounced knee action, as well as being taller—up to 16.3 h.h.—and is finally becoming more accepted.

In 1987, the Real Escuela Andaluza Del Arte Equestre (the Royal Andalusian School of Equestrian Art) in Jerez was awarded its Royal prefix, and has become a great ambassador for the Spanish horse. Rapidly gaining recognition, the School sent a team of riders to the 1996 Olympics; the Spanish team then went on to finish in fourth

place at the 1997 European Dressage Championships. This short-coupled, strong, active breed, which has such enormous presence combined with a docile temperament and an exceptional talent for executing the *piaffe* and *passage*, will perhaps one day earn a deserved Olympic gold medal.

THE GENETIC JIGSAW

THE EVOLUTION OF HORSES, particularly in the past 300 years since the development of the Thoroughbred by the use of Arabian stallions (see pages 34 and 38) at the end of the seventeenth century, has largely been determined by the skill of the horse breeders.

In the case of the Thoroughbred, the emphasis has been on breeding in order to produce the unique combination of speed, stamina, and beauty that are the strengths of the breed.

For most of the mainstream breeds (see Part Two, page 32), there are stud books of registered animals. To ensure the continuity and purity of the breed, most breed societies conduct annual gradings of breeding stock and have strict requirements on entry to their registers so that all animals "with papers" meet not only the basic standards of height, color, and conformation but carry some of the more indefinable qualities that characterize the breed as well.

For those breeders less concerned with one particular breed and whose objects are to produce a certain "type" of horse such as a hunter or event horse, the skills required in assessing the gene pool are no less exacting. The dreams of producing a show hunter that will win in the show ring at top level, is a project that can take years and several generations from the first pairing to get just right. The process of crossing breeds to produce good quality part-bred stock is most favored around the world for the creation of riding horses. A typical example of a well-known and sought after cross-bred type is that of the native British mare (a New Forest and Connemara being typical examples) and a Thoroughbred sire. The resultant progeny should be up to height but with good bone and should possess not only the sure-footed and calm nature of a native pony, as well as its intelligence, but also carry forward the stamina and bearing of the Thoroughbred.

right: *Of the two basic coat colors, bay and chestnut, bay is dominant and so the chances of a bay mare producing a chestnut foal, as in this case, are rare.*

Particularly in the Thoroughbred world, breeding to produce the best quality young stock that will carry the hopes and dreams of owners to the racetrack, has long been something of a science. At the top level the Thoroughbred yearling sales are still dominated by some of the world's richest men. However, the fascination of breeding horses lies in its unpredictability—it is not simply a question of pairing the best with the best to get the best.

The science of genetics is expanding rapidly in this modern era. Opinion is divided as to whether such advances are actually a good thing or not, but knowledge of the way in which heredity works can help to explain phenomena that our forebears could only observe and wonder at. Why, for instance, can the mating of two bay horses produce a chestnut foal? Or why does the union of two champions not necessarily result in another?

Genes, passed down from parent to offspring, are what shape an individual before environment and opportunity enter the equation. They have a definite physical existence, and there is a different gene for each discrete characteristic—for example, hair color—owned by every individual. Every living creature has two genes—one from each parent—for any given characteristic. Each of the parents, therefore, has an equal opportunity to shape his or her offspring.

Genes are carried—like beads on a string—on chromosomes, which are rod-like structures found deep within each of a body's cells. Chromosomes occur in pairs, and one member of each gene pair is located on each of the paired chromosomes. Each species has a characteristic number of chromosomes per cell. In the horse, this is 64, or 32 pairs.

Inherited genes

In each egg and sperm cell there are only 32 chromosomes so that, when fertilization occurs, the full complement is restored to the new creature, with one member of each pair, together with its genes, coming from each parent. However, when these germ cells are formed, the 32 single chromosomes are not handed on as an intact set exactly as they were inherited. Instead, a shuffling of chromosomes and even a splitting and re-combination of parts of pairs takes place, in a process known as "crossing over." The result is that each egg and sperm cell carries a random combination of genes, some derived from the father and some from the mother, which are different from that of any previous generation.

Although genes for different characteristics are inherited separately, certain genes may have a tendency to be inherited together; this occurs if the genes are carried together on the same chromosome. This phenomenon is not invariable, because crossing over can result in linked genes being separated. However, the closer the genes are on the chromosome, the less likely it is that such separation will occur.

In some species—such as productive farm stock—chromosomes have been mapped, and the position and identity of their genes have been established, but our knowledge of equine genetics—although improving—is still in relative infancy. Any progress that will aid health and soundness must be welcomed, but it should be remembered that the vast majority of horses are bred to perform and excel as individuals, not as producers of, for example, a uniform milk yield.

Genetics and coat color

The way in which a characteristic shows itself in an individual will depend on the dominant or recessive behavior of the two genes (called alleles) in a pair. This concept

above: Sadler's Wells, a superb racing Thoroughbred sire and an example of a double-bay genotype; he is incapable of siring a chestnut foal.

below: Embryo transfer can be performed in the horse. In this procedure the uterus (womb) of the mare, called the donor mare, is flushed with several liters of fluid. The recovered fluid is then searched for the presence of the embryo, which at this stage will be about the size of a pin-head.

above: Stallion sperm can be stored for many years in liquid nitrogen. The semen is frozen in small straws and must be thawed in warm water before it is used.

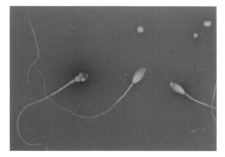

above: Stallion sperm cells being examined under a microscope. Normal stallion sperm, as shown here, consist of a flattened, oval-shaped head attached to a long tail.

is most easily illustrated by touching briefly on the inheritance of color, the most instantly obvious physical characteristic of a horse.

Of the two basic coat colors—bay and chestnut—the gene for bay is dominant, while that for chestnut is recessive. Thus, a horse with two bay genes must be bay; a horse with a bay gene and a chestnut gene must also be bay, but a horse with two chestnut genes can only be chestnut (the technical term for what the eye sees is the phenotype; the underlying genetic "hard-wiring" is the genotype). It follows that the mating of two chestnut horses can produce only a chestnut foal; but two bay horses can also produce a chestnut foal, if both possess a bay and a chestnut gene, and if both happen—and it is random chance that decrees this—to pass on their chestnut genes to their offspring.

Equine ability and prepotency

A horse's color is immaterial as far as its athletic ability or progenitive prepotency is concerned. In the past 50 years, 69 percent of Epsom Derby winners have been bay, or its close genetic relative, brown—however, so have 69 percent of Derby runners. As an example, the superb Thoroughbred racing sire Sadler's Wells is a double-bay genotype (and so cannot sire a chestnut foal), but there are numerous true-breeding bays which are bad stallions.

Observations about the way in which color is transmitted can illustrate how other physical characteristics which may affect a horse's performance are able to progress from generation to generation. This makes it impossible for us to be dogmatic about the source of ability.

PRINCIPAL HORSE BREEDS Europe

Britain

Cleveland Bay

size:	*16–16.2 h.h. (160–165 cm)*
main colors:	*bay*
characteristic:	*longevity*
uses:	*driving & light draft work*

The oldest and purest of the indigenous British horse breeds, the Cleveland Bay was used in the seventeenth and eighteenth centuries as a pack animal. It originated in Cleveland—where it evolved from the bay-colored Chapman horse of Cleveland—and has remained relatively free from external influences, although some Thoroughbred blood was introduced into the breed around the end of the eighteenth century.

The Cleveland Bay is a handsome horse with a large convex head, good shoulders, a deep girth, and a strong, fairly long back. The hindquarters are powerful, and the legs short with good bone and feet. Notable characteristics of the breed include its intelligence, strength, and stamina. Due to the shortage of pure-bred mares, it is currently classified as critical by the Rare Breeds Survival Trust.

Clydesdale

size:	*16.2 h.h. (165 cm)*
main colors:	*usually bay or brown, although gray and black also occur*
characteristic:	*active paces*
uses:	*heavy draft work*

The Clydesdale is a heavy horse that originated in the Clyde Valley in Lanarkshire, Scotland, as a result of crossing local mares with heavier Flemish stallions first imported at the beginning of the eighteenth century. The considerable demand for a strong draft horse suitable for farm work and for transporting coal from the Scottish mines meant that the breed quickly flourished, and great emphasis has always been given to breeding individuals with sound legs and good feet.

The Clydesdale is smaller than the Shire horse and, for such a large animal, has active paces. The various coat colors usually include a good deal of white on the face and on the legs—the latter carrying profuse feathering—and sometimes also on the body.

Hackney Horse

size:	*15 h.h. (150 cm)*
main colors:	*bay, brown, black, & chestnut*
characteristic:	*high, floating action*
uses:	*driving*

The Hackney Horse is a descendant of the now extinct Norfolk Roadster, a renowned trotting horse developed in the eighteenth century. The best Roadsters were descendants of a horse called Shales, who was a son of the Thoroughbred, Blaze, by Flying Childers, and can thus be traced back to The Darley Arabian (see page 38). The Hackney, therefore, has both Thoroughbred and Arab blood in its veins.

In the nineteenth century the breed was in demand as a good-quality military and carriage horse, but today is chiefly seen being driven in the show ring—an activity for which its extravagant, elevated trot and spirited disposition are ideally suited. The neat head, carried high on an arched neck, and the high-set tail, add to the overall impression of vigor and alertness.

Shire

size:	*18 h.h. (180 cm)*
main colors:	*bay, brown, black, & gray*
characteristic:	*strength*
uses:	*showing & heavy draft work*

One of the largest horses in the world, the Shire is a descendant of the Old English Black horse, whose forebear was the "Great Horse" of Medieval times. An immensely strong, big-barreled horse, with long legs carrying much feathering, the Shire has a fine head in comparison to its overall size. Despite this great size, and its strength—an average Shire weighs 1 ton and is capable of moving a 5-ton load—members of the breed are gentle in temperament and are easily managed.

With the ever-increasing mechanization that occurred during the twentieth century the breed could have died out, but the Shire remains remarkably popular. However, it is now much more likely to be seen in the show ring than working in the fields.

Suffolk

size:	*16–16.2 h.h. (160–165 cm)*
main colors:	*chestnut*
characteristic:	*longevity*
uses:	*heavy draft work & showing*

The Suffolk is a heavy draft horse that originated in East Anglia at the beginning of the sixteenth century. This is the purest of the British heavy breeds, and every Suffolk in existence today may be traced back to one individual, Thomas Crisp's Horse of Ufford (Orford), foaled in 1768.

The modern Suffolk is a compact horse with a large body set on short, clean legs. Despite weighing approximately one ton it is an active animal, and is still used on the land as well as appearing in the show ring. Although members of this breed are without exception chestnut in color, this may be one of seven shades ranging from almost brown to a pale "mealy" color.

The Suffolk is noted in particular for its long life, for its ability to thrive on meager rations, and for its exceptionally gentle nature.

Thoroughbred

size:	*up to 16.1 h.h. (162 cm)*
main colors:	*all solid colors*
characteristic:	*speed and stamina*
uses:	*riding (especially racing)*

Arguably one of the most beautiful horses in the world, the Thoroughbred is also the fastest and the most valuable, supporting a multi-national breeding and racing industry. The breed evolved in England in the seventeenth and eighteenth centuries, when native "running horses" (horses used in early racing contests) were crossed with oriental stallions.

The foundation sires (see pages 34–7) were The Byerley Turk (imported in 1689), The Darley Arabian (1705), and The Godolphin Arabian (1728). These three horses produced the four principal Thoroughbred lines: Herod, Eclipse, Matchem, and Highflyer (Herod's son).

The Thoroughbred excels in all branches of equestrian sport in which speed, courage, and stamina are prerequisites. It has a fine head set on an elegant neck, good sloping shoulders, a deep girth to allow for maximum lung expansion, powerful hindquarters, fine limbs with large, flat joints, and strong legs with plenty of bone.

Anglo-Arab

size:	*16–16.3 h.h. (160–167 cm)*
main colors:	*all solid colors*
characteristic:	*toughness & versatility*
uses:	*riding*

A cross between a Thoroughbred and an Arab, the Anglo-Arab originated in Britain (although it is now bred on a much larger scale in France). In the former, the requirement for stud-book entry is a minimum of 12.5 percent Arab blood, while in the latter the requirement is at least 25 percent.

The modern Anglo-Arab is a tough, hard, athletic, and versatile horse. The outline tends towards the Thoroughbred, with a straight head profile, well-sloped shoulders, and prominent withers. However, the frame is more solid than that of the Thoroughbred, and the croup is longer. Although the Anglo-Arab is not as fast as the Thoroughbred, it has greater jumping ability and is also well suited to dressage.

Ireland

Irish Draft

size:	*15–17 h.h. (150–170 cm)*
main colors:	*gray, bay, brown, & chestnut*
characteristic:	*free action*
uses:	*harness work*

The origins of this light draft horse are uncertain, but the first Irish Draft Stud Book was opened in 1917. The breed suffered serious losses during World War I, with many of the best mares requisitioned by the British Army. More recently, the export of Irish Draft horses to the European continent caused further depletion in numbers until legislation to curb this trade was passed in the mid-1960s.

The Irish Draft horse is an excellent farm worker, but its chief value lies in producing top-class hunters and show jumpers when mares are put to Thoroughbred stallions. The best examples of this breed have excellent shoulders and good, sound legs; there is only a little feathering on the fetlocks. The action is free and straight, and most Irish Draft horses are naturally capable jumpers. They make excellent sports horses and hunters.

France

Ardennais

size:	*15.3 h.h. (157 cm)*
main colors:	*roan, bay, & chestnut*
characteristic:	*hardiness*
uses:	*all types of draft work*

The Ardennais is a stocky, compact draft horse with very large bones. It originated in the Ardennes region of France, where the severe climate of the region still produces immensely tough horses of medium height that are ideally suited to farm work (see also the Belgian Ardennes).

The breed was developed during the nineteenth century when various outcrosses developed two specific types. The lighter Postier-type, now rare, was developed from Arab, Thoroughbred, Percheron and Boulonnais, whereas the heavier draft was a result of Brabant blood.

The Ardennais is a horse of tremendous gentleness and docility. The Ardennais horse is also bred for its meat.

Auxois

size:	5.2–16 h.h. (155–160 cm)
main colors:	bay & red roan
characteristic:	hardiness
uses:	draft work

This is the modern version of the old Burgundian heavy horse, which is known to have existed at least as far back as the Middle Ages. Since the nineteenth century, infusions of Percheron, Boulonnais, and Ardennais blood have been added and the present-day breed—called the Auxois—is a heavier type than the old horse of northeast Burgundy. Selective breeding also produces the predominantly bay or red roan coloring.

Like its near relatives, the Auxois is an extremely hardy and willing worker, with the equable temperament typical of this type of draft horse. In appearance it resembles the Ardennais and the Trait du Nord, being strongly built with relatively little feathering on the legs.

Boulonnais

size:	6–16.3 h.h. (160–167 cm)
main colors:	gray, bay, & chestnut
characteristic:	prominently veined skin
uses:	draft work

The Boulonnais comes from northern France and is a descendant of the ancient north European heavy horse. It is thought to have received infusions of eastern blood as early as the time of the Roman invasion of Britain, when Numidian cavalry was stationed on the coast of Boulogne. Eastern blood was certainly also introduced during the times of the Crusades; the Andalusian, too, has had its effect on the breed. Although it is a heavy draft horse, the Boulonnais also has great intelligence and is a very active animal. The influences of its infusions of eastern blood are apparent in its oriental characteristics, which include a refined, graceful head and a well-proportioned physique.

Breton

size:	Draft Breton: 16 h.h. (160 cm); Breton Postier: 15 h.h. (150 cm)
main colors:	blue & red roan, chestnut, & bay; occasionally black
characteristic:	calm temperament
uses:	draft & light agricultural work

The original Breton horse was a small draft or carriage horse indigenous to Brittany in northwest France, but cross-breeding with various other breeds has resulted in the emergence of three distinct types. These are the Draft Breton, containing infusions of Percheron, Ardennais, and Boulonnais blood; the Breton Postier, which is a horse with a good, active trot, and containing Norfolk Roadster and Hackney blood; and the Corlay (now rare, if not actually extinct), a lighter type of carriage or riding horse containing Arabian and Thoroughbred blood.

The Draft Breton, an early maturing horse, is bred for its meat as well as being used for agricultural work; the Postier is used for light agricultural work and for improving less developed stock. Both are active animals and have a good disposition.

Comtois

size:	14.3–15.3 h.h. (147–157 cm)
main colors:	roan
characteristic:	hardiness
uses:	light draft work

The Comtois is a light draft horse of the Franco-Swiss borderland, where it is thought to have existed since the sixth century A.D. It is related to the Ardennais and the environment it has lived in has made it sure-footed, active, and extremely hardy as well as making it ideally suited to working in hill country. The Comtois is rather a plain-looking horse, with a large head set on a straight neck; it has a long back, and the strong hindquarters typical of a hill-bred animal.

French Trotter

size:	16.2 h.h. (165 cm)
main colors:	black, brown, bay, & chestnut
characteristic:	toughness
uses:	harness racing and riding

A world-class harness racehorse, the French Trotter was developed in the nineteenth century by putting Thoroughbred, half-bred, and Norfolk Roadster stallions—all imported from England—to Norman mares. Two particularly influential English horses were Young Rattler and The Heir of Linne, both foaled in the first half of the nineteenth century, and 90 percent of modern French trotters trace back to five descendants of these two prepotent stallions: namely, Conquerant, Lavater, Normand, Phaeton, and Fuchsia.

More recently, American Standardbred blood has been introduced, but the French Trotter is a larger and more upstanding horse than the American Standardbred—and necessarily so, for ridden trotting races are still popular in its native country. This is a raw-boned type of horse, with the typically sloping, muscular quarters of the trotting horse.

Percheron

size:	16–17 h.h. (160–170 cm)
main colors:	gray & black
characteristic:	hardiness
uses:	draft work

Originating in the Perche region of France, only those horses actually bred in the Departments of Perche—Sarthe, Eure et Loir, Loir et Cher, and Orne—are admitted into the Percheron Stud Book, while those bred in other regions have their own stud books. It is still possible to discern in the modern Percheron's physical appearance its Arabian ancestry; it is also more highly strung than the other heavy horses.

The Percheron is well proportioned and, despite its size, has both beauty and grace of movement. It has a fine head for a horse of such a powerful build, and combines stamina and endurance with considerable freedom of movement. This is a popular breed, particularly in the United States and in Britain.

Poitevin

size:	*16–17 h.h. (160–170 cm)*
main colors:	*usually dun, although some bays & browns occur*
characteristic:	*poor conformation*
uses:	*breeding mules*

The Poitevin derives from horses imported from several countries, including the Netherlands and Denmark, and was originally used for work on the marshlands of the Poitou region, for which its large feet made it extremely suitable. However, its chief use today is in the production of mules, which are obtained by mating jack asses with the best of the Poitevin mares. The Poitevin is considered to be a poor equine specimen, combining many conformational defects with very limited mental capacity. Its head is heavy, its neck short and straight, its shoulders straight, its back long, and its hindquarters sloping.

Selle Français

size:	*15.2–16.3 h.h. (155–167 cm)*
main colors:	*predominantly chestnut, although all solid colors may be found*
characteristic:	*good jumping ability*
uses:	*riding*

The name Selle Français (French Saddle Horse) dates only from 1965, although the stud book for the breed is a continuation of the Anglo-Norman stud book: in the nineteenth century, Norman breeders used Thoroughbred and half-bred stallions from England to cross with their useful—but common—Norman stock. More recent infusions of Thoroughbred, French Trotter, and Arabian blood have resulted in the good-quality Selle Français. This is a strong horse of good conformation and temperament, which is well suited to competitive sports such as show jumping and eventing.

Trait du Nord

size:	*16–17 h.h. (160–170 cm)*
main colors:	*gray & black*
characteristic:	*hardiness*
uses:	*draft work*

A horse of fairly recent origin (a stud book was first opened in 1919 after the breed had been fixed at the beginning of the twentieth century), the Trait du Nord comes from the same part of France as the Ardennais (see page 52) and contains Ardennais, Belgian, and Dutch blood. A powerful but gentle draft horse and—like the Ardennais—exceptionally hardy, it is in fact a bigger, heavier version of that breed. It has a large head set on a huge neck, and a strong, muscular body and hindquarters.

Germany

Bavarian Warmblood

size:	16 h.h. (160 cm)
main colors:	chestnut
characteristic:	calmness
uses:	riding

Although not the best known of the German Warmbloods, the Bavarian is probably the oldest, as its origins can be traced back to before the time of the Crusades. Until recently the breed was known as the Rottaler because it originated in the Rott Valley of Bavaria, a region noted for horse-raising, and as a war horse it was considered the equal of the Friesian. Various types of British blood—including Cleveland Bay and Thoroughbred—were introduced during the eighteenth century, and Norman and Oldenburg horses (see below) have also influenced the breed. Today it is a heavyweight riding horse with a steady, reliable temperament.

Hanoverian

size:	16–17 h.h. (160–170 cm)
main colors:	all solid colors
characteristic:	correct movement & strength
uses:	riding

The foremost German Warmblood, the Hanoverian traces back to the seventeenth century when Spanish, oriental, and Neapolitan stallions were imported into Germany and crossed with local mares. Members of the House of Hanover promoted the breed and in 1735 George II of England opened the Celle Stud, at which 14 black Holstein stallions were installed. For a time Thoroughbred blood was used to produce horses of better quality; and since the mid-1940s, the aim has been to produce good competition horses, so Trakehner (see page 57) and additional Thoroughbred blood have been used to upgrade the breed.

Today, strictly selective breeding produces Hanoverians of exceptional strength with notably correct movement. This is a big, strong, upstanding horse, of good conformation. Active and bold, it is in great demand both for show jumping and dressage. The Westphalian is another (regional) name for the Hanoverian.

Holsteiner

size:	16–17 h.h. (160–170 cm)
main colors:	black, brown, & bay
characteristic:	bold jumping style
uses:	riding

The Holsteiner is a heavier stamp of riding horse than the Hanoverian, and the modern breed is based on horses that lived in the marshes surrounding the river Elbe in the fourteenth century. The introduction of Spanish and eastern blood made it lighter in build, and in the nineteenth century Yorkshire Coach Horses and English Thoroughbreds were imported into Germany to upgrade the breed and produce stock suitable for light harness and saddle work.

Additional Thoroughbred blood has been introduced since World War II and the modern Holsteiner is a good all-rounder, being particularly noted as a show jumper. It is powerfully built, with strong quarters, a good depth of girth, and short legs with plenty of bone. It is a good-tempered, intelligent, and willing horse.

Oldenburg

size:	*16.2–17.2 h.h. (165–175 cm)*
main colors:	*all solid colors*
characteristic:	*early age of maturing*
uses:	*riding & driving*

This is the heaviest of the German Warmbloods and may be traced back to the seventeenth-century Oldenburg, when the latter was based on the Friesian. The breed was originally developed as a good, strong carriage horse. Over the years Spanish, Neapolitan, and Barb blood were introduced, followed at a later stage by Thoroughbred, Cleveland Bay, Norman, and Hanoverian blood.

When the need for carriage horses dwindled during the twentieth century, additional Thoroughbred and Norman blood was introduced, resulting in the production of an all-purpose saddle horse. The Oldenburg is a short-legged horse with plenty of bone, a strong back, and a good depth of girth. The breed is ideally suited for dressage and driving, and has a kind, yet bold nature.

Trakehner

size:	*16 –17.2 h.h. (160–175 cm)*
main colors:	*all solid colors*
characteristic:	*excellent conformation*
uses:	*riding*

King Friedrich Wilhelm I founded the Trakehnen Stud in 1732, and it was here that the East Prussian Horse—known today as the Trakehner—was developed. At the beginning of the nineteenth century, Arab and Thoroughbred blood was introduced and by the early twentieth century over 80 percent of the stud's mares were by Thoroughbred stallions. The East Prussian horse made an excellent cavalry remount and was renowned for its great endurance. At the end of World War II, when the Germans retreated from Poland, some 1,200 of the 25,000 horses registered in the Trakehner Stud Book reached West Germany after a three-month trek from

East Prussia (now part of Poland, where the breed's influence is still to be found in the Wielkopolski).

Today, selective breeding has ensured that the Trakehner is a top-class saddle horse, with extremely good conformation; members of the breed are particularly renowned for their excellence in dressage and show jumping.

Württemberg

size:	*16 h.h. (160 cm)*
main colors:	*black, brown, chestnut, & bay*
characteristic:	*excellent action*
uses:	*riding & harness work*

The Württemberg traces back to the end of the sixteenth century, and was developed by putting local mares to Arab stallions from the German state-owned stud farms at Marbach. In order to produce the type of horse needed for working the small mountain farms of the Württemberg area, East Prussian and Norman blood was later introduced, followed by infusions of Oldenburg and Nonius. A stud book was not opened until 1895, when the required type had eventually been achieved—largely through the influence of the Anglo-Norman stallion named Faust.

In recent years, still more East Prussian blood has been introduced, and the present-day Württemberg is a strong, "cobby" type, suitable for work both in harness and under saddle. It is a strongly built horse, and is noted both for its sound legs and feet, and for the fact that it is highly economical to feed.

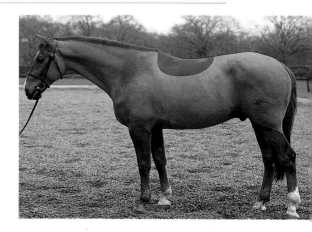

Hungary

Furioso

size:	16 h.h. (160 cm)
main colors:	black & brown
characteristic:	versatility
uses:	riding & driving

This is a handsome saddle or carriage horse based on two English foundation sires—the Thoroughbred Furioso (foaled in 1836), and the Norfolk Roadster North Star (foaled in 1844)—which were mated with the local mares of Nonius type. Originally developed at the

Mezöhegyes Stud, Hungary, infusions of Thoroughbred blood continued to be used to upgrade the breed. The result is a horse of sufficient quality to take part in all equestrian sports—including steeplechasing—at European level; it also goes well in harness. The Furioso is a horse of reasonably good conformation, with a free, slightly exaggerated action.

Murakoz

size:	16 h.h. (160 cm)
main colors:	usually chestnut with flaxen mane & tail, although bays, browns, grays, & blacks do occur
characteristic:	fast movement
uses:	light agricultural work

A draft horse bred in the river Mura region of Hungary (and also in Poland and the former Yugoslavia), this breed has been developed during the twentieth century by crossing native mares with Percheron, Belgian Ardennes, and Noriker stallions, as well as with home-bred horses.

In the 1920s, as many as 20 percent of all horses in Hungary were Murakoz, but the breed suffered many losses during World War II and it has never succeeded in regaining the strength of its former numbers.

The Murakoz is a fast-moving horse of some quality and is also a good agricultural worker. It is noted, too, for being good-tempered, reliably sound and an economical feeder.

Nonius

size:	15.3–16.2 h.h. (157–165 cm)
main colors:	bay & brown
characteristic:	good all-rounder
uses:	riding and driving

The precursor of the Furioso, the Nonius was also developed at the Mezöhegyes Stud in Hungary. The foundation sire is said to have been a French stallion called Nonius (foaled in 1810), itself the result of a mating between an English half-bred stallion and a Norman mare. Nonius was captured during the Napoleonic wars and taken to Hungary, where he sired 15 outstanding stallions from a variety of mares, including Arabian, Holsteiner, Lipizzaner, and Anglo-Norman.

This breed makes a good riding or carriage horse of medium to heavy weight, and has an equable temperament. It is a late developer and is, consequently, a horse of some longevity. It is tough and compact in build, and is used in competitive sports as well as for light agricultural work.

Shagya Arabian

size:	*15 h.h. (150 cm)*
main colors:	*often gray, but all solid colors may be found*
characteristic:	*notably correct hind legs*
uses:	*ridden, harness*

A product of the great Hungarian studs, the Shagya Arabian was originally bred as a riding horse for the light cavalry of Hungary. The modern Shagya is equally practical, performing well in harness and under saddle. The breed takes its name from a Syrian horse called Shagya, who was imported to the Babolna Stud in Hungary along with several other Arabs in 1836 for restocking purposes, and became a prepotent sire.

The breed possesses the usual Arabian characteristics and temperament, but is bigger and has more substance and bone than many modern Arabs. The Shagya has pronounced withers, a more sloping shoulder, and notably correct hind legs.

Austria

Lipizzaner

size:	*15 h.h. (150 cm)*
main colors:	*often gray, but all solid colors may be found*
characteristic:	*notably correct hind legs*
uses:	*ridden, harness*

This breed is noted for its docility and intelligence, and has become world-famous for its connection with the Spanish Riding School of Vienna (see page 19). The modern Lipizzaner traces back to the Spanish Andalusian horses imported into Yugoslavia by the Archduke Charles, who founded a stud at Lipizza in 1580; later, other blood was introduced—notably that of the Arabian stallion, Siglavy. Today Lipizzaners are bred at the famous Piber Stud in Austria—which supplies the Spanish Riding School—and extensively in Hungary, Romania, Slovakia, and Slovenia.

The Lipizzaner is a compact horse, with a strong back and quarters and short, strong legs. Many foals are born black or brown and can take up to 10 years to acquire their distinctive gray coats. Lipizzaners mature slowly, with many High School horses performing difficult movements in their twenties; they also make excellent carriage horses.

Noriker

size:	*15 h.h. (150 cm)*
main colors:	*often gray, but all solid colors may be found*
characteristic:	*notably correct hind legs*
uses:	*ridden, harness*

The Noriker, or South German Coldblood, takes its name from the state of Noricum, which formed part of the Roman Empire and in outline corresponded approximately to modern Austria. The Noriker is probably descended from the tough ponies of the Hafling district of Austria, but owes its present size to later infusions of Neapolitan, Burgundian, and Spanish blood. The term Noriker now includes the Pinzgauer, a spotted horse which was formerly designated a separate breed.

The present-day Noriker is a sure-footed draft horse of equable temperament, with a broad chest, a heavy head set on a short, thick neck, good feet, and clean legs. This hardy and economical breed is found throughout Germany and Austria; it is well suited to working in mountainous regions, and careful selection of stallions ensures that the standard of the breed is maintained and improved.

Bulgaria

Pleven

size:	15.2 h.h. (155 cm)
main colors:	chestnut
characteristic:	versatility
uses:	riding & light agricultural work

This breed is of comparatively recent origin. It was developed at the state-owned Dimitrov farm near Pleven, and resulted from the crossing of Russian Anglo-Arabs with local Arab and cross-bred horses; Hungarian Arab blood of the Gidran type was added in the early part of the twentieth century. The breed was deemed fixed in 1938, although since that time some carefully selected English Thoroughbred blood has been introduced.

The Pleven has an "Araby" appearance and makes a bold, spirited ride. It is a dual-purpose animal and is used both for light agricultural work and for riding. Its natural jumping ability makes it a good competitive horse.

Slovakia

Kladruber

size:	16.2–17 h.h. (165–170 cm)
main colors:	gray, black
characteristic:	strength
uses:	harness

The big, upstanding Kladruber is similar in appearance to the Andalusian, with the same convex face shape. The Emperor Maximilian II founded a stud at Kladruby in Bohemia in 1572, using Spanish foundation stock. The horses that were bred there became known as Kladrubers and were used for drawing the imperial carriages. Much inbreeding took place, although infusions of Neapolitan blood were also made from time to time, but it was not until the 1920s that the first successful cross—with a Shagya Arabian—was made.

Since that time the Kladruber—which originally stood at around 18 h.h. (180 cm)—has become smaller and more active, and, although it is still a harness horse, it is also used to produce cross-bred riding horses. Only gray and black Kladrubers have been bred since the early nineteenth century, and today the Kladruby Stud solely produces grays, the black horses being kept at a nearby stud.

Switzerland

Einsiedler

size:	15.3–16.2 h.h. (157–165 cm)
main colors:	all solid colors, although chestnut & bay are most common
characteristic:	good all-rounder
uses:	riding & driving

Also sometimes known as the Swiss Anglo-Norman, this is a dual-purpose horse closely related to the Anglo-Norman. Its name derives from the stud of Kloster Einsiedel. The Einsiedler is a versatile horse, of good temperament. Its active and true paces make it a good all-rounder for riding and driving, and it was particularly noted as a cavalry mount. The conformation is usually good, with plenty of depth through the girth, powerful quarters, and strong legs.

Franches-Montagne

size:	*15 h.h. (150 cm)*
main colors:	*all solid colors*
characteristic:	*good temperament*
uses:	*light draft work*

This small draft horse came originally from the Jura region of Switzerland, when Anglo-Norman stallions were imported and crossed with local mares in the nineteenth century. There may also have been some infusions of English half-bred hunter and Ardennes blood during the early days of the Franches-Montagne but, since that time, the breed has remained remarkably pure.

Being small, active and sure-footed, this horse is ideally suited to working on the hill farms of the region and is a popular and versatile agricultural horse. It is a heavily-built cob-type with a powerful body set on short, strong legs, and invariably possesses a good temperament.

Freiberger

size:	*15.2–16 h.h. (155–160 cm)*
main colors:	*all solid colors*
characteristic:	*stamina*
uses:	*harness*

The Freiberger is a mountain-bred horse that has been developed in the Jura region of western Switzerland. The Freiberger has a strong Norman background with many of the breed tracing back to Valliant, born 1891, who was a great grandson of Leo I, a half-bred German hunter. Valliant's granddam on both sides were of Thoroughbred/Anglo-Norman stock.

The Freiberger is an attractive riding horse with an Arabian-looking head, good shoulders and hindquarters, a short back, a deep girth, and strong legs with plenty of bone. It is an active, intelligent horse and is renowned for its great powers of endurance.

Poland

Malapolski

size:	*15 h.h. (150 cm)*
main colors:	*all solid colors*
characteristic:	*soundness*
uses:	*riding*

A recently developed breed containing a good deal of oriental blood, the Malapolski is similar to the Wielkopolski, but lighter. It is bred mainly in the south-west of Poland and has similar regional variations to the Wielkopolski. The Malapolski is a quality riding horse that averages 15 h.h. (150 cm), although the Sadecki—which may be bigger—is capable of undertaking light draft work. It is an exceptionally sound horse, with great stamina and an equable temperament.

Wielkopolski

size:	16 h.h. (160 cm)
main colors:	all solid colors
characteristic:	good paces
uses:	riding & driving

Wielkopolski is a composite name for what were formerly two separate breeds, the Poznan and the Masuren. The Poznan contained Arabian, Hanoverian, and Thoroughbred blood, while the Masuren was based on the Trakehner. Although all the Polish Warmbloods are now known as Wielkopolskis, those bred in certain areas are still regarded as being of specific types.

The Wielkopolski is a good quality riding horse, of sound constitution and sensible temperament; it can also be used in harness. Members of the breed are noted for their paces: long, easy walk, a low, level trot, and a ground-covering canter and gallop.

Italy

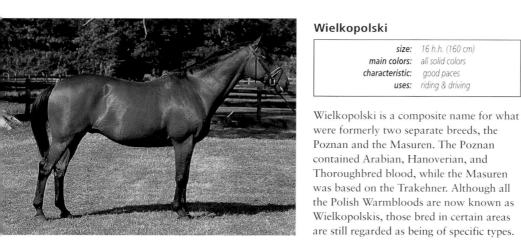

Italian Heavy Draft

size:	15–16 h.h. (150–160 cm)
main colors:	often a striking dark liver chestnut with flaxen mane & tail, although other colors—notably roan & chestnut—do occur
characteristic:	strong quarters
uses:	meat and draft work

A medium-sized draft horse with a Breton ancestry, the Italian Heavy Draft used to be a popular agricultural worker. Today, it is bred as much for meat—throughout central and northern Italy—and its numbers are decreasing. This is an active animal, whose head is fine for so heavy a build and is set on a short neck. Other characteristics include a deep chest and girth, and a compact body; the feet tend to be boxy.

Maremmana

size:	15.3 h.h. (157 cm)
main colors:	all solid colors
characteristic:	hardiness
uses:	riding and agricultural work

A rather common heavy saddle or light draft horse, the Maremmana is indigenous to Italy. Its chief uses are as a mount for the Italian mounted police and for Italian cattle herdsmen, the *butteri*. It is a hardy horse and an economical feeder, and, being a good steady worker, makes a useful farm horse.

Murgese

size:	*15–16 h.h. (150–160 cm)*
main colors:	*usually chestnut*
characteristic:	*versatility*
uses:	*riding & light agricultural work*

The modern Murgese horse, which takes its name from the famous horse-breeding region of Murge near Puglia, dates from the 1920s, the old breed having died out 200 years ago. It is a light draft or riding horse in which oriental blood is obviously present, although this cannot be positively identified. The breed has active movement despite its short stride. When Murgese mares are put to Thoroughbred and Arab stallions, they produce a good stamp of riding horse.

Salerno

size:	*16 h.h. (160 cm)*
main colors:	*all solid colors*
characteristic:	*jumping ability*
uses:	*riding*

A good saddle horse bred in the Maremma and Salerno districts, this breed was formerly the favorite mount of the Italian cavalry. It is one of the most attractive of the Italian Warmbloods, although today its numbers have greatly decreased. The Salerno is a sensible horse possessed of intelligence and good jumping ability and,

although there is now less demand for it as a cavalry mount, it makes a good, all-round riding horse. The breed traces back to the Neapolitan and is a horse of very good conformation.

The Netherlands

Dutch Draft

size:	*16.3 h.h. (167 cm)*
main colors:	*chestnut, bay, and gray*
characteristic:	*stamina*
uses:	*draft work*

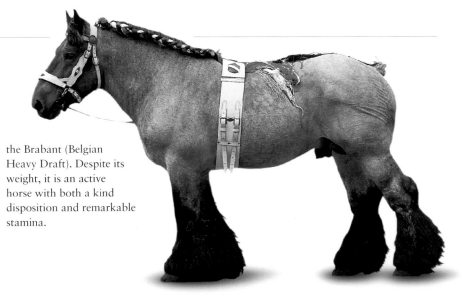

This heavy draft horse has been developed since the First World War specifically as a suitable horse for working on the sand and clay lands of agricultural Holland. Zealand-type mares were chosen and crossed with Brabant (Belgian Heavy Draft) stallions, and later with Belgian Ardennes; the resultant Dutch Draft is a massively built horse that closely resembles the Brabant (Belgian Heavy Draft). Despite its weight, it is an active horse with both a kind disposition and remarkable stamina.

Friesian

size:	15.3 h.h. (150 cm)
main colors:	always black, with no white markings
characteristic:	pleasant nature
uses:	harness work

The Friesian is one of Europe's oldest breeds and takes its name from Friesland, where a heavy horse existed as far back as 1000 B.C. Throughout the seventeenth century, the Friesian was popular as a weight-carrying saddle horse, but the popularity of trotting races in the nineteenth century—coupled with the Friesian's trotting prowess—led to the production of a lighter, faster horse that was less suited to the agricultural work hitherto required of it.

The breed went into something of a decline as a result of this change, although a breeding plan was subsequently adopted and—with the aid of imported Oldenburg stallions—it was revived and is now flourishing. The Friesian is an excellent horse, both attractive and sweet-natured, and its willingness and active paces make it an ideal all-round working horse. Small in stature, it is both compact and muscular, with a fine head, a strong body, short legs with some feathering on the heels, and hard feet.

Gelderland

size:	15.2–16.2 h.h. (155–165 cm)
main colors:	chestnut
characteristic:	versatility
uses:	riding, harness work, & light draft work

Along with the Groningen, the Gelderland is the principal component in the makeup of the Dutch Warmblood. This popular horse traces back to the last century, when a variety of imported stallions—notably Norfolk Roadsters and Arabians—were mated with native mares in the Gelderland province to produce an upstanding carriage horse. Later, East Friesian, Oldenburg, and Hackney blood was added, and in this century infusions of Anglo-Norman blood have also played their part.

The modern Gelderland is a strong, active sort. As well as being a first-class carriage horse, with its great presence and eye-catching action, it is a useful heavyweight riding horse with some jumping ability.

Groningen

size:	15.2–16.2 h.h. (155–165 cm)
main colors:	bay & brown
characteristic:	good bone
uses:	light draft work

Similar in appearance to the Oldenburg from which it derives, the Groningen—together with the Gelderlander—provides the base stock for the evolution of the Dutch Warmblood. Crossing the original Groningen, now rarely seen in its early form, with Friesians, East Friesians, and Oldenburgs, has produced an attractive carriage horse with a great depth of girth, powerful quarters, and shoulders set on short, strong legs. An economical feeder, the Groningen is a horse of sound constitution and equable temperament.

Belgium

Belgian Ardennes

size:	15.3 h.h. (157 cm)
main colors:	bay, roan, & chestnut
characteristic:	kind nature
uses:	draft work

The modern Ardennes horse is thought to be the descendant of the draft horses praised by Julius Caesar in his *De Bello Gallico*, although it has in more recent times received infusions of Brabant (Belgian Heavy Draft) blood. This is a compact, heavily built horse, with a wide, deep chest, a big broad head, and a huge barrel carried on short, massively built legs. There is a pronounced crest to the neck and the legs carry a good deal of feathering. The Belgian Ardennes has an exceptionally gentle temperament and makes a willing draft horse, well suited to hilly country.

Brabant (Belgian Heavy Draft)

size:	16.2–17 h.h. (165–170 cm)
main colors:	roan & chestnut
characteristic:	notably deep barrel
uses:	draft work

Originally known as the Flanders horse, the Brabant—or Belgian Heavy Draft—horse is the product of several centuries of selective breeding. Today it is a handsome, powerful horse, with a short back, a deep girth, and short legs with a good deal of feathering. The head is square in shape, and small in proportion to the body. A willing, good-tempered draft horse, with a notably active walk, the Brabant has exerted a tremendous influence on other European heavy horses and is particularly popular in the United States.

Norway

Døle Gudbrandsdal

size:	14.2–15.2 h.h. (145–155 cm)
main colors:	black & brown
characteristic:	power
uses:	light draft & harness work

The Døle Gudbrandsdal makes up nearly 50 percent of the Norwegian horse population, and has some resemblance to the British Dales and Fell ponies (see pages 83 and 84). Bred in the Gudbrandsdal valley in Norway, members of the breed were used as pack animals and for light agricultural work, and are noted for their speed at trot. The Gudbrandsdal is a hardy horse, and powerful in relation to its size.

A somewhat lighter offshoot of the breed—called the Døle Trotter—was also developed for harness racing; the Thoroughbred stallion, Odin, imported from Britain in 1834, had significant influence on this type.

Sweden

North Swedish

size:	*15.3 h.h. (157 cm)*
main colors:	*all solid colors*
characteristic:	*apparent immunity to most common equine diseases*
uses:	*light draft work*

Closely related to Norway's Døle Gudbrandsdal, the North Swedish is a small, compact and active draft horse. It is a powerful animal with a large head set on a short neck, and a long, deep body. Its legs are short and strong with plenty of bone, and it has a good, lively, long-striding action.

The North Swedish is long-lived and has a kind temperament. It is exceptionally resistant to equine disease, and this quality—coupled with the fact that it is an economical feeder—make the breed a popular choice for farm and forestry work. The main stud is at Wangen and, since the beginning of this century, stringent performance testing has been in force.

Swedish Ardennes

size:	*15.2–16 h.h. (155–160 cm)*
main colors:	*black, bay, chestnut, & brown*
characteristic:	*energetic paces*
uses:	*draft work*

This heavy draft horse was bred from imported Belgian Ardennes horses crossed with the North Swedish horse, after the first Belgian Ardennes had been introduced into Sweden approximately 100 years ago. A fixed type was quickly developed, with the Ardennes becoming the dominating influence. The breed's numbers have declined over the years, but it remains a popular horse, both in its country of origin and in those countries to which it has been imported since.

The Swedish Ardennes is a good-natured horse and is quiet to handle although energetic in its paces. It has a crested neck, and a deep and muscular body, which is set on short, strong legs carrying little feathering.

Swedish Warmblood

size:	*max 16.2 h.h. (165 cm)*
main colors:	*all solid colors*
characteristic:	*good conformation*
uses:	*riding*

The Swedish Warmblood is a saddle horse of some quality, and represents the result of selective breeding going back some 300 years. In the early years, Spanish, Friesian, and oriental blood was imported, and more recently infusions of Thoroughbred, Arab, Hanoverian, and Trakehner have been added. This is a strong, sound, riding horse of good temperament. It is a big, imposing horse of good conformation, with plenty of depth through the girth and short strong legs. It makes a good competition horse and has a particular aptitude for dressage.

Denmark

Frederiksborg

size:	15.3 h.h. (157 cm)
main colors:	chestnut
characteristic:	high carriage action
uses:	riding & light draft work

King Frederik II set up the Royal Frederiksborg Stud in 1562, stocking it with Andalusian horses imported from Spain. Later, Neapolitan, Eastern, and British blood was added and the Frederiksborg was developed. This elegant saddle horse became renowned as a military charger and was also used in light harness. Although King Frederik II's stud closed in 1839, private breeders kept the

Frederiksborg in existence, and today it is found all over Denmark.

This is a strong active horse and has retained a high carriage action, and its good temperament makes it a useful working as well as a riding horse. It has a particularly powerful chest and shoulders, as well as good limbs with plenty of bone. The face is often convex in outline, showing it to be a horse of Spanish origin.

Jutland

size:	15.2–16 h.h. (155–160 cm)
main colors:	predominantly chestnut, although roan, bay, & black are also seen
characteristic:	willingness to work
uses:	draft work

The Jutland horse takes its name from the island of Jutland, and has existed for some 1,000 years; in the Middle Ages it was used to carry heavily armored knights into battle. The modern breed—greatly influenced by a Suffolk stallion called Oppenheim LXII, who was exported from Britain to Denmark in 1860—is a heavy

draft horse of massive proportions. It has a great depth of chest and girth, and short, feathered legs, but in spite of its enormous strength the Jutland is gentle, co-operative and easy to handle when working. Although numbers of the breed have declined, it can still be seen hauling brewers' drays.

Knabstrup

size:	15.2 h.h. (155 cm)
main colors:	spotted
characteristic:	intelligence
uses:	riding

The Knabstrup traces back to a spotted mare called Flaebehoppen which, in 1808 was put to a Frederiksborg stallion and founded a line of spotted, more lightly built horses.

The original Knabstrups were raw-boned horses, although intelligent and quick to learn, but they deteriorated as a result of injudicious breeding for color—

rather than conformation—and are now rarely found. The modern type of Knabstrup—which is closer in character to the Appaloosa—is a quality animal of some substance, and with a greater range of colors than the earlier breed.

Finland

Finnish

size:	15.2 h.h. (155 cm)
main colors:	chestnut, bay, brown, & black
characteristic:	longevity
uses:	light draft work & riding

The Finnish is the only officially recognized equine breed in Finland. It is descended from two closely related breeds, the Finnish Draft and the Finnish Universal: these two breeds contain a mixture of many Warm- and Coldblood types that were imported into Finland and crossed with the country's native ponies.

The present-day Finnish horse is a good all-rounder, being used as a draft horse as well as under saddle and excelling at such diverse occupations as timber-hauling and trotting races. The breed has strong shoulders, clean legs with little feathering, and uniformly correct limbs with good bone; it has great stamina and is long-lived.

Spain

Andalusian

size:	15.2 h.h. (155 cm)
main colors:	usually gray or bay
characteristic:	long, often wavy, mane & tail
uses:	riding

This famous long-established breed traces back at least to the Moorish occupation of Spain, when Barb horses from north Africa were introduced to the Iberian peninsula. The horse that resulted from this mingling of the invaders' Barbs with the indigenous stock was to become the foremost horse of Europe, remaining as such until the eighteenth century. The Andalusian also exerted a great influence on other European breeds—most notably the Lipizzaner.

Córdoba was an early center of organized breeding and is still one of the principal centers, together with Seville and Jerez. The Andalusian is an active horse of enormous presence, combining agility and athleticism with a gentle, docile temperament. It has a characteristic hawk-like profile, a luxuriant mane and tail—which is often wavy—and a spectacular, high-stepping action.

Hispano (Spanish Anglo-Arab)

size:	16 h.h. (160 cm)
main colors:	usually bay, chestnut, or gray
characteristic:	amenable temperament
uses:	riding

The Hispano, or Spanish Anglo-Arab, is the result of putting Spanish Arab mares to English Thoroughbreds; such a cross produces an attractive saddle horse with more highly pronounced Arabian characteristics than the average Anglo-Arab. The breed's attributes of intelligence, great courage, and agility have made it a popular competition horse, and it is also used as a mount in the *acoso y derribo* contests, in which riders test the fighting bulls by bringing them down with a thrust from a long pole. Despite being a spirited animal, the Hispano has a pleasantly tractable disposition.

Portugal

Alter-Real

size:	*15–16 h.h. (150–160 cm)*
main colors:	*usually bay, brown, or gray*
characteristic:	*high, showy action*
uses:	*riding*

This horse is based on the Andalusian, and is very similar to it in appearance. It originated in the mid-eighteenth century at the Vila de Portel Stud in Portugal's Alentejo province, which imported some 300 mares from the Jerez region of Spain. The breed flourished until the Napoleonic invasion of 1821, when the stud was

sacked by the French invaders and the stock was dispersed.

In subsequent years, the remaining Alter-Reals were crossed with an assortment of horses ranging from Arabians to Hanoverians, but at the beginning of the twentieth century steps were taken to reintroduce Andalusian blood and to re-establish the former type. In spite of its history, the Alter-Real has survived all these vicissitudes. It is a compact horse and, with its extravagant, high, showy action, is especially suited to High School work.

Lusitano

size:	*15–16 h.h. (150–160 cm)*
main colors:	*predominantly gray*
characteristic:	*elevated action*
uses:	*riding and harness work*

A Portuguese version of the Andalusian, the Lusitano is a handsome, compact horse with an alert expression and a wavy mane and tail.

A highly intelligent, agile animal of great courage, it was formerly in demand as a cavalry horse and is today much prized in the bull ring. The Portuguese

mounted bullfighters—known as *rejoneadores*—require highly schooled, athletic mounts, since the entire fight is carried out on horseback. The Lusitano breed is also popular both in Britain and in the United States.

North America   United States

American Quarter Horse

size:	*15–16 h.h. (150–160 cm)*
main colors:	*all solid colors*
characteristic:	*powerful quarters*
uses:	*riding*

The American Quarter Horse was developed by early English colonists in Virginia and the Carolinas, and is the result of crossing mares of Spanish descent with imported English stallions. The breed was used as a riding and harness horse—taking its name from the quarter-mile sprints at which it was so adept—and was also used as a cow pony, developing a remarkable

instinct for herding and cutting out cattle (separating individuals from the herd).

The future of the American Quarter Horse breed now seems assured, with over 3,000,000 individuals registered with the American Quarter Horse Association. This is an intelligent, agile, and compact horse with good conformation, including strong shoulders, a short, muscular back, and massive hindquarters.

American Saddlebred

size:	*15–16 h.h. (150–160 cm)*
main colors:	*chestnut, bay, brown, & black*
characteristic:	*elevated action*
uses:	*riding and harness work*

An elegant saddle horse, originally known as the Kentucky Saddler, this breed was developed as a riding horse by the Kentucky plantation owners of the nineteenth century. The breed was developed from the English Thoroughbred and the Old English Ambler (and old Narragansett Pacer blood). Selective breeding has produced a showy horse with easy gait and great stamina. A horse that performs the walk, trot, and canter with a high, elevated action is described as three-gaited; gaits exhibited by a five-gaited horse also include the four-beat prancing slow gait and the full-speed rack. This gait achieves speeds of up to 38 mph, involving total smoothness for the rider. The American Saddlebred has a small, elegant head set on a long, muscular neck, and a strong back, shoulders, and quarters. Although the breed is mainly seen in the show ring, is also used for pleasure riding.

American Standardbred

size:	*15.2–16 h.h. (155–160 cm)*
main colors:	*bay, brown, black, & chestnut*
characteristic:	*toughness and courage*
uses:	*harness work*

One of the world's finest harness racehorses, the Standardbred traces back to an imported English Thoroughbred called Messenger (a descendant of The Darley Arabian—see page 38), who was crossed with the Narragansett Pacer. The resulting offspring possessed a marked trotting ability, and it was one of Messenger's descendants—the prepotent Hambletonian 10—who was responsible for Messenger being designated the breed's foundation sire; Hambletonian himself sired 1,335 offspring between 1851 and 1875.

The term Standardbred derives from the time standard, which was adopted to test the ability of harness racers before they were admitted into the American Trotter Register. The Standardbred can cover 1 mile (1.6 km) in 1 minute 55 seconds. It is courageous and tough with a longish body, a great depth of girth, and powerful hindquarters. The legs are fairly short and strong, and the action is free and straight. Standardbreds either trot or pace, employing the lateral, swaying gait (see also pages 172–3).

Appaloosa

size:	*15.2 h.h. (155 cm)*
main colors:	*spotted*
characteristic:	*stamina*
uses:	*riding*

Bred by the Nez Perce Indians in the Palous Valley of northwest United States, the Appaloosa is descended from horses taken to South America by the Spanish conquistadors during the sixteenth century. It is noted for its spotted coat, which may be an all-over spotted pattern consisting of dark spots on a white background (leopard); light spots on a dark background (snowflake); or spots only on the loins and hindquarters (spotted blanket). Other variations include marble (red or blue roan with dark colorings on the edges of the body and a frost pattern in the middle), and frost (white speckling on a dark background).

The usual ground color of the Appaloosa is roan. The skin of the nose, lips, and genitals is mottled, and the sclera (the membrane around the iris of the eye) is white. The feet are often vertically striped, and the mane and tail are sparse. The Appaloosa is agile and tractable; it has powerful quarters and is known for its speed and stamina.

Missouri Fox Trotter

size:	14.2 -15.2 h.h. (145-155cm)
main colors:	all solid colors
characteristic:	Fox Trot gait
uses:	riding

The Missouri Fox Trotter is descended from Thoroughbred, Arabian, and Morgan horses. Selective inbreeding produced a saddle horse with a peculiar broken gait known as the "fox-trot," from which the breed takes its name.

The horse walks briskly with its forefeet and trots with its hind feet, and can achieve speeds of up to 10 mph (16 km per hour). The gait is a comfortable one, and the Fox Trotter was originally used as an all-purpose mount in the hill country of Missouri and Arkansas.

This is a strong, compact horse with an attractive head, a short strong back, and plenty of depth through the girth. It is used as an all-round pleasure and show horse, and is usually ridden in western tack (see page 138).

Morgan

size:	15.2 h.h. (155 cm)
main colors:	bay, chestnut, brown, & black
characteristic:	stamina
uses:	riding and driving

Possessing great physical strength, the Morgan descends from one prepotent stallion called Justin Morgan. Named after his second owner, who acquired him in 1795, Justin Morgan is thought to have been of Thoroughbred and Arabian extraction, although it is possible that he also had some Welsh blood. He was a horse of quite incredible endurance, used as a farm horse, in harness, and for timber hauling, and, although he stood only 14 h.h. (140 cm), he excelled in weight-pulling contests.

The Morgan makes an ideal all-round pleasure horse and, with its good conformation, strong shoulders, short strong legs, hard feet, and attractive head set on a muscular, crested neck, is shown both under saddle and in harness. It is active and versatile, and has great powers of endurance.

Mustang

size:	13.2–15 h.h. (135–150 cm)
main colors:	all solid colors
characteristic:	hardiness
uses:	feral

The Mustang is a scrub type of horse, and is descended from the sixteenth-century horses of the Spanish conquistadors. As these wild herds increased in number, so they spread through many states and became favorite mounts for the Indian tribes. They were also used by the first settlers to mate with their imported horses to provide the foundation stock for producing various subsequent breeds.

Formerly much used as cow ponies, Mustangs have now largely been replaced by better-quality animals; their numbers have declined as a result, although they are now protected by law. In type, the Mustang is a small, inelegant, lightweight horse. It is extremely hardy, and an economical feeder.

Tennessee Walking Horse

size:	*15–15.2 h.h. (150–155 cm)*
main colors:	*black, bay, & chestnut*
characteristic:	*bounce-free gaits*
uses:	*riding*

One of the most popular breeds in the United States, this horse was developed in the nineteenth century by plantation owners. The Walking Horse derives from the old Narragansett Pacer and Thoroughbred and American Saddlebred blood. The foundation sire of the breed was a Standardbred called Black Allan (foaled in 1886), whose peculiar four-beat gait was inherited by his progeny.

The Walking Horse has three bounce-free gaits: a flat walk, a running walk (which has four beats and in which the head nods in time to the movement), and the smooth, "rocking-chair" canter. The breed is said to be the most comfortable ride in the world because of its rapid, four-beat smooth gait. It is a naturally good-tempered horse with good conformation, powerful shoulders, and strong limbs.

Colorado Ranger

size:	*15.2 h.h (155 cm)*
main colors:	*most have a patterned coat*
characteristic:	*stamina*
uses:	*riding and harness work*

This breed takes it names from the state in which it was developed, although its evolution actually began in Virginia and Nebraska. An American General visiting the Sultan Abdul Hamid of Turkey in 1878 received a token of a two horses: Leopard, a pure Siglavy-Gidran Arab; and a Barb named Linden Tree. Originally used as the foundation sires for a breed of light harness horse, these two also sired stock from native mares in Nebraska. A.C. Whipple of Colorado later chose Tony, a white stallion with black ears, to head the herd.

The modern Ranger is the creation of Mike Ruby, who brought Patches (a son of Tony), and a Barb called Max (a son of

Waldron Leopard), and used them as foundation sires for the breed, which showed a lot of unusual coloring. These Rangers were bred as working horses, being tough and possessing great stamina. Today, this is still a very compact animal with powerful limbs and hindquarters.

Canada

Canadian Cutting Horse

size:	*15.2–16.1 h.h. (155–162 cm)*
main colors:	*all solid colors*
characteristic:	*intelligence*
uses:	*riding*

This is the Canadian equivalent of the American Quarter Horse, from which the breed was developed and which it closely resembles in appearance. It is a highly intelligent horse with an innate talent for working cattle, and its prowess as a cutting horse (i.e., for "cutting out," or separating, individual cattle from a herd) has led to its being highly developed for skilled competition work.

South America Peru

Peruvian Paso

size:	*14–15 h.h. (140–150 cm)*
main colors:	*principally bay & chestnut, although all solid colors may be found*
characteristic:	*natural gait (the Paso)*
uses:	*riding*

Also known as the Peruvian Stepping Horse, the Peruvian Paso shares a common ancestry with the Criollo. It has been systematically developed for its characteristic gait—the Paso—in which the forelegs display extravagant action and the hind legs are driven powerfully forward with the quarters lowered (to allow for this movement, the hind legs and hind pasterns are long, and the joints are unusually flexible). The gait can best be described as resembling the amble, and is a comfortable pace for the rider. Possessing great stamina, the Paso can achieve and maintain a steady speed of about 11 mph (18 km per hour) over the roughest of country.

Puerto Rico

Paso Fino

size:	*5 h.h. (150 cm)*
main colors:	*all solid colors*
characteristic:	*Paso gaits*
uses:	*riding*

The Paso Fino resembles the Andalusian, and is descended from the sixteenth-century Spanish horses taken to South America by the conquistadors. It is also bred in Peru and Colombia, and displays unusual gaits that have been perpetuated by selective breeding. These are the Paso fino, a collected, highly elevated, four-time gait; the Paso corto, a similar, but uncollected, four-time gait that is used for traveling long distances; and the Paso largo, an extended four-beat gait that can achieve speeds of up to 16 mph (25 km per hour). These four-time gaits—which are inherited instinctively and do not have to be taught—make the Paso Fino a comfortable ride. It is an intelligent horse of good temperament.

Asia Iran

Tchenarani

size:	*15 h.h. (150 cm)*
main colors:	*all solid colors*
characteristic:	*stamina*
uses:	*riding*

The Tchenarani—bred in the north of Iran, where it has been known for over 2,000 years—was originally produced by crossing Plateau stallions with Turkmene mares. This is still the favored cross, since stock tends to deteriorate if Tchenarani is mated to Tchenarani, and also if Turkmene stallions are mated with Plateau Persian mares. The different strains of Arabian-type horses that have for many centuries been bred on the plateaus of Iran—formerly Persia—are now collectively termed Plateau Persian, and today both the Darashomi and the Jaf also come under this blanket heading.

Popular for a long time as a cavalry mount, the Tchenarani is a wiry little saddle horse. In appearance, it is rather similar to the Arabian, and possesses much the same characteristic toughness and stamina as other horses from this part of the world.

Darashomi

size:	*15 h.h. (150 cm)*
main colors:	*gray, chestnut, brown, & bay*
characteristic:	*good temperament*
uses:	*riding*

The Darashomi—also known as the Slurazi—is a horse of uncertain origin, but its physical appearance suggests that it had oriental forebears. Bred in southern Iran, this is a spirited riding horse, with similar physical characteristics to the Arabian. It is noted for its good temperament.

Jaf

size:	*15 h.h. (150 cm)*
main colors:	*bay, brown, chestnut, & gray*
characteristic:	*stamina*
uses:	*riding*

Like the Darashomi, the Jaf is an oriental-looking saddle horse. It is bred in Kurdistan and has all the characteristics of the desert horse, being tough, wiry, and possessed of great stamina. It is particularly noted for its tough, hard feet. Although a spirited horse, it has a gentle disposition.

Turkoman

size:	*15.2 h.h. (155 cm)*
main colors:	*predominantly bay*
characteristic:	*floating action*
uses:	*racing and general riding*

Like the Tchenarani, the Turkoman is also a descendant of the ancient Turkmene and is bred in northern Iran, where it is prized as a racehorse and excels in long-distance races. The Turkoman is an oriental-looking horse of some distinction. It is slow to mature and has great speed and endurance.

Turkey

Karacabey

size:	*16 h.h. (160 cm)*
main colors:	*all solid colors*
characteristic:	*versatility*
uses:	*light draft work and riding*

This dual-purpose horse originated at the Karacabey Stud, which was in existence long before it was brought under the control of the Turkish Government in recent times. The breed was based on local mares that were mated to imported Nonius stallions, and the modern Karacabey still shows its Nonius ancestry. It is a highly versatile horse, strong enough to undertake light farm and draft work as well as making a good saddle horse. Noted also as being a good cavalry mount, it has a calm temperament and is a willing worker.

Australasia Australia

Waler

size:	*16 h.h. (160 cm)*
main colors:	*all solid colors*
characteristic:	*willing nature*
uses:	*all-purpose riding horse*

This breed is named after its place of origin, New South Wales, which in the early days of settlement was the name given to all newly inhabited areas of Australia. Horses were not indigenous to the continent, and the first individuals were imported by European settlers in the late eighteenth century. These initially came from South Africa and subsequently from Europe, with the English Thoroughbred and the Arabian being much in demand by Australian breeders.

The Waler is the result of crossing hack mares with Arabian, Thoroughbred, and Anglo-Arab stallions, and the best specimens have many of the characteristics of the Thoroughbred. Members of this

breed have an equable disposition and make good, general-purpose mounts.

The CIS

Akhal-Teké

size:	*15.2 h.h. (155 cm)*
main colors:	*"metallic" golden dun*
characteristic:	*endurance*
uses:	*riding*

The Akhal-Teké is a strain of the ancient Turkmene or Turkoman horse; it traces back over 2,500 years and is bred around the oases of the Karakum Desert. This horse is noted for its outstanding powers of endurance: Akhal-Tekés took part in the trek from Ashkabad to Moscow in 1935, a distance of 2,580 miles (4,152 km) that included 225 miles (360 km) of desert and was completed in 84 days on minimal rations of feed and water.

The Akhal-Teké is a distinctive, wiry horse that has a long, thin neck set very high and carried almost vertically to the body. The body is long and narrow, and the legs long and slender with joints set high off the ground. The mane and tail are sparse and fine in texture. Members of the breed are popular long-distance performers, but they are also used for competing in dressage, show jumping, and racing.

Budenny

size:	*16 h.h. (160 cm)*
main colors:	*all solid colors, especially chestnut*
characteristic:	*endurance*
uses:	*riding*

This horse was developed in the early part of the twentieth century as a cavalry mount and named after Marshall Budenny, the Russian cavalry general who instigated the breed. The Marshall based his breeding program on Don mares and Thoroughbred stallions, and the best of the resultant progeny were interbred.

Still bred today in the Rostov region where it originated, the Budenny possesses great powers of endurance and good jumping ability. No longer required as a cavalry mount, it is used in competitive sports—including steeplechasing.

This lightly built horse has an acceptable conformation, with short shoulders and a strong body that is deep through the girth. The limbs—reflecting the quality of the base stock—are not its best feature, but the Budenny breed is none the less incredibly tough.

Don

size:	*15.3 h.h. (157 cm)*
main colors:	*chestnut & brown*
characteristic:	*hardiness*
uses:	*light agricultural work & riding*

Traditionally associated with the Cossack cavalry, the Don was founded on a mix of Steppe-bred Mongolian horses, Akhal-Tekés, and Persian Arabians. Orlovs, Thoroughbreds, and part-bred Arabs were introduced during the early nineteenth century to upgrade the breed but, since the beginning of the twentieth century, no new infusions of other blood have been made.

Centuries of life on the frozen Don steppe has produced an exceptionally tough horse. It is still herded on the plains and makes a useful working horse,

although it also excels in long-distance races despite its restricted, stilted action. The shoulders are short and straight, and the forelimbs usually well-muscled (although the forelegs also have a tendency to calf knees and upright pasterns).

Kabardin

size:	15.2–16 h.h. (155–160 cm)
main colors:	bay, brown, & chestnut
characteristic:	versatility
uses:	riding, and light draft and harness work

This mountain horse originated in the Caucasus some 400 years ago, when the indigenous mountain breed received infusions of Arab, Turkmene, and Karabakh blood. The resultant progeny has produced a strong horse of equable temperament, with the sure-footedness and homing instinct that make it an ideal animal for tackling the tortuous mountain tracks of its native land. The Kabardin is exceptionally hardy and is a popular sports horse in its local areas (it is performance-tested on the racetrack). The breed is also used in harness.

The Kabardin's ears have a tendency to turn inward. It has strong legs and good feet, although the hindquarters are often of poor conformation and sickle hocks are prevalent.

Karabair

size:	15 h.h. (150 cm)
main colors:	bay, chestnut, & gray
characteristic:	endurance
uses:	light agricultural and harness work, and riding

The region now called Uzbekskaya, the home of the Karabair, has been renowned for producing quality horses for 2,500 years. The exact origins of this breed are unknown, but its distinctly Arabian appearance—the breed resembles a rather stocky Arab, although with less refinement—would suggest oriental influence. The Karabair is a spirited but tractable horse with the boundless endurance typical of the Russian mountain breeds. The heaviest individuals make good agricultural workers, while the lighter-framed animals can either be ridden or driven.

Kirghiz

size:	14.1–15.1 h.h. (142–152 cm)
main colors:	often bay, although all solid colors may be seen
characteristic:	toughness and versatility
uses:	riding and transport of goods

Also known as the Novokirghiz, the modern Kirghiz is a relatively recent development of the native Kirghiz horse. In the last 100 years or so infusions of Don and Thoroughbred blood to the old Kirghiz stock have produced a small but immensely tough riding and pack horse, ideally suited to working at the high altitudes of its native Tien Shan mountains. It is sure-footed, with a longish back and straight shoulders, and short, strong legs with plenty of bone and good feet. This is a good-tempered and active horse, and is used for both work and leisure purposes.

Latvian

size:	16 h.h. (160 cm)
main colors:	all solid colors, especially chestnut
characteristic:	endurance
uses:	riding

The Latvian breed derives from the ancient forest horse of northern Europe, that dates back to a time prior to the existence of historical records. However, the modern Latvian is known to date from the seventeenth century, when Warmblood horses were crossed with the native stock. Several breeds were used, among them the Oldenburg. Coldblood crosses were also made to add greater substance to the breed, and these included both the Ardennes and the Finnish Draft Horse.

The result of all this is a sturdy, all-purpose draft horse that can also be ridden or put in harness. The Latvian is a strong worker that is also sensible and willing, with active paces and a kindly temperament. The conformation of the Latvian is also good, with depth through the girth and good bone; the legs have a little feathering.

Orlov

size:	*16 h.h. (160 cm)*
main colors:	*gray, black, & bay*
characteristic:	*longevity*
uses:	*harness racing & other sports*

The Orlov is named after Count Alexis Orlov, who founded the Khrenov Stud in 1778 and thereby lay the foundations of what was to become one of the world's most renowned trotting breeds. The Orlov derives from Arabian and Dutch blood, and by the beginning of the nineteenth century was one of Russia's leading breeds.

Trotting races were held in Moscow as far back as 1799 and, as the sport developed during the nineteenth century, so the Orlov prospered and became faster. It was also a popular carriage horse.

The Orlov is a tall, lightly built horse, characterized by its strong, powerful shoulders, a long back but plenty of depth through the girth, strong legs with good bone, and a rather heavy but attractive head. It is a long-lived horse and, although it is bred for racing in harness, it is sometimes also used under saddle in other sports.

Russian Trotter

size:	*15.3–16 h.h. (157–160 cm)*
main colors:	*bay, black, chestnut, & gray*
characteristic:	*early maturity*
uses:	*harness racing*

The Russian Trotter—which was only recognized as a breed as recently as 1949—was created in the second half of the nineteenth century by crossing the Orlov with the American Standardbred. This was a period when the Standardbred was outclassing all other trotting breeds, and Russian breeders made the cross in the hope of improving the Orlov's performance. The resulting offspring were indeed faster—although smaller and less elegant—than the Orlov. A program of interbreeding the crossbreds was subsequently initiated, and gradually the height increased and the frame, body measurements, and overall conformation improved.

Today, the breed has stringent breed standards imposed, with a height of 15.3 h.h. (157 cm) specified for mares and 16 h.h. (160 cm) for stallions. The modern Russian Trotter has pronounced muscular development, and hard, clean limbs. It is quick to mature, but the maximum trotting speeds are not attained by these horses until they reach the age of five or six.

Russian Heavy Draft

size:	*14.2 h.h. (145 cm)*
main colors:	*predominantly chestnut*
characteristic:	*strength*
uses:	*draft work*

This is a small draft horse with a distinctly "cobby" appearance. Developed during the past 100 years or so, principally in the Ukraine, local draft mares were crossed with Ardennes, Percheron, and Orlov stallions; the best of the progeny were then interbred to create a fixed type. The Russian Heavy Draft is an active but kind little horse, and is noted for its great pulling power. It is compact in build, with a powerful back, shoulders, and quarters, set on fairly short, strong legs. It is a popular work horse on the farms of the Ukraine and in the Urals.

Tersky

size:	15 h.h. (150 cm)
main colors:	silver gray & white
characteristic:	stamina
uses:	riding

The Tersky was developed between 1921 and 1950 in an attempt to preserve the old Strelets Arab, which had virtually died out during the First World War. The Strelets was an Anglo-Arab rather than a pure-bred Arabian—the result of crossing pure-breds with Anglos from the Orlov and Rastopchin Studs. The Strelets had thrived successfully during the nineteenth century, but by 1921 only two stallions remained, both of which had the characteristic silvery-gray coloring.

Pure and part-bred Arabs were mated with these two stallions and, by a careful system of selection, a new Strelets-type horse was developed. It was named the Tersky after the Tersk Stud in the Caucasus which, along with the Stavropol Stud, was its birthplace. Today the Tersky resembles a large Arabian, although with a little less refinement. The silver gray or white coloring often has a rosy tint, caused by

the pink skin beneath. This is a good-natured, active horse with plenty of stamina, and makes a good all-round riding horse.

Toric

size:	15–15.2 h.h. (150–155 cm)
main colors:	usually bay or chestnut
characteristic:	good constitution
uses:	light draft work

This "cobby" type of work horse traces back to a Norfolk Roadster stallion called Hatman, who was imported into Estonia in 1894 and mated with the local mares, known as Kleppers. Initially the progeny were interbred to some extent, but blood from other breeds—including that of the Orlov Trotter (see page 77)—has at various times been introduced. The Toric is an active, fast-moving, light draft horse of good constitution and temperament. It takes its name from the Toric Stud at which the breed originated, and is still used for agricultural work in Estonia.

Lokai

size:	15 h.h. (150 cm)
main colors:	gray, bay, & "metallic" chestnut
characteristic:	stamina
uses:	riding and transport of goods

Bred in Tajikistan on the western edge of the Pamirs, the Lokai is a mountain horse. The breed was developed in the sixteenth century by the Lokai people. In the beginning it was a mix of central Asian blood, but later was more specifically improved by additions of Iomud blood and by the Karabair. In more recent times there have also been outcrosses to Tersk, Arabian, and Thoroughbred stallions. This lightly built, wiry horse is tough and has very hard feet. It has immense powers of endurance and is a versatile animal, being used for racing, as a pack horse, and for the national game of Kokpar, which is a galloping game using a goat's carcass in place of a ball.

Karabakh

size:	14 h.h. (140 cm)
main colors:	chestnut, bay, & dun
characteristic:	speed
uses:	riding

The Karabakh originated in the Karabakh uplands between the rivers of Araks and Kura in Azerbaijan. Descended from the Mongolian-type Steppe horse of primitive origin, the breed has been open to the influence of Eastern stock from Turkey, Iraq, Kurdistan, and Iran. The breed is also heavily influenced by the Akhal-Teké, from which it has inherited its striking "metallic" chestnut coat. The Karabakh is noted for its speed and agility, and is performance-tested on the racecourse.

It has a refined head that is well-set on an arched neck. The legs are slender with good, hardwearing feet, and the shoulders are upright.

Africa   Egypt

Arabian

size:	14.2–15 h.h. (145–150 cm)
main colors:	all solid colors
characteristic:	beauty and endurance
uses:	riding

Regarded as the fountainhead of the world's breeds, the Arabian has played a significant part in the evolution of almost every recognized breed and is acknowledged as the principal foundation of the Thoroughbred. The breed's genetic purity has meant that it is remarkably prepotent, stamping its stock with its own powerful character. Horses of recognizable Arab type existed on the Arabian Peninsula at least 2,000 years before the Christian era, and Arab blood was spread throughout the known world by Muslim conquests in the seventh century.

The Arab is a horse of exceptional beauty and refinement. Its delicate head—with the characteristically dished profile, small tapered muzzle, broad forehead and large, wide-spaced eyes—is carried high on an elegant neck. The body is compact and muscular, the legs slender but strong, and the coat, mane, and tail are silky, the latter being carried high. The Arab is unsurpassed in stamina, has a floating movement and, although fiery and intelligent, has the gentlest of dispositions. It excels at long-distance work, but is a popular all-round mount and is also seen competing in Arab racing.

Libya, Algeria & Morocco

Barb

size:	15 h.h. (150 cm)
main colors:	all solid colors
characteristic:	stamina
uses:	riding

Another horse of ancient origin, the Barb comes from the Barbary coast, which has been noted for its horses for some 2,000 years. Like the Arabian, the Barb has exerted considerable influence on other breeds: it was used in the development of the Andalusian during the Moorish occupation of Spain, and through that breed has influenced many others; it was also imported into Europe in large numbers during the seventeenth century.

The Barb is the all-purpose riding horse of north Africa. While it is not a particularly impressive-looking horse—having a long, plain head, and sloping hindquarters with a rather low-set tail—it is immensely tough and combines considerable speed over short distances with great endurance over longer ones. It is also an economical feeder.

Principal **Pony Breeds**

PRINCIPAL PONY BREEDS

Przewalski
(Equus przewalskii przewalskii poliakof)

size:	12–14 h.h (122–143 cm)
main colors:	bright yellowish-brown at birth, changing to shades of dun at maturity; mealy markings around eyes & muzzle; black mane and tail; black eel stripe along back with zebra markings on legs

The Mongolian wild horse takes its name from Colonel N.M. Przewalski, a Russian explorer who in 1881 discovered a small herd of these animals in the Tachin Schara Nuru mountains at the western edge of the Gobi desert. They are the last truly wild type of horse or pony, on which no attempts at domestication have been made. It is debatable whether any of them still exist in the wild, as extensive hunting has driven them back into the desert and mountain regions and into China, but many are preserved in zoos. The Przewalski has great powers of endurance and was able to exist on the poorest of vegetation in the salty steppe and mountain regions of Mongolia, where it withstood severe climatic conditions.

The Przewalski is powerfully built, with a broad chest, straight shoulders, and a short back with virtually no wither. The neck is short and the head large and heavy, with long ears. The quarters are underdeveloped and the legs short and strong with large, shallow hooves. The mane is erect and the tail hairs are long.

Tarpan
(Equus przewalskii gmelini antonius)

size:	13 h.h (133 cm)
main colors:	brown or mouse dun with black eel stripe along back; black mane and tail; zebra markings on legs &, occasionally, stripes on body; coat may turn white in winter

This is the last survivor of the primitive horse that lived on the southern Russian steppes in eastern Europe. It would appear that there are two strains of Tarpan, one living on the steppes and the other a forest type, but both were extensively hunted for meat and were finally killed off during the nineteenth century. The Tarpan is now technically extinct, but survives in a maintained herd in Poland.

This horse has a long, broad head with a straight or convex profile and a bulge around the nostrils, longish ears, a short thick neck, and good shoulders. The back tends to be long with high withers, the quarters are weak and sloping, and the tail is set low. The legs are fine, long, and hard.

Experiments at cross-breeding undertaken by Professor Lutz Heck at the zoo park at Hallabrunn, Munich, using Przewalski stallions and Polish Konik mares—to which breed the Tarpan bears a likeness—have produced a horse that strongly resembles the steppe Tarpan.

Europe   Britain

Connemara

size:	13–14.2 h.h. (133–148 cm)
main colors:	gray, bay, black, dun, & brown
characteristic:	hardiness
uses:	riding

Originally a native of Ireland, the Connemara pony is also bred extensively in England and has been exported all over the world. It descended from the Celtic pony, but over the years has had infusions of Andalusian and Clydesdale blood. Rather more recently, Arabian stock has been introduced to add quality and refinement, and, when the Connemara is put to a Thoroughbred, a rather larger, very good all-round riding horse is the result.

The Connemara is a sturdy, useful general-purpose pony, with a free action, a quality pony head, a good length of neck, depth through the girth, and good sloping riding shoulders. The back is straight, the quarters well developed, and the tail well set on; the feet are hard and the legs have plenty of bone. Members of this breed are superb jumpers—sure-footed and agile—and have a kindly, tractable nature.

Dale

size:	*14.2 h.h. (148 cm)*
main colors:	*black & dark brown;*
	occasionally gray
characteristic:	*sure-footedness*
uses:	*riding & harness work*

Similar to the Fell pony, the Dale, together with the Highland, is the heaviest of Britain's native ponies and is bred on the eastern side of the Pennines in Northumberland, Co. Durham, and Yorkshire. It also shows a likeness to the Welsh Cob, and modern Dales can, in fact, be traced back to a Welsh Cob stallion called Comet, who competed in trotting contests and was used extensively to cover Dale mares toward the end of the nineteenth century.

The trotting aspect is still present in the modern Dale, making it a particularly good harness pony that is capable of pulling great weights. It is also used for trekking, being sound, active, and sure-footed, with a docile and sensible temperament. The Dale has a quality pony head and an abundance of mane, tail, and feathering on the legs.

Dartmoor

size:	*12.2 h.h. (128 cm)*
main colors:	*black, bay, & brown (only a*
	small amount of white
	marking is acceptable for
	registration/showing purposes)
characteristic:	*long, low action*
uses:	*riding*

A native of Dartmoor in Devon, this tough little breed has inhabited the moorlands for thousands of years. The type has varied during the ages, with infusions of Arabian and Welsh blood having been introduced at the beginning of the twentieth century.

The Dartmoor makes an ideal first pony for a young child, as it is small and narrow in build, but has a fairly high head carriage. It is also a very sensible and sure-footed horse, with an equable, kindly temperament. The Dartmoor has a reputation, too, for being a naturally good jumper. It has a fine, pretty, intelligent-looking head, large eyes, small pricked ears, and a good front and sloping shoulders. The short, compact body has strong quarters, a well set-on tail, and good hard legs and feet.

Exmoor

size:	*12–12.3 h.h. (122–130 cm)*
main colors:	*bay, brown, & mousey dun;*
	mealy muzzle and markings
	around eyes, on underbelly
	& between thighs
characteristic:	*"toad" eyes (heavy top lids*
	give a hooded look); "ice" tail
	(thick with fan-like growth at
	the top); great powers of
	endurance
uses:	*riding*

Currently on the Rare Breeds Survival Trust's critical list, the Exmoor is the oldest of Britain's native breeds and one of the oldest equine breeds in the world, probably being the last survivor of the Celtic pony. Comparisons of fossilized remains of the original Celtic ponies found in Alaska with the Exmoor have revealed the same-shaped jaw bones and the beginnings of a seventh molar tooth found in no other equine breed. There are now only three principal herds on the moor and, although some ponies are bred elsewhere, they tend to lose type away from their natural habitat.

The Exmoor pony is intelligent and independent, and may be willful if not correctly handled. It has a short head with a straight profile, well set on to a neck of good length.

The shoulders are good and sloping, and there is depth through the girth, a short back, powerful quarters, short legs with plenty of bone, and good hard feet. The coat is short, springy, and virtually waterproof. Although when properly trained the Exmoor makes a good child's pony, it is strong and quite capable of carrying a fully grown man.

Fell

size:	*13–14 h.h. (133–143 cm)*
main colors:	*black, dark brown, dark bay, & occasionally gray; very few white markings*
characteristic:	*hard feet of blue horn*
uses:	*riding & driving*

Slightly smaller and lighter than its close relation, the Dale, the Fell is bred on the northern side of the Pennine range and in the Cumberland and Westmorland areas of the Lake District. It was extensively used in the eighteenth century as a pack pony for carting lead from the mines, and also for the local sport of trotting.

Having much better riding shoulders than the Dale, the Fell pony produces a good stamp of hunter when a stallion is mated with a Thoroughbred mare. It is deep through the girth, compact in build, and has plenty of bone, moving well from the shoulder, and has an excellent head carriage. The Fell is sensible in temperament, hardy, strong, and sure-footed, and therefore makes an excellent all-round pony and is good both in harness and under saddle. It is currently recognized as a minority breed by the Rare Breeds Survival Trust.

Highland

size:	*13–14.2 h.h. (133–148 cm)*
main colors:	*gray, black, bay, & shades of dun*
characteristic:	*exceptional strength*
uses:	*riding & driving*

The Highland pony is a native of the north of Scotland and the Western Isles, and would appear to comprise two distinct types: the bigger and rather heavier mainland type, and the lighter, more active Western Isles pony. Both have had infusions of outside blood: French and Clydesdale in the mainland type, and Arab in the Island type.

Although originally bred for working the crofts—the Highland pony is very sure-

footed and is still used today to carry shot deer down from the hills—it is also used in harness and is a popular general-purpose riding pony, being docile, very strong, steady, hardy, and up to weight. The Western Isles type, in particular, produces good hunters when crossed with the Thoroughbred. The legs have fine silky hair, and most true Highland ponies have a dark eel stripe down the center of the back which tends to disappear on aged, gray ponies.

New Forest

size:	*12.2–14.2 h.h. (128–148 cm)*
main colors:	*various shades of bay are usual, although all solid colors are possible*
characteristic:	*exceptional riding shoulders; long, low action*
uses:	*riding*

Native to the New Forest area of Hampshire, this breed has had many infusions of outside blood. As far back as the thirteenth century, it is recorded that Welsh mares were turned out in the Forest, and since then Dartmoors, Exmoors, Highlands, Fells, Dales, Hackneys, Clydesdales, and Arabs have all been introduced in an effort to improve the size and substance of the breed. At present there are about 3,000 ponies running in the Forest, with their owners carrying out an annual round-up to select individuals for sale. The New Forest is bred at studs throughout Britain and abroad.

This breed has an excellent temperament and makes an ideal family pony. It is noted for its sure-footedness and adaptability, and usually has a good riding action, made possible by nicely sloping shoulders with free, straight movement. Most individuals have plenty of bone, good feet, a short back, and strong quarters, and are deep through the girth. There is a tendency toward a rather large head and shortish neck.

Shetland

size:	*10.3 h.h. (107 cm)*
main colors:	*all, including spotted (this is not accepted for registration/ showing)*
characteristic:	*hardiness; profuse growth of mane and tail hair for weather protection*
uses:	*riding & harness work*

The Shetland pony is the smallest of Britain's nine native pony breeds, and originates from the Shetland Islands some 100 miles (160 km) off the north coast of Scotland. It has been used by the island's crofters to work their land, as a pack pony to collect peat from the moor, and as a means of transport for many years. In the mid-1800s many Shetlands were exported to the mainland for use in the coal mines: being both strong and low to the ground, they proved ideal pit ponies and were soon bred selectively for this purpose. There are currently around 100 Shetland ponies on the islands, but they are also bred extensively on the mainland as well as in Europe, Australasia, and the Americas.

The Shetland breed is extremely strong and hardy, with a short, strong back, and considerable depth through the girth. Although it is very strong-willed, it is also a popular child's riding pony and, with its active paces, makes a particularly good driving pony.

Welsh Mountain

size:	*12 h.h. (122 cm)*
main colors:	*all solid colors*
characteristic:	*hardiness & hereditary soundness*
uses:	*riding*

The Welsh Mountain pony (Section A in the Welsh Pony and Cob Society Stud Book) has roamed the mountains and moorlands of Wales since Roman times, although over the years certain outcrosses have been introduced. Julius Caesar formed a stud in Merionethshire at Bala, and later introduced oriental blood to upgrade the stock, while in the nineteenth century there were infusions of Arab blood as well as of the Norfolk Roadster (the now extinct predecessor of the Hackney). At about the same time the Thoroughbred Merlin was introduced.

The Welsh Mountain is the base from which the Welsh Pony (section B) and Welsh Cobs (C and D) evolved. It is intelligent and courageous, yet kind and

gentle. An excellent child's riding pony, its good free movement combined with some knee action make it equally suitable for harness work. It has a fine, slightly dished head, large wide-spaced eyes, small pricked ears, and is tough and hardy with a true pony character. The shoulders are sloping, the body is deep and compact, and the tail is well set on and carried high. The legs are short and hard with plenty of substance.

Welsh Pony

size:	*13.2 h.h. (138 cm)*
main colors:	*all solid colors*
characteristic:	*elegance*
uses:	*riding*

The Welsh pony (Section B) is known as the riding pony of the Welsh breeds; it is derived from the Welsh Mountain pony and the Welsh Section C Cob, with an infusion of Thoroughbred blood. Successful crosses with small Thoroughbreds or Arabs often produce the larger show-pony type, but care must be taken in this case that the hardiness and substance of the breed are not lost.

The characteristics of the Welsh Pony are similar to those of the Welsh Mountain, although its movement is lower to the ground and there is less knee action. It is a courageous and intelligent pony, with a small neat head, a neck with a good length of rein, good sloping riding shoulders, rounded and well-muscled quarters, and a tail set high and carried gaily. The legs should be strong and hard with flat joints and hard feet.

The Welsh Pony of Cob Type

size:	13.2 h.h. (138 cm)
main colors:	all solid colors, & piebald & skewbald (not permitted for showing)
characteristic:	toughness and hardiness
uses:	riding

Also descended from the Welsh Mountain pony, the Welsh Pony of Cob Type (Section C) has in the past had infusions of blood from the Andalusian, and from the now extinct Pembroke cart horse and the Norfolk Roadster, as well as—in more recent years—from the Hackney.

This breed is courageous, kind, intelligent, and very sound and hardy. It is the smaller edition of the Welsh Cob, and combines strength with quality and common sense. An ideal pony for a child—or for a small adult—its good, free trotting action also makes it suitable for harness

work. Individuals of the breed should have an abundance of pony character, well-laid-back shoulders, and a neck giving a good length of rein; together with a compact, "stuffy" body that is deep through the girth, powerful quarters, and good bone. The mane and tail hair should be silky and there should only be a small amount of feathering on the heels.

Welsh Cob

size:	no smaller than 14.2 h.h. (148 cm)
main colors:	all solid colors
characteristic:	exceptional hardiness
uses:	riding & driving

The Welsh Cob (Section D) is the largest of all the Welsh breeds and, uniquely for the British native ponies, has no upper height limit for showing purposes. This breed follows the conformation of the Welsh Mountain pony, but outcrosses to Norfolk Roadsters and Yorkshire Coach Horses in the eighteenth and nineteenth centuries

resulted in the modern Cob. The breed is courageous with great powers of endurance, and is famed for its trotting ability as well as for for its performance in harness.

However, it is just as good under saddle and, being a naturally good jumper, it makes an excellent hunter. Indeed, as a general, all-round riding horse, there is little to beat the inherently sound and hardy Welsh Cob. A cross with the Thoroughbred is the basis for the Welsh part-bred which has grown in popularity over recent years and produces a useful competition horse.

Hackney pony

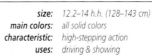

size:	12.2–14 h.h. (128–143 cm)
main colors:	all solid colors
characteristic:	high-stepping action
uses:	driving & showing

The Hackney pony is a real pony with pony character, but it shares the stud book with the Hackney horse. The Hackney breed is essentially the creation of Christopher Wilson of Cumbria who, in the 1880s, succeeded in producing a distinctive type based on the Fell pony with Welsh outcrosses.

The Hackney pony has a remarkably hardy constitution, which is the result of being left on the fells during the winter to fend for itself. It has a naturally high-stepping action in harness, it possesses plenty of stamina, and it has a lot of courage. The modern Hackney Pony is largely confined to the show ring, where its spectacular action is demonstrated to its best advantage.

France

Camargue

size:	15 h.h. (153 cm)
main colors:	foals are born black, dark gray, or brown, lightening to gray or white
characteristic:	strength and endurance
uses:	herding

The Camargue area of southern France, in the Rhône delta between the town of Aigues-Mortes and the sea, is the swampland home of the Camargue, which was only recognized as a breed in 1968. There are currently only about 30 herds, or manades, of Camargue ponies in the area. Known as the "white horse of the sea," the coat color is the most striking thing about this hardy pony, which thrives on a diet of tough grass and saltwater.

The conformation of the Camargue is generally poor—it has a large square head, a short neck and upright shoulders—although it is noted for its depth through the girth and short, strong back. It also has plenty of bone and good hard feet, and a long, thick mane and tail.

The action of the Camargue pony is principally noted for its high-stepping walk, for its gallop and for its characteristic ability to twist and turn—these being the paces and movements most used to work the famous black bulls of the Camargue area for the bullring.

Austria

Haflinger

size:	14.2 h.h. (148 cm)
main colors:	chestnut with flaxen mane & tail
characteristic:	exceptional strength in relation to size
uses:	draft work and riding

The Haflinger is a hardy mountain breed that originated in the Austrian Tyrol. Tough and thick-set with plenty of bone and substance, its breeding can be traced back to the Arabian on one side and to the cold-blooded heavier breeds on the other. This combination makes it ideal for both draft and ridden work in its native land; its sure-footedness and placid temperament also make it suitable for beginners to ride.

The breed's name was taken from the village of Hafling (the center of an area in what is now northern Italy), where the Haflinger was extensively bred. State studs were later established at Piber and Ossiach, but ponies are now widely bred throughout Austria. The breed has been exported to various countries but is particularly popular in Germany, Switzerland, and Holland. All stallions are owned by the state and kept at government

stud farms, and colt foals are subjected to rigorous inspection before being chosen as possible future stallions.

Germany

Dülmen

size:	12.2 h.h. (128 cm)
main colors:	any, although brown, black, & dun are most usual
characteristic:	upright shoulders
uses:	ornamental, they are privately owned by the Dukes of Croy and live on the family's estate

Germany has only two breeds of native ponies: the Dülmen and the Senner. Although the latter—which was once found in the Teutoburg Forest of Hanover—is now virtually extinct, both of these breeds have had a significant influence on the Hanoverian. The Dülmen today is a rather mixed breed, having run in the Meerfelder Bruch in Westphalia in a semi-wild state since the fourteenth century.

Not unlike the New Forest in overall appearance, the Dülmen tends to have upright shoulders, a short back, and poor hindquarters with a neck that is a little on the short side.

Poland

Hucul

size:	*12–13 h.h. (122–133 cm)*
main colors:	*most colors may be seen, although dun, bay, & piebald are usual*
characteristic:	*hardiness*
uses:	*transport of goods & draft work*

The Hucul is a native of the Carparthian region of Poland, where herds have wandered the mountain regions for thousands of years and where the breed is known locally as the Carparthian pony. It is probably a direct descendant of the primitive Tarpan, which it resembles more than any other breed. In fairly recent times, however, Arab blood has been introduced to improve its quality, and selective breeding is now carried out at several studs throughout Poland, the principal one being at Siary near Gorlice.

The Hucul makes an ideal pack and draft pony and, being very hardy and having good endurance, is widely used on the mountainous farmlands of southern Poland. Sure-footed, docile, strong and willing,

it has a characteristic short head, rather poor quarters, and a low-set tail.

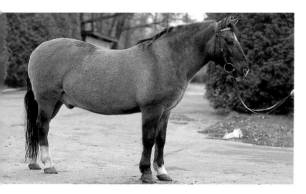

Konik

size:	*13 h.h. (133 cm)*
main colors:	*varying shades of dun*
characteristic:	*easily kept*
uses:	*farm work*

Similar to the Hucul and with a common ancestor in the Tarpan, the Konik is used to work the lowland farms in Poland, as well as in eastern Europe, to which area a number of these ponies have been exported. It has also had infusions of Arab blood and, although fairly small in stature, has lost a degree of its "pony" qualities, resembling instead a little horse.

The Konik is bred selectively at the two Polish state studs at Popielno and Jezewice, as well as by numerous small farmers for use on their land. It is a very tough and hardy pony, works willingly on a limited diet and is easily managed.

Spain

Sorraia

size:	*12.2–13 h.h. (128–133 cm)*
main colors:	*usually dun, but may also be gray or palomino; black eel stripe along back & zebra markings on legs*
characteristic:	*primitive appearance*
uses:	*(formerly) light agricultural work*

Spain's only native pony, the Sorraia, originates from the western area of the country, in the regions bordering the Sorraia river and its tributaries, and on into Portugal. It is an extremely hardy breed—able to survive on the poor vegetation available in its habitat while withstanding the extreme climatic conditions—and was formerly used for agricultural work. The Sorraia is a true "primitive" type, having characteristics both of the Przewalski and of the Tarpan.

The Sorraia's head tends to be large with a straight or convex profile, the ears long with black tips, and the eyes set a little high. The neck is usually long and the shoulders upright, the hindquarters are poor and underdeveloped with the tail set low, and the legs tend to be rather long and lacking in bone.

Portugal

Garrano

size:	*10–12 h.h. (100–122 cm)*
main colors:	*almost always dark chestnut*
characteristic:	*sure-footedness*
uses:	*haulage & light agricultural work*

Also known as the Minho, this native breed of Portugal comes from the mountain valleys of the Garrano do Minho and Traz dos Montes areas. Arab blood has been introduced by the selective breeding of certain ponies, and the result is a lightly built animal with good conformation and noticeable quality. The Garrano pony also has a luxuriant mane and tail.

Members of the Garrano breed of pony are characteristically strong, hardy, and sure-footed, and are used extensively for hauling timber as well as for light agricultural work. They also make excellent riding ponies, and are in great demand as pack animals.

Greece

Peneia

size:	*14 h.h. (143 cm)*
main colors:	*usually bay, brown, chestnut, or gray*
characteristic:	*sturdiness*
uses:	*light agricultural work*

Today, Greece has only three remaining breeds of native pony (those such as the Thracian, Thessalian, and Achean having long since disappeared). Of those still surviving, the Peneia is the local pony bred in the district of Eleia in the Peloponnese, where it is used for light agricultural work and as a pack pony. It is a sturdy animal and can live on fairly meager rations.

Pindos

size:	*12–13 h.h. (122–133 cm)*
main colors:	*usually dark gray; may also be brown, bay, or black*
characteristic:	*ability to exist on frugal diet*
uses:	*riding & light agricultural work*

Bred in the mountainous regions of Thessaly and Epirus, the Pindos pony is another individual of "oriental" type. It is used for light farm work, being a popular choice with farmers because of its strong constitution and its ability to live very frugally; it is also used for riding. Pindos mares are frequently mated with donkey stallions in order to breed hardy mules.

Skyros

size:	*11 h.h. (110 cm)*
main colors:	*almost any color, although brown, gray, & dun are usual*
characteristic:	*willing temperament*
uses:	*transport of goods; children's riding*

The Skyros pony comes from the island of Skyros in the Aegean sea. It is the smallest—and probably the oldest—of the Greek breeds, and is of "primitive" Tarpan type. On the island, the Skyros is used principally as a pack pony, but on the Greek mainland it is a popular choice as a child's riding pony, being very quiet and amenable by nature.

A hardy breed, and able to exist frugally, the Skyros is small and very light in terms of bone with a weak neck, upright shoulder, poor hindquarters, and a tendency towards cow hocks.

Norway

Fjord

size:	*13–14.2 h.h. (133–148 cm)*
main colors:	*dun, with dark eel stripe along back & zebra markings on legs*
characteristic:	*versatility*
uses:	*agricultural work, driving, & riding*

The mount of the Vikings, and used by them for the "sport" of horse fighting, the Fjord or Westlands pony originated in western Norway. It has since spread throughout the whole of Scandinavia, as well as Germany, and is particularly popular in Denmark—especially Jutland—where it was imported at the beginning of the twentieth century for performing light agricultural work.

The Fjord is a "primitive" type of pony and has the characteristic coloring and markings. The mane, which—like the tail—consists of black hairs in the center and silver around the outside, stands upright and is cut in an attractive, characteristic crescent shape. The head is small, neat, and pony-like with widely spaced eyes, and the neck is well-muscled.

The Fjord pony is known to be strong, hardy, and sure-footed with short, strong legs and good feet. It is a tireless worker and is used extensively in the mountain areas for farm work; it also performs well both in harness and under saddle.

Sweden

Gotland

size:	*12–12.2 h.h. (122–128 cm)*
main colors:	*brown, black, dun, chestnut, gray, & Palomino*
characteristic:	*jumping ability*
uses:	*light agricultural work, harness racing, and riding*

The oldest of the Scandinavian breeds, the Gotland, or Skogruss, pony is now bred extensively on the mainland as well as on Gotland Island, from where it originated in the Stone Age. It is probably a descendant of the Tarpan, and a number of ponies still run wild in the forest lands of Lojsta. About 100 years ago oriental blood was introduced into the breed, but they still retain their "primitive" characteristics and are not unlike the Hucul and Konik of Poland and the extinct Lofoten pony.

The Gotland is now in demand for light agricultural work and, with the current interest in trotting races, is also selectively bred for this purpose. It is a hardy and easily managed pony, although inclined to be obstinate. It is small, rather light and narrow, with a small head,

straight profile, and short neck, long back, sloping quarters, poor hind legs, and a low-set tail. Although light of bone, Gotland ponies are fast and capable jumpers.

Iceland

Icelandic

size:	*12–13 h.h. (122–133 cm); larger ponies are occasionally found*
main colors:	*all, but primarily gray or dun*
characteristic:	*toughness*
uses:	*riding & harness work*

Introduced into Iceland from Scandinavia (from Norway in particular), this Celtic pony has since interbred with individuals imported later from Scotland, Ireland, and the Isle of Man to form what is now known as the Icelandic pony.

From subsequent selective breeding, two distinct types have emerged: one rather heavy pony used for draft and pack work, and a lighter type for riding. Both were used extensively until the 1920s, when they formed the only transport in the country. Until the turn of the twentieth century, ponies were exported from Iceland to work in the British coal mines, where their extreme hardiness, courage, strength, small size, and great endurance made them highly popular.

The Icelandic pony is small and stocky, deep through the girth, and has a rather large head set on a short, thick neck. There is an abundance of mane and tail hair, and of feathering on the heels. One of the toughest of the pony breeds, the Icelandic is extremely intelligent and docile, and is noted for its independence and homing instinct. The usual pace is a fast, running walk known as the tølt, which covers a great deal of ground.

Italy

Avelignese

size:	*13.2–14.2 h.h. (138–148 cm)*
main colors:	*always chestnut (possibly with white facial markings), with flaxen mane & tail*
characteristic:	*hardiness*
uses:	*transport of goods; farm and draft work*

A native of central and northern Italy, the Avelignese is bred principally in the hill regions surrounding Venetia and Tuscany, where it is used extensively for light agricultural and draft work. In the Alps and Apennines, it is popular as a pack pony. Similar to the Haflinger, to which it is related—both breeds share a common ancestor in the now extinct Avellinum-Haflinger—the Avelignese is believed to contain a degree of Arabian blood, having descended from an imported Arabian called El Bedavi.

This breed of pony is extremely hardy and sure-footed, and is able to pick its way over mountain trails in the most treacherous of winter conditions. It is also noted for its pleasantly docile disposition and its longevity. It is deep through the girth with a wide chest, a well-muscled neck and quarters, short legs, and a short broad head, with plenty of bone and good hard feet.

North & Central America   United States

American Shetland

size:	11.1 h.h. (113 cm)
main colors:	any colors
characteristic:	high, exaggerated trot
uses:	riding and harness racing

Although developed in the United States by crossing imported Shetlands with Hackney Ponies, the American Shetland—which is bred throughout the country—bears little resemblance to its British counterpart. It is a useful child's mount, as well as being popular as a harness pony in trotting races, hitched to a lightweight racing sulky (see also pages 136–7). The action of the breed—especially at the trot—is high and exaggerated, testifying to the infusion of Hackney blood.

Chincoteague/Assateague

size:	12 h.h. (122 cm)
main colors:	any (many are piebald or skewbald)
characteristic:	heavy shoulders
uses:	riding

These two breeds are inhabitants of Chincoteague and Assateague, small islands off the coast of Maryland and Virginia in the United States. It is uncertain how the ponies came to be living on the islands, where their diet consists of whatever they can find on the sandy marshland, and where there is no shelter from the Atlantic storms. One theory is that they are descended from animals that survived shipwrecks during the English and Spanish colonial period, and that their size has become stunted on account of the sparse vegetation. They are more like small horses than ponies, and a recent infusion of Arab blood has improved their quality.

Assateague is uninhabited by people, but once a year all the ponies are rounded up and swum across to Chincoteague for round-up, branding and/or sale; those that are not sold are swum back to Assateague the next day.

Pony of the Americas

size:	11.2–13.2 h.h. (115–138 cm)
main colors:	Appaloosa colors (any of six are acceptable for registration purposes)
characteristic:	ease of management
uses:	children's riding

A breed founded in the 1950s by crossing a Shetland stallion and an Appaloosa mare, the Pony of the Americas is popular throughout the United States and Canada as an ideal riding pony for young children, which has plenty of substance. Members of this breed are versatile and easy to manage, and have a straight, free action. The head should be small and "Araby" with a dished profile, large eyes, and small ears; the shoulder is sloping, the chest wide, and the body deep, with well-rounded quarters and tail set high. The legs are short and have plenty of bone.

Mexico

Galiceno

size:	*12–13.2 h.h. (122–138 cm)*
main colors:	*all solid colors*
characteristic:	*natural agility*
uses:	*harness work, ranch work, & riding*

Descended from the Garrano (Minho) ponies of Portugal, and from the Spanish Sorraia, the Galiceno's ancestors are thought to have been those brought over to America by the Spaniards from Hispaniola. Although a native of Mexico, this pony has spread throughout the United States, and was recognized as a breed in 1958. It is used in harness and for ranch work as well as for riding.

A lightly built, compact pony, the Galiceno has a fine head, large well-spaced eyes, upright shoulders, and a short back. The pony's chest tends to be narrow, but the limbs and feet are good and the pony moves with the characteristic natural gait of a fast, comfortable running walk. It is both hardy and intelligent, and has a pleasing tractable disposition.

Canada

Sable Island Pony

size:	*14 h.h. (143 cm)*
main colors:	*chestnut, bay, brown, black, & gray*
characteristic:	*narrow body shape*
uses:	*riding & light draft work*

A descendant of the principally French stock taken to Canada by the French in the mid-seventeenth century, the Sable Island Pony is also supposed to have been introduced to Sable Island—a sandbank some 200 miles (320 km) off Nova Scotia in the Atlantic Ocean—early in the eighteenth century. There are at present some 300 ponies, most of them scrub stock, running on the 25-mile (40-km) long island, and they are extremely hardy, tough and wiry, living on the poor vegetation that the island offers.

South America

Criollo

size:	*14–15 h.h. (143–153 cm)*
main colors:	*usually dun, with black points, eel stripe along back, & zebra markings on legs*
characteristic:	*powers of endurance*
uses:	*riding*

Descended from Spanish stock—a mixture of Arab, Barb, and Andalusian, brought over to South America by the sixteenth-century conquistadors—the Criollo has now spread all over this continent, acquiring slightly different characteristics according to its environment. In Argentina it is known as the Criollo, in Brazil as the Crioulo, in Chile as the Caballo Chileno, and in Venezuela as the Llanero; while in Peru there are three types—the Costeno, the Morochuco, and the Chola.

Essentially, the Criollo is sturdy, compact, and muscular, with a short broad head, a straight profile, and wide-set eyes. The neck and quarters are well-developed, the chest wide, the back short, and the shoulder fairly sloping. The legs are short with plenty of bone and hard feet. This is a tough pony with great powers of endurance and an ability to carry a great deal of weight.

Falabella

size:	*7 h.h. (70 cm)*
main colors:	*all*
characteristic:	*intelligence*
uses:	*showing & occasional harness work*

The Falabella is really a miniature horse rather than a pony, and is the smallest horse in the world. It was first bred by the Falabella family on their ranch near Buenos Aires in Argentina, by initially crossing a small Thoroughbred with small Shetland ponies and by in-breeding thereafter. The Falabella is not suitable for riding, but may be shown in hand and is sometimes used in harness in the United States. Falabella studs are now established worldwide.

Asia Myanma (formally Burma)

Burmese

size:	*13 h.h. (133 cm)*
main colors:	*all*
characteristic:	*hardiness*
uses:	*transport of goods and riding*

Also known as the Shan pony, this breed is very similar to the Manipur but is a native of Myanmar and the Shan States, where it is bred by the hill tribes. It is strong and active, and is used as a pack animal as well as for riding.

The Burmese is generally a bad-tempered pony. It is also very hardy and sure-footed, and is rather plain in appearance. It has a small head, a longish back, and rather underdeveloped quarters with poor hind legs.

India

Bhutia

size:	*13–13.2 h.h. (133–138 cm)*
main colors:	*usually gray*
characteristic:	*sturdiness*
uses:	*transport of goods*

A thick-set pony from the Himalayan mountain area of India, the Bhutia is principally used as a pack pony on the mountain passes. It is intelligent, sure-footed, and extremely hardy, with plenty of stamina and the ability to live frugally. It

has a strong and sturdy build, with muscular hindquarters and plenty of bone.

Indonesia

Batak

size:	*12–13 h.h. (122–133 cm)*
main colors:	*all*
characteristic:	*ease of maintenance*
uses:	*riding & transport of goods*

The Batak is bred selectively on the Indonesian island of Sumatra, where Arabian imports have been introduced to the studs to upgrade the rather common native pony and lend a little quality to the breed. The Batak is a kindly, gentle pony, easy to manage and economical to keep, and makes a good general-purpose animal. The Arabian blood has added a touch of spirit and elegance that is lacking in most of the other Indonesian breeds (the Sandalwood being an exception).

Java

size:	*12.2 h.h. (128 cm)*
main colors:	*all*
characteristic:	*hardiness but poor conformation*
uses:	*harness work*

The Java—a native of that island—is slightly larger than some of the other Indonesian ponies. Although lightly built it is tough, hardy, and apparently tireless, capable of working all day in tropical conditions. Its principal function is to pull the two-wheeled Sados that serve as taxis on the island. The Java generally has poor conformation with a weak neck and hindquarters, a long back, rather long legs and, often, cow hocks.

Sandalwood

size:	*12–13 h.h. (122–133 cm)*
main colors:	*all*
characteristic:	*well-shaped head*
uses:	*mainly racing*

A native of the islands of Sumba and Sumbawa, the Sandalwood is the quality pony of Indonesia, being finer than the others and with an "Araby" head. Named after the island's principal export, it is used mainly for bareback racing, even though it is only small in size. It has a delicate, well-shaped head with large eyes; the chest is wide and the girth deep. The legs and feet are good and hard, and the coat is very fine in texture.

Sumba/Sumbawa

size:	12.2 h.h. (128 cm)
main colors:	dun, with black eel stripe along back
characteristic:	primitive appearance
uses:	riding

As the likeness of the Indonesian pony breeds to the wild Mongolian and Chinese ponies is so apparent, it is possible that the ancient Chinese may have originally brought the former to Indonesia. The native ponies of Sumba and Sumbawa— which are almost identical—are tough but somewhat primitive in appearance, with their coloring and upright manes. They are very agile ponies, which makes them ideal for Indonesia's national sport of lance-throwing.

Timor

size:	11–12 h.h. (110–122 cm)
main colors:	usually black, brown, or bay
characteristic:	docile temperament
uses:	riding

The native pony of the island of Timor is the smallest of the Indonesian breeds, and is used by the islanders as a "cow pony." It is exceptionally agile and strong in spite of its small size, and has great powers of endurance coupled with a high level of common sense.

Being both docile and sure-footed, the Timor makes an excellent child's pony, and has been imported to the Australian mainland for this purpose. The Timor is finely made with a small head, short back, strong hindquarters, and good hard legs and feet.

Iran

Caspian

size:	10–12.h.h (100–122 cm)
main colors:	gray, brown, bay, & chestnut
characteristic:	exceptional jumping ability
uses:	riding

At one time the Caspian pony—a native of the area around the Elburtz mountains and Caspian Sea in Persia—was thought to be extinct, but in 1965 a number of them were discovered pulling carts in the coastal towns and wandering along the shores of the Caspian Sea in northern Iran. This was an important discovery, as members of the breed today are believed to be the direct descendants of the earliest equine animals that roamed the region in around 3,000 B.C.; a breeding program was subsequently set up to safeguard their future.

More like a small horse than a pony, with a wonderful natural action, the Caspian pony is sure-footed and intelligent. It also has a remarkable jumping ability, and is a popular mount for children. It has a small, fine, Arab-type head with wide-set eyes; in body shape it has a narrow chest, a short back, and poor hind legs, and is light of bone.

Australasia Australia

Australian Pony

size:	*12–14 h.h. (122–143 cm)*
main colors:	*usually gray or chestnut*
characteristic:	*good build*
uses:	*riding*

The native pony of Australia is controlled by the Australia Pony Stud Book Society, formed in 1929, and has derived principally from imported Welsh Mountain ponies with a mixture of Arabian, Thoroughbred, Hackney, Timor, and Shetland blood; it is, therefore, not indigenous. Members of the breed make a popular choice for children to ride, as they are quality ponies of correct conformation and have a good, free action. The Australian pony is also intelligent, hardy, and sound.

The CIS

Kazakh

size:	*12.2–13.2 h.h. (128–138 cm)*
main colors:	*usually gray, bay, chestnut, or black*
characteristic:	*hardiness*
uses:	*riding and food*

An ancient pony originally bred in the region of Kazakhstan, the Kazakh is exceptionally hardy and able to withstand extremes of climatic conditions. Crosses with the Don or Akhal-Teké have produced good cavalry mounts, although the principal use of the breed is as a "cow pony." The Kazakh makes a strong, willing mount and has good hard limbs and feet. The mares are used to produce milk, and many of the young stock are fattened for their meat.

Africa Lesotho (Basutoland)

Basuto

size:	*14.2 h.h. (148 cm)*
main colors:	*usually bay, brown, gray, or chestnut*
characteristic:	*versatility*
uses:	*riding & transport of goods*

The Basuto pony is derived principally from the Arab and Barb horses imported to the Cape Province of South Africa from Java in 1653 that, by various crossings with Thoroughbreds, produced the Cape Horse. Following raids in the early nineteenth century, the Cape Horse found its way into Basutoland, where a combination of interbreeding with local scrub stock and the unfavorable climatic conditions caused it to degenerate into what is now known as the Basuto pony; it is, therefore, not an indigenous breed.

This exceptionally tough, hardy, and enduring pony is well up to carrying weight and was used extensively during the Boer War. Today it proves its versatility by being favored for polo and racing, as well as for general-purpose riding and for use as a pack animal. The Basuto is thick-set in build, frequently with a quality head, a long neck and back, and upright shoulders. It has very hard hooves and is extremely sure-footed.

Part Three: Equestrian Sports and Recreation

DRESSAGE

previous page: *Mary King on Star Appeal, on their way to a second place at Badminton in 1997.*

right: *Former Olympic champions Dr. Reine Klimke and Ahlerich demonstrate "piaffe."*

right: *Germany's Nicole Uphoff-Becker and Rembrandt on course for gold at the Olympic games.*

THE ORIGIN OF TRAINING HORSES for the most classical form of riding can be traced at least as far back as the fifth century B.C., when its value and basic principles were established by the Greeks—notably a cavalry general called Xenophon (see page 16). However, the term dressage did not come into use to describe this training and riding until the early eighteenth century, and is derived from the French verb *dresser* (to train, adjust, or straighten out).

Aside from the dressage practiced by individuals for their own pleasure, and for the improvement of their horses, there are two forms in which it is known and enjoyed by the public. The first is in the world of competitive events, and the second—and more popular—is that of dressage displays, the most famous of which are given worldwide by the Spanish Riding School in Vienna (see page 19).

The twentieth century has seen the transition of dressage from a mainly military and aristocratic activity to an almost entirely civilian sport. By the beginning of this century the royal courts—at which the riding schools were maintained, and of which the Spanish School is the last—were dwindling rapidly. All the cavalry schools had also disappeared by the end of the Second World War, and the lead passed to civilians and to the few retired soldiers who had received their training before the war. Interest became more widely spread, and quickly found its expression in the expanding world of competitive sport.

Competition dressage

For the first 40 years of the twentieth century competitive dressage was pursued throughout continental Europe, giving these countries a head start in the competitive arena. One significant innovation was the emergence of women riders at the highest levels and, from a previous standpoint of non-participation in the sport, they soon proved themselves well able to challenge men on equal terms. The first woman to win an Olympic dressage medal was Denmark's Liz Hartel, who had been severely disabled by poliomyelitis. Riding Jubilee, Hartel won the silver medals at Helsinki and Stockholm in 1952 and 1956.

Competition dressage covers a wide range of standards, from riding-club events to the Olympic Games. Competitions are controlled by the Dressage Bureau of the International Equestrian Federation (FEI) which was founded in 1921 and is based in Lausanne, Switzerland. The Bureau lays down rules to cover performance standards, qualifications, and rules for judges and competition organizers, and all other factors affecting the sport internationally. Each federated nation also has a dressage bureau to control its national affairs. The highest priority is given to maintaining the purity of the classical concept, and to preventing the growth of potentially false methods of training that would lead to lower standards.

There are various grades of dressage training, each of which is subdivided into two or more degrees of difficulty. The advanced grades in all countries are distinguished from the early grades by the inclusion of flying changes of leg and pirouettes and, at the highest level, the High School "Airs" of *piaffe* and *passage*. Airs above the ground—such as the *levade* and *courbette*, which are the ultimate achievement at academies such as the Spanish Riding School—are never included in competitions.

Dressage tests

Each country's national federation is responsible for devising a set of tests for all levels of national competition. The FEI publishes the standard advanced international tests (the lowest being the Prix St. Georges,

left: *Long-reining, a method of training from the ground, is used in the early education of young horses as well as to teach more advanced work, as seen here.*

above: *Dressage always involves perfect timing—the need for precision is heightened in the "Pas de Deux" here.*

then the Intermediaire I, Intermediaire II, Grand Prix, and Grand Prix Special), as well as the requirements of Freestyle tests, and these form the basis of all international competitions. Five judges are recommended for each test, although this number has varied; for national contests, one to three judges are normally required.

The tests are revised regularly to prevent the horses from becoming over-familiar with them, and usually take 8–12 minutes to perform. The program at national and international level frequently includes a Freestyle competition to music (or Kür), in which competitors devise their own display; this must include a set of movements required for that level.

Dressage contests are ridden in a rectangular arena. The standard size for this arena is either 66 x 131 ft. (20 x 40 m), which is required by the international tests, or 66 x 197 ft. (20 x 60 m). All arenas use a conventional lettering system to indicate to both riders and judges where each movement should begin and end, although the origins of this somewhat illogical system are, in fact, obscure.

Dressage judging

Dressage judges are required to allocate a mark from a maximum of 10 for each movement or combination of movements (in the dressage phase of eventing, this is reversed to become a system of penalty marks, with the lowest scores indicating the best performance, and the competitor with the fewest overall penalties going forward to the next phase in the lead). Each judge is accompanied by a writer, who records the allotted marks together with a summary of the judge's comments on the judging sheet; this is later made available to the competitor. The marks given by each of the presiding judges are collected and totaled, and the competitor with the fewest penalties is deemed the winner.

A judge must have a thorough knowledge of the principles of dressage and of the problems involved in training a horse, as well as memorizing the test, making his or her task almost as difficult to carry out as that of the riders. The FEI maintains its own panel of judges who may officiate at international competitions; each nation also maintains its own list of judges, graded according to the standard of dressage for which they are qualified.

Developments in competitive dressage

At the Olympic Games, and at Continental and World Championships, it is usual to award prizes for teams of four from any one nation, in addition to the individual awards. The dressage contest at Stockholm in 1912—the first Olympic Games at which the sport was included—was staged in a 66 x 131 ft. (20 x 40 m) arena; it was in the form of a Freestyle competition, and the degree of difficulty was extremely modest by later standards. No lateral movements were required, nor *piaffe*, *passage*, or sequence changes of leg. The contest also included a jumping section, comprising five jumps, and an obedience test. By the following Olympics, held in Antwerp in 1920, a much more comprehensive set test had been devised, including sequence changes of leg up to one-time, and various coefficients were used for what were considered the most important movements. The *piaffe* and *passage* were first introduced into the Olympic dressage test in Los Angeles in 1932, and—with the exception of the postwar Games held in London in 1948—have remained ever since. Canter pirouettes were required for the first time in Berlin in 1936.

As Freestyle tests to music became more popular, a World Cup dressage series was set up in 1985, with points-gaining qualifying competitions contributing toward an annual final. In addition, to make the sport more appealing to a wider audience, the

above: The High School movement passage, an element of Grand Prix dressage tests performed here by Germany's Balkonhol and Goldstern.

1991 European Championships included dressage to music, awarding two sets of individual medals for the Freestyle and Grand Prix Special. However, as it was thought unsatisfactory to have two champions, a new championship formula was introduced at the 1995 European Championships, based on the addition of the individual percentage points from the Grand Prix, Grand Prix Special, and Kür; this was also used for the first time at the Olympic Games in Atlanta in 1996.

Qualities of the dressage horse

Despite the enormous expansion of interest in pleasure riding and equestrian sports, the number of truly first-class international horse-rider combinations from any country (with the exception of Germany) seldom exceeds four or five at any one time. However, when one considers the principles of modern dressage, it becomes easier to understand why most countries can boast only a few top-class horses.

Firstly, it is required that a horse should be active and free, but still display all the power and speed that are its inherent characteristics. It must be light in the hand, allowing the rider to control its movements with no visible effort, and it must be calm but keen, giving the impression of always wanting to go forward when asked. It should be supple and submissive, adjusting its paces without resistance; should remain perfectly straight when moving in a straight line; keep a regular rhythm and correct sequence of footfall at all paces; and accept a light but continuous contact through the reins, remaining confident and diligent so that, in effect, it appears to be doing of its own accord what is asked of it. Together, the horse and rider should create an impression of total harmony.

It is generally felt that most breeds are able to produce excellent dressage horses, provided that the individuals have good conformation and are well handled and well ridden. However, there has always been a tendency for certain breeds to be credited with the best qualities for this highly disciplined sport, with the most popular and successful currently appearing to be the German-, Swedish-, and Dutch-bred horses. The Hanoverian, Trakehner, Westphalian, and Holstein studs all produce fine horses of substance and quality, and their breeding is carefully controlled so as to eliminate lines that do not come up to the required standards of movement and temperament. Swedish horses have been almost as successful as their German counterparts, and are mainly a mixture of German and Thoroughbred blood. Over the past 20 years dressage horses have generally become lighter, with more Thoroughbred blood and, more recently, other breeds—such as the Andalusian—are also becoming more accepted at international level.

International competition

Germany—with its seemingly endless supply of good horses, riders and trainers—leads the world in dressage, with its riders' impressive achievements at the Olympic Games showing their overwhelming domination during the twentieth century. The sport is helped by the strong support given to it throughout the country, which is further upheld by government interest. The state-run school at Warendorf, for example, acts as a central training venue and home for national and Olympic federations.

Dressage training in France has mainly been based at, and fostered by, the long-established, one-time cavalry school at Saumur (see page 17). However, as the school's output has dwindled, it has been overtaken by individual civilians.

France's neighbor, Switzerland, has ideal conditions for dressage, which it owes in part to the severe winters which encourage indoor riding and, therefore, dressage. The leading Swiss riders were formerly soldiers based at the cavalry school at Berne, but its closure tilted the balance in favor of civilian riders. During the 1950s and 1960s, they developed a distinct style of dressage which owed more to the teaching of Saumur than to that of Vienna or to the more precise and forceful German style. The Swiss have always looked to other countries—and to Sweden in particular—for their best cavalry (and therefore dressage) horses. However, one of their most successful and famous horses, Granat, owned and ridden by Christine Stückelberger, was a Holsteiner, and was trained with the help of Georg Wahl, the Austrian ex-Oberbereiter of the Spanish School of Vienna. Granat is considered by many to be one of the finest dressage horses in living memory.

The Scandinavian countries—notably Sweden—have long been prominent on the dressage map. Sweden's inspiration came from the cavalry school at Stromsholm; its northern climate, like that of Switzerland, has also always encouraged indoor riding. The country played a leading role in the development of modern dressage throughout the first half of this century. Its riders completely dominated the competition world dressage arenas for the first 25 years, and have remained a strong force. Possibly their most famous rider has been Major Henri St. Cyr, who took the Olympic gold medals in 1952 and 1956, riding Master Rujus and Juli.

Dressage in the former USSR owes its origins to the work of Englishman James Fillis, who was *écuyer en chef* at the cavalry school at St. Petersburg from 1898 to 1910 and is considered one of the greatest High School riders (see page 18). The sport in this part of the world was inevitably eclipsed by the Bolshevik Revolution in 1917, but gradually began to be practiced again in the state riding schools of the bigger cities after the Second World War. The CIS riders first achieved major international status in the Rome Olympics of 1960, and since then have been consistently to the fore in their annual excursions to the European championships and at the Olympic Games.

One nation that has emerged in the 1990s is Holland, spearheaded by Anky van Grunsven and Olympic Bonfire. This combination challenged the individual gold medals, finishing second at the 1996 Olympics, and at the 1995 and 1997 European Championships, to Germany's Isabell Werth and Gigolo—by a whisker and amid much controversy over the judging. The criticism endured by judges of this highly subjective sport is sure to continue, although dressage is now changing with the times.

It has always been considered an intellectual activity, and was once dominated by mature riders with many years' experience. However, this all changed in the 1980s when the 21-year-old German rider Nicole Uphoff-Becker rode the great Rembrandt to individual and team gold honors at the 1988 Olympic Games. She went on to repeat this feat at the 1992 Olympics with record scores, marking the start of a trend that looks set to continue.

right: Classical equitation at its best, as performed by the Spanish Riding School of Vienna. The "courbette," seen here, is one of the "Haute Ecole" airs performed above the ground.

right: "Haute Ecole" or High School is demonstrated around the world by the Spanish School of Vienna's quadrille team.

SHOW JUMPING

PEOPLE HAVE BEEN RIDING horses for over 3,000 years, but persuading them to jump obstacles is a comparatively new idea. Show jumping, which grew out of this, is, therefore, also a fairly recent innovation in comparison with other equestrian activities. Only in the second half of the eighteenth century did jumping on horses begin to achieve recognition, and then it was slow to gain ground. The first mention of it in a cavalry manual was in France in 1788 and, even though the British foxhunter imagines his or her predecessors crossing country from time immemorial, it was the Enclosure Acts of the eighteenth century—which increased the number of hedges and fences enclosing fields—that set them jumping.

It was about another 100 years before jumping (as opposed to steeplechasing) was officially recorded, and then it sprang up rapidly in various parts of the world. Ireland, where steeplechasing had its infancy, was also a front-runner in show jumping, and at the 1865 Royal Dublin Society's annual show there were competitions for both "high" and "wide" leaps. There were contests in Russia at about the same time, and in Paris in 1866, although here the competitors paraded at the show and then went out into the country to jump fences. Nine years later the famous School at Saumur (see page 19) included jumping in its High School display. In Britain, jumping was primarily a part of agricultural shows and first officially recorded in London in 1876; in the United States the National Horse Show began at Madison Square Garden, New York, in 1883; and a few years later shows were being held all over Germany.

International competition

By the turn of the century the sport was established internationally. In the second of the Modern Olympic Games, at Paris in 1900, three jumping competitions—a High Jump, a Long Jump, and Prize Jumping—were included. The following year in Turin saw the first recorded official international show jumping, with German Army officers pitting their skill against their Italian counterparts. The first International Horse Show was held at Olympia in London in 1907; high and wide jumps were included, and the prize money was quite considerable.

Show jumping was included in the Olympic Games at Stockholm in 1912 under complicated rules. Each fence carried 10 marks, with deductions made for faults: for example, a first refusal cost two marks; a second refusal, or a fall of horse and rider, four marks; and a third refusal, or a fall of the rider only, six marks. There were also marks for hitting a fence with the fore- or hind legs, or for landing on or within the demarcation line of a spread fence. One of the great appeals of show jumping today as a spectator sport is the fact that each person can see for themselves when a horse has hit a fence or brings it down, but in the early days it was so complicated that every fence had its own judge, who would send his marks back to a main judging box to be added up to establish the winner.

In the 1912 Olympics, eight countries—Belgium, Britain, Chile, France, Germany, Norway, Russia, and Sweden—entered a total of 31 riders for the individual show jumping competition, which was won by Captain Cariou of France; Sweden won the team gold medal with France in second place. The following year, Germany founded its own Olympic Equestrian Committee, but of course the war brought the sport to a standstill in Europe. In the United States, the American Horse Shows Association (AHSA) was founded in 1917, and was to be the official representative body for the United States in international affairs.

The Fédération Equestre Internationale

Although equestrian sports were by this time a recognized part of the Olympic program, they had no ruling body of their own. Sweden and France were the prime movers in establishing the Fédération Equestre Internationale in 1921, to bring uniformity to the sport worldwide; the other six founder members were Belgium, Denmark, Italy, Japan, Norway, and the United States. Germany became affiliated to the FEI in the same year, and Switzerland joined in 1922.

Nor was show jumping confined to countries in the northern hemisphere—the first international show had been held in Buenos Aires in 1910, and two Chilean riders competed in the 1912 Olympics. A record entry of 99 riders from 17 countries at the first Olympic event held under FEI rules in Paris, in 1924 (where Sweden again won the team event), showed that the sport was continuing to grow in popularity.

Britain's fairly chaotic show jumping situation was gradually sorted out following the foundation of the British Show Jumping Association in 1923 which, by improving judging and the courses,

right: Strength and athleticism shown by Michel Robert and Miss San Patrignano.

below: Early days for the novice show jumping horse at home. Getting the basics right will go a long way to establishing confidence in future competition.

began to produce top-quality British competitors. The country joined the FEI in 1925 and, the following year, the Royal Dublin Society—having helped to get the sport off the starting blocks some 60 years earlier—introduced international jumping.

Olympic equestrian events were held outside Europe for the first time when the Games went to Los Angeles in 1932, but international travel for horses was an arduous and expensive business, and only 34 riders from six countries competed. The Berlin Olympics in 1936 proved a showcase for German superiority, and their riders won the individual and team gold medals at show jumping, dressage, and the three-day event.

1945 onward

After the Second World War, show jumping restarted throughout Europe. The 1948 Olympic Games were held in London, where Britain gained its first show jumping medal—a team bronze—while Mexico took gold ahead of Spain. Also in that year, the first official FEI Championship for Juniors (from 14–18 years) was introduced. Gradually the FEI introduced other championships, beginning with the Men's World Championship, held for the first time in Paris in 1953, which was won by the Spaniard Francisco ("Paco") Goyoaga. In 1955 Hans Gunter Winkler won the first of two successive World titles on Halla— arguably the greatest show jumping mare of all time, on whom he went on to win the

individual Olympic gold in Stockholm in 1956. Winkler was also a member of the winning team, a feat he repeated in Rome, Tokyo, and Munich to give him a total of five gold medals. The next two World titles were won by the Italian Raimondo d'Inzeo. By this time the World Championship— originally held every year—had settled down to a four-year cycle interspersed with the European Championship (now held every other year).

There is a fundamental difference in these two championships. The European contest is decided on a basis of three rounds, with points from each accumulating to decide the champion, while the World Championship has three qualifying rounds: a speed competition, a Nations Cup, and a Grand Prix. These produce the top four riders, who, in the final round, all ride one another's horses.

A European Championship for women was introduced in 1957, and the British rider Pat Smythe achieved a hat-trick in the years 1961–3 on Flanagan, before the competition was amalgamated with the men's title in 1975. In that year the competition was open to amateur riders only but, from 1977, the European Championship was open to both amateur and professional riders; in 1979 the format was revised again and is still used today.

Pat Smythe was the first woman rider to compete in the Olympics, at Stockholm in 1956, where the British team took the bronze medal behind Germany and Italy. Four years later, in Rome, British rider David Broome won another bronze medal in the individual competition while Germany took the team honors. Germany repeated this feat four years later at the Tokyo Olympics, finishing ahead of France, but then lost its domination of the event to Canada, which won its first team show jumping gold at Mexico in 1968, ahead of France and Germany. The French team in

left, above:
*Ludger Beebaum and
Sprehe Rush On,
Calgary 1995.*
left, below:
*The forerunners of these
contemporary competitors
took part in contests for
"high" and "wide" leaps.
The competitions at Dublin,
Ireland were among the
earliest recorded.*

Tokyo included 18-year-old Janou Lefèbvre (now Tissot), who was also a member of the silver-medal-winning team in Mexico and holds two of the only three women's World Championships to be held.

The first of these was in 1965 at Hickstead in Sussex, England. With its exciting permanent obstacles and gradually improving facilities, Hickstead had a profound effect on show jumping in Britain, introducing the type of course previously only seen in continental Europe. The American Kathy Kusner was expected to take the first World title, but in the end she finished second to the British rider Marion Coakes (now Mould) and her brilliant pony Stroller; this team also won the silver in Mexico in 1968 behind the American Bill Steinkraus, who gave the United States its first individual show jumping gold medal.

The course for the team competition in Mexico was generally condemned as one of the worst ever for an Olympic Games—the awkward placing of fences produced astronomical scores, and the contest was finally won by Canada with 1023/4 faults. By this time Britain was becoming a major show jumping force, experiencing its heyday when David Broome and Harvey Smith came first and third respectively in the 1970 World Championship at La Baule. Four years later, Germany's Hartwig Steenken added to his 1971 European title by winning the World title at Hickstead.

Post-1975

In 1975, all equestrian competitions were opened to men and women (which made sense because Olympic competition was mixed), but changes in that year to the various championships separated amateurs from professionals. Thus the European Championship—which was won by Alwin Schockemöhle of Germany—was for amateurs only, as a result of which, after some arguing, no British riders took part. The British Federation was the only one that had placed its top riders into professional status, putting the country at a great disadvantage in Olympic competition. The World Professional championship of 1975 was never held, because the FEI refused to allow the sponsors to append

their name to it. The 1976 Montreal Olympics were also characterized by a lack of top professional riders, and France won its first Olympic show jumping team gold medal while Alwin Schockemöhle took the individual honors.

Gerd Wiltfang won the 1978 World Championship on home ground in Aachen, where Britain won the team title ahead of Holland, which had emerged as a strong force the year before when winning the European title in Vienna, with team member Johan Heins also taking individual

gold. Britain reclaimed the team honors in 1979 in Rotterdam, the site of the substitute Olympic Games the following year where Canada topped Britain for the gold medal, and Austria's Hugo Simon won individual gold from Britain's John Whitaker.

Paul Schockemöhle, following in brother Alwin's footsteps, won the next three European titles, in Munich (1981), Hickstead (1983), and Dinard (1985). His compatriot Norbert Koof claimed the World title in 1982 in Dublin, Ireland, while France finished ahead of Germany in the team competition. However, the United States successfully challenged Germany's dominance at the 1984 Los Angeles Games, winning the team title over Britain and Germany, and also taking the individual gold and silver medals. The United States remained in its winning team position in the 1986 World Championship in Aachen, where Canada's Gail Greenhough became the first female individual winner since the amalgamation of the Championship.

Britain won the European team title at St. Gallen (1987) and again in Rotterdam two years later, where British rider John Whitaker also took the individual gold. At the Seoul Olympics the following year, Germany again took the team gold, followed by the United States and France. Individual honors went to Pierre Durrand of France, while Greg Best from America took silver ahead of Germany's Karsten Huck. Greg Best also went on to win the World title two years later in Stockholm,

beating Eric Navet of France and Britain's John Whitaker, while France took the team title ahead of Germany and Britain.

Holland came to the fore in the 1992 Barcelona Games, the year after winning the European team championships in La Baule, finishing ahead of Austria and France, although Germany remained on top in the individual competition with Ludger Beerbaum winning gold ahead of Holland's Piet Raymakers. Two years later, at the World Championship in The Hague, Germany had regained its domination and headed the team competition ahead of France, while Franke Sloothak won individual gold from France's Michel Robert.

Switzerland claimed the European Championship team titles ahead of Britain in Gijon (1993) and two years later in St. Gallen, with its team member Willie Melliger winning individual gold in 1993; Irishman Peter Charles took the honors in 1995, while Switzerland won the team gold.

At the Atlanta Olympics in 1996 Germany claimed both team and individual gold medals with Ulrich Kirchhoff, while Willie Melliger finished in the silver-medal position ahead of France's Alexandra Ledermann. Germany, the reigning Olympic and World Champion, claimed the triple crown on winning the European team Championship at Mannheim in 1997—its first success here since 1981. Holland won the silver ahead of Britain, while Ludger Beerbaum won individual gold from Austria's Hugo Simon and Willie Melliger.

EVENTING

THE EXHILARATING SPORT of eventing is considered by many to be the most complete test of a horse, as it incorporates the three disciplines of dressage, cross-country, and show jumping, and calls on the full extent of a horse's ability and its rider's skill. Smaller competitions, especially for novice horses, may be one-day events (in fact, high numbers of entrants sometimes dictate that the three phases of the competition are spread over two days), but all major competitions are three-day events. In the mid-1990s, the name of the sport was changed to "Horse trials" but was then dropped again in favor of the term "Eventing"; this is now used worldwide except in France, where the sport is known as the "Cours Complet."

The origins of eventing

The three-day event was designed originally as a trial for military chargers, and was known as the "Military." The requirements of a charger were that it should be fit to cover long distances at a good average speed and to travel over open country, being bold enough to negotiate any obstacles in its path; while the rider had to judge the paces to reach his target safely and quickly—but without exhausting his horse, because a new day would bring fresh demands. With these principles in mind, the "Military" consisted of an endurance test undertaken at working pace, with a section across country negotiating natural obstacles and a steeplechase course to be ridden at speed. A dressage test was subsequently added to demonstrate the charger's physical development, mastery of the basic paces, and obedience to its rider's unspoken commands. Finally, a show jumping course represented the everyday life to which a charger must be fit to return after an exceptionally demanding exercise.

Although international competition for most sports began with the foundation of the modern Olympic movement in 1896, equestrian events were not introduced until the Stockholm Games in 1912. Entries for these events were exclusively from the military at first, but gradually civilians also started to take part. The framework of the "Concours Complet" (or complete competition, as it was then known) was fairly fluid at first, but settled down between the First and Second World Wars into more or less the form that it takes today.

The three-day event today

The competitors, following one another in succession, complete three different tests—dressage, speed, and endurance, and show jumping—on three consecutive days.

The dressage comprises a set program of about 20 different movements of medium difficulty, to be performed at the walk, trot, or canter, in an arena measuring 197 x 66 ft. (60 x 20 m). Marks are awarded by a panel of three judges, who assess the fluency and accuracy of the performance, and the balance, impulsion, rhythm, and suppleness of the horse, as well as the rider's seat and application of the aids.

The speed and endurance is a four-phase test consisting of: Phases A and C, held over roads and tracks totaling 6–12 miles (10–20 km) to be ridden at the trot or slow canter; Phase B, a steeplechase course of 1–2.5 miles (2–4 km) with 8–12 fences, to be ridden at the gallop; and Phase D, a cross-country course of 3–5 miles (5–8 km) with 20–32 fixed obstacles, to be ridden at the gallop. Penalties are incurred for falls or refusals at the obstacles and for exceeding the maximum time allowed for each phase.

The show jumping consists of a course of 750–1,000 yds. (700–900 m) with 10–12 obstacles. Penalties are incurred for falls or refusals at the obstacles, and for exceeding the time allowed.

There are five levels within eventing, based on a system of points accumulated in competition: Pre-novice (involving courses generally intended to introduce young horses to eventing), Novice, Intermediate, Open Intermediate, and, finally, Advanced (within which there is also a system of one to four stars for different levels—four stars being given to top-class events such as Badminton).

All horses must undergo a veterinary inspection before the start of the competition, another during the speed and endurance test, and a final check before the show jumping. The same horse-and-rider combination must complete all three tests, and the competitor with the lowest number of overall penalties is the winner. In a team competition, there may be three or four team members, and the best three final scores will count for the final placing of the team, with the fourth being discarded.

The cross-country course

The roads and tracks of Phases A and C, and the steeplechase course for Phase B, are quite straightforward (although riders must time these phases carefully to conserve their horses' energy), but the crux comes in Phase D, the cross-country. No two events are alike because of the variation in the natural terrain where they are built. It is this factor, together with the state of the going, the altitude and the weather—quite apart from the different obstacles to be negotiated—that provides the unique challenge. The permutations are endless, and the horses must be fit and bold enough to cope with them all as they gallop and jump over a course they

have never seen. Riders are permitted to walk the course on the previous day in order to work out the speed, the line of approach to the obstacles, the angle and the exact point at which to jump them (there is often a choice, with one or more alternatives being easier but more time-consuming than the most demanding route).

The course-builder's job is to test the riders' judgment and nerve, and the horses' scope, courage, and obedience, but without making unnatural demands. His or her course must produce a worthy winner without destroying the losers, and course-building—undoubtedly a job that calls for considerable skill—has developed into a challenging career. Certain obstacles have become bywords in the sport, and are found in a similar form on many courses: the Coffin (a narrow trough at the bottom of a ditch, with a post-and-rails fence on banks to either side), the Trakehner (a tall post-and-rails set in the bottom of a ditch), and the Helsinki Steps (rails forming the outline of steps dropping down a hillside, which first appeared in the 1952 Olympic Games) are all good examples.

International competition

The first Olympic three-day event at Stockholm in 1912 began with speed and endurance tests, followed by show jumping and then dressage. Sweden won both the team and the individual gold medals, as happened again at Antwerp in 1920, when the dressage phase was replaced by a second endurance test.

For the 1924 Olympics in Paris, the three-day event adopted the format we know today, with dressage first, speed and endurance second, and show jumping last, and Holland won both team and individual

competitions. Four years later, a record 20 nations took part in the Amsterdam Games, including Japan, Argentina, and the United States; Holland won both titles once again, the individual gold medal going to Lt. C.P. Mortanges, who also won in Los Angeles in 1932 where only six nations were represented—largely because of the difficulty and cost to European countries of transporting their teams.

At Berlin in 1936 the cross-country course was particularly demanding, with the fourth obstacle—a sloping pond swollen with rain—causing havoc, and Germany won both team and individual gold medals. After the war, the recently formed British Horse Society organized the three-day event at Aldershot for the London Games in 1948—the first time Britain had ever held such an event. The United States won the team competition and Capt. Chevallier of France won the individual, but this was a turning point for Britain in the history of the sport because the Duke of Beaufort, then Master of the Horse, decided that eventing was something at which Britain should excel. He invited the British Horse Society to hold a national three-day event at Badminton, his Gloucestershire estate, in spring 1949, and this soon gained a reputation as the world's leading three-day event.

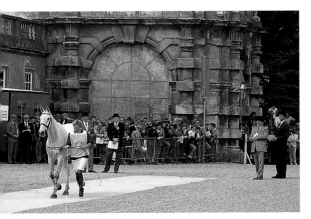

above: Stringent veterinary testing is carried out throughout a three-day event.

left: The standard required of the dressage phase of a horse trial is lower than the specialty sport. Here, New Zealand's Mark Todd partners Bertie Blunt, to embark on a famous victory at Badminton.

above left: *Part of the cross-country stage.*
above right: *The steeplechase phase is the "speed" element of the testing three-day event.*
left: *The young horse is carefully introduced to natural obstacles like water.*

right: *Walking the course; measuring distances, working out the optimum routes are all part of the skill of a successful event rider.*

The 1950s onward

In 1954, Switzerland held the first European Championship at Basle, where Britain's Bertie Hill was the winner and British riders filled four out of the next six places, also taking the team competition; among them were Margaret Hough and Diana Mason, the first women riders to compete internationally. In 1955 Britain successfully defended its title at Windsor and, the following year at the Stockholm Olympic Games, won its first team gold medal, with Sweden taking the individual honors. Sheila Wilcox became the first female European Champion on High and Mighty at Copenhagen in 1957, but at the European Championships at Harewood, England, two years later, Britain's star was waning and Germany won the team championship. Australia captured the team title at the Rome Olympics in 1960, while Italy

won both team and individual titles at Tokyo four years later.

The first World Championship was scheduled for Burghley, England, in 1966, but an outbreak of African Horse Sickness prevented the movement of horses throughout Europe. However, Ireland, the U.S.S.R., and the United States overcame the ban by flying their horses directly to Britain, and the gallant Argentinian team made the mammoth journey by sea—an effort that proved worthwhile, as the country's Tokyo silver medalist, Carlos Moratorio, became the first World Champion. Ireland took the team title.

Treacherous rain at the Olympic Games in Mexico—over a fairly straightforward course although at unprecedented altitude—in 1968 caused a number of falls, but did not deter Britain from winning the team gold medal, with Derek Allhusen finishing

as individual silver medallist behind Jean-Jacques Guyon of France. Britain repeated this feat four years later in Munich, where Richard Meade also won the country's first individual gold medal. Germany won the team and Russia the individual title at Kiev in 1973, while the United States took the World Championship at Burghley by storm in 1974; the American Bruce Davidson also won the individual title. The United States continued its domination at the 1976 Montreal Olympics, taking the team gold and the individual gold and silver with Tad Coffin and Mike Plumb. Bruce Davidson continued the run by winning the individual gold medal at the World Championship at Lexington in the United States in 1978, where Canada took the team title. The U.S.S.R. won the team title at the 1980 Moscow Games, which were boycotted by a number of countries.

The emerging southern hemisphere

It was later in the 1980s that the domination of riders from the southern hemisphere—particularly from New Zealand and also, to an extent, Australia—began to emerge. Meanwhile Britain's Lucinda Prior-Palmer (later Green) became the first all-conquering female event rider, winning Badminton six times on six different horses, together with two European golds and one silver medal, and a World title at Luhmuhlen, Germany in 1982. Her mantle was next taken by another British rider, Virginia Elliot (formerly Holgate and Leng), who won an Olympic bronze medal in Los Angeles, 1984, behind the New Zealander Mark Todd and American Karen Stives. The United States also took the team gold ahead of Britain and Germany before the latter moved into gold-medal-winning position in Seoul four years later. Virginia Leng won her first World title in Gawler, Australia, in 1986, ahead of New Zealander Trudy Boyce, where Britain also won the team title; she went on to win European championship gold medals at Burghley (1985); Luhmuhlen (1987), and Burghley (1989).

Mark Todd of New Zealand won his second individual Olympic gold medal at Seoul, encouraging the explosion of the sport in his country and the beginning of Kiwi and Australian riders basing themselves and their horses in Europe to prepare for the major championships. Britain was the most popular place for overseas riders to choose because of its numerous one-day events, which are ideal for novice horses. Another New Zealander, Blyth Tait, emerged as the World Champion at Stockholm in 1990, while he and his compatriots won the team title ahead of Britain, whose dominance in the sport was by this time being severely challenged.

Matt Ryan, an Australian based in Britain, secured the team and individual gold medals at the Barcelona Games in 1992, while New Zealand took the team silver ahead of Germany. New Zealander Vaughn Jefferis won the subsequent World title in The Hague in 1994, while Britain took the team title from the United States, which emerged from a lean spell to become once again a major force in the sport. Indeed, the United States—together with Canada, Mexico, and Argentina—have always had a strong equestrian tradition, and these four countries provide the mainstay of the Pan-American Three-day Event, which has been held at regular intervals since 1955.

Eventing rule changes

Rule changes implemented by the International Olympic Committee in 1996 in Atlanta meant that, for the first time, riders could not represent their country in the team and individual competition on the same horse; instead the competitions were divided and ridden over slightly different cross-country courses. Australia took the team title ahead of the United States and New Zealand, while the individual honors—albeit with some of the world's best horse-and-rider partnerships missing—were awarded to Blyth Tait ahead of his compatriot Sally Clark.

Rule changes from the Fédération Equestre Internationale (FEI) also affected the European Championship, run every two years, which, after Ian Stark's individual and team victory for Britain in Punchestown, 1991, and Sweden's gold medal in Achselschwang, Germany two years later, were made open to the world. Britain won the first team title over France at the 1995 "open" European Championship in Pratoni Del Vivaro, Italy, while Ireland's Lucy Thompson took the individual title ahead of Marie-Christine Duroy of France. At Burghley in 1997, Mark Todd won the competition itself but the European individual gold medal went to Germany's second-placed Bettina Overesch-Boeker, ahead of Britain's William Fox-Pitt. Britain won the team gold. After this competition, the FEI decided to revert to the original format of the European Championship, which has once again become "closed" to the rest of the world. This is a change which can only lower both the standard and the prestige of the competition.

One other change to affect the sport is that of the withdrawal of the weight system in the speed-and-endurance phase, whereby lighter riders were required to make up the difference with saddle weights. Research proved that this "dead" weight made the task of these horses more difficult (since human weight can obviously be moved to assist the horse), and its requirement was lifted internationally in February 1998. This is, inevitably, the subject of ongoing debate because, whereas the weighted system was perhaps prejudicial against lighter riders, these same riders could now be said to have a considerable advantage over their heavier competitors.

RACING

left: Eclipse, one of the most famous racehorses of all time, captured by one of the most famous equestrian artist George Stubbs.

O N JULY 23, 1985, two of the world's major names in flat racing—trainer Wayne Lukas and owner Robert Sangster—battled to acquire an unraced yearling colt at the Keeneland Sales in the United States. Robert Sangster eventually won the battle with a record bid of $13.1 million. The colt in question, Seattle Dancer, demanded such a price because his pedigree indicated him to be a prime example of that swiftest of all equine breeds, the Thoroughbred. He was by Nijinsky, European Horse of the Year, and his grandsire was Northern Dancer, the most influential Thoroughbred stallion on either side of the Atlantic.

The Thoroughbred (see also pages 38–41) was established in seventeenth-century Britain, perfected through a judicious program of selective breeding in many of the countries to which it subsequently spread, and is now the basis of an international industry linking five continents, providing some superb talent for excellent racing throughout the world.

Flat racing

The person responsible for turning racing into the sport that we recognize today was King Charles II of England. Horse racing was one of his passions, and he developed the sport around the town of Newmarket in Suffolk, where his father, Charles I, had endowed the first cup race in 1634.

Until this time, horses used for racing—which was generally in the form of two horses racing to settle a wager between owners—were nearly all native-bred. However, from the reign of Queen Elizabeth I, more and more horses were imported into Britain, initially from Italy and Spain. These, together with later arrivals from North Africa and the Eastern Mediterranean—the so-called Barbs (from the Barbary Coast), Turks, and Arabians—achieved little actual racing success, but

their blood, mixed with that of native stock, was to have a profound effect on the breed of horse, and led to nothing less than the establishment of the Thoroughbred as a breed in its own right.

All Thoroughbreds in the world today are descended from three famous eastern stallions—the Byerley Turk, the Darley Arabian, and the Godolphin Arabian (see page 38). The second of these, described as "a horse of exquisite beauty," sired Flying Childers—the first truly great racehorse—and, through the latter's brother, became the great-great grandsire of perhaps the most famous racehorse of all time, Eclipse.

Bred in 1764 by the Duke of Cumberland, Eclipse was never beaten, with 26 races to his credit. At stud, he produced 344 individual winners, one of his most celebrated descendants being St. Simon, the 1884 Gold Cup winner at Ascot. His offspring won 571 races in Britain alone, where he headed the winning sire's list nine times. From St. Simon descends one of the greatest of modern racehorses, the Italian champion Ribot, also unbeaten in a lengthy career and twice successful in the Prix de l'Arc de Triomphe.

British racing and the Jockey Club

Racecourses began to spring up all over Britain in the early eighteenth century, but—with the exception of Newmarket, where King Charles made and kept the rules—overall control was lax. It was for this reason that, in about 1750, a group of sportsmen at Newmarket formed the Jockey Club. This became the supreme authority over its corner of Suffolk, and its right to "warn off" anyone whom it considered undesirable was recognized by the courts in 1827. The influence of the Jockey Club was gradually extended until all racecourses in the country came under its aegis. It assumed responsibility for sanctioning tracks, approving programs, licensing officials, and framing the regulations, and it was not until 1993, with the formation of

right: The world's most challenging steeplechase, the Grand National, held every year in April at Aintree racecourse, England.

above left: Racehorses in training on the gallops. Training usually takes place early in the morning.

above right: The National Hunt Festival at Cheltenham, England. Racing amid the beautiful setting of the Cotswolds.

the British Horseracing Board, that the responsibility for the administration of British racing was eventually removed from the jurisdiction of the Jockey Club.

During the late eighteenth and nineteenth centuries, the Jockey Club's power had often rested in the hands of a single forceful personality. One of the first of these men was Sir Charles Bunbury, under whose rule the Club was sufficiently strong, in 1791, to warn off the Prince of Wales (later George IV) after an inquiry into suspicious circumstances concerning the running of a horse called Escape. Bunbury was the owner of Diomed, winner of the first race run at Epsom in 1780, when racing younger horses was becoming more fashionable. This was to become the world's premier classic race—the Derby—which led to the development of today's five Classic races: the 1,000 Guineas (for fillies) and 2,000 Guineas (for colts), both over 1 mile (1,500 m); the Oaks (for fillies) and the Derby (for colts), both over 1½ miles (2,2500 m); and the St. Leger, run over 1 mile, 6 furlongs and 127 yds. (1,500 m).

The United States

Throughout this period of progress in Britain, racing had also been developing in other lands. In North America racing took hold after the revolutionary war, when Sir

Charles Bunbury's Diomed was among many influential horses imported from Britain. A failure at stud in England, Diomed was 21 before arriving in America, where he soon began to produce offspring of fine quality. Another horse, Medley, who reached the country in 1784, also had an enormous effect on the evolution of the American Thoroughbred, while two of the most successful sires in the history of racing in the New World were Leviathan, who arrived in 1830 and was five times leading sire, and Glencoe, who left an indelible mark on both sides of the ocean.

The greatest American-bred stallion of the nineteenth century was Lexington, champion sire on no fewer than 16 occasions, whose career spanned the Civil War. The war shattered racing and breeding in the southern states, but development continued apace in the north—where New York became a major center—together with the mid- and far west, as well as the "border" states of Maryland and Kentucky. The classic three-year-old races were all instituted in the decade following the Civil War. First came the Belmont Stakes in 1867 which, since 1905, has been run at Belmont Park, the New York course, over 1½ miles (2,400 m). This was followed by the Preakness Stakes of 1 mile, 1½ furlongs (1,900 m) established in 1873 on the

Pimlico course near Baltimore, Maryland; and in 1875 by the Kentucky Derby, run over 1¼ miles (2,000 m) at Churchill Downs, Louisville in Kentucky.

However, the image of the sport was becoming increasingly tarnished through the malpractices of those concerned solely with making money—and as quickly as possible. Even after the formation of a Jockey Club in 1894, the rising tide of public indignation led to racing being banned or curtailed in many states. Today, with the Jockey Club and its associated bodies exercising overall control, the situation is very different and the United States holds the premier position on the world racing stage.

The main breeding area for racehorses is in Kentucky, the world-renowned "blue grass" country near Lexington. American breeding is heavily inclined toward satisfying the needs of owners anxious for quick returns, which has resulted in a high production of sprint-bred stock designed to win as two-year-olds. However, a rigorous testing program, plus a voracious acquisition of representatives of the world's best bloodlines, has brought American-bred racehorses to an ascendancy seen in the English Derby successes of such horses as Sir Ivor (1968), Mill Reef (1971), Golden Fleece (1982), and Shahrastani (1986).

left: Under floodlights at
the Happy Valley racetrack
in Hong Kong.

above: Racing in the snow
at St. Moritz, Switzerland.

France

In recent years there has been a resurgence of the French-bred racehorse. The sport did not begin to get underway in France in any recordable manner until more than 20 years after the establishment of the Jockey Club across the Channel in England, and then what little organization there was disappeared during the Revolution and the Napoleonic Wars.

It was an Englishman, Lord Henry Seymour, who was largely instrumental in the renaissance of French racing in the second quarter of the nineteenth century. Together with the Duc d'Orleans, he founded the Jockey Club in 1833 and, when it became apparent that their fellow members were more interested in the social aspect of the club than in racing, they led a breakaway group to form the Société d'Encouragement pour l'Amélioration des Races de Chevaux en France.

In 1836 a new racecourse was opened not far from Paris at Chantilly, and the training center that has grown up around it now rivals that of Newmarket. The 1 mile, 4 furlongs (2,400 m) Prix du Jockey Club—the equivalent of the Epsom Derby—was founded there in the course's inaugural year, and was followed within 10 years by the other classic French races, the Poule d'Essai des Pouliches and the Poule d'Essai des Poulains (equivalent to the 1,000 and 2,000 Guineas respectively), the Prix de Diane (the French Oaks), and the Prix Royal Oak (the St. Leger). The Prix de l'Arc de Triomphe, now the greatest of all the international flat races, was founded at Longchamp in 1920.

Italy

Italy is the most important of the other European racing countries, but again it was a late starter. Regular race meetings in Milan—today the principal center of the sport—were held only from the 1840s, and racing in Rome did not begin until 1868.

Although the Italian breeding industry is small, it has had a disproportionately large international influence, primarily due to one man, Federico Tesio, who founded what is now the Dormello-Olgiata Stud in 1898. Between 1911 and his death in 1954, Tesio produced 20 winners of the Italian Derby, and two world-beaters, Nearco and Ribot—both of them undefeated throughout their careers.

Australia and New Zealand

The horse was unknown in Australia and New Zealand when the early English settlers landed there in the late eighteenth century, but in numerical horse terms the Antipodes today rank second only to United States.

In Australia the policy has always been to produce tough horses with endurance and as much speed as possible. Each state has its individual classic program, but these races are supplemented by valuable long-distance handicaps, such as the 2 mile (3,200 m) Melbourne, Sydney, and Brisbane Cups, which carry big prize money and offer attractive betting opportunities.

Jump racing

Racing on the world stage is flat racing. In the United States this operates all year round, while in Europe the season runs only from March to early November. However, in Europe there is also the "winter game" of National Hunt racing, which is staged over fences or hurdles and, in Britain and Ireland at least, attracts almost as large a following as racing on the flat.

These races are run either over fences of birch or gorse (called steeplechases) or hurdles; they are longer than flat races (the minimum distance is 2 miles (3,200 m) and

right: The betting ring: part and parcel of the racing world.

are contested by older horses. Hunting is the direct ancestor of the steeplechase, which began when the British Enclosure Acts of the eighteenth century caused the spread of hedges, ditches, fences, and other obstacles to enclose areas of land, making it essential for followers of the chase to teach their horses to jump if they were to stay with the hunt. Enthusiasts so enjoyed this new development that matches were held over natural country, from one landmark to another; this was usually from the steeple of one village church to another, hence the name of the race.

The first half of the nineteenth century brought a gradual division of the sport, one part retaining the essentially amateur, hunting-based element that was to become the foundation of point-to-pointing, and the other gathering an increasingly professional aura, with jumping races held on regular public courses. The first annual jumping meeting was inaugurated at St. Albans in 1830, and nine more years saw the first running of what has become the greatest steeplechase of all, the Grand National at Aintree, near Liverpool. This race—"a sweepstakes of 20 sovereigns each, 5 forfeit, with 100 sovereigns added"—was won by a 16 h.h. bay horse called Lottery. In this race, each horse carried 168 lbs. (76 kg), and the 4 mile (6,400 m) course, most of it over plowed earth, contained 29 obstacles.

Since that first race, some truly magnificent horses have won the Grand National. Golden Miller, for example—claimed by many to have been the finest of all winners, and successful in five consecutive Cheltenham Gold Cups—won in 1934. Reynoldstown became a dual winner in 1935 and 1936, a feat that remained unsurpassed until Red Rum triumphed in 1973, 1974, and 1977.

By the 1960s the Grand National was no longer out on its own in the prize-money stakes. With the advent of commercial

left: Racing in Maryland over wooden fences.

sponsorship, there is now a series of rich prizes to be won by steeplechasers and hurdlers—especially at the three-day National Hunt Festival at Cheltenham, which hosts some famous jumping races such as the Gold Cup and the Champion Hurdle.

However, this sport has never really caught on in countries other than Britain and Ireland. Early American jump racing was, like its British counterpart, based on the hunting that took place on the eastern seaboard, but on regular tracks it had a later beginning and it was not until 1865 that the first American steeplechase was recorded. Another 30 years brought the formation of the National Steeplechase Association, but the sport never achieved the enormous public following accorded to flat racing, and jump racing gradually diminished.

Today, however, the United States calendar includes races such as the Maryland Hunt Cup, held over 4 miles (6,400 m). Fields are small, all riders must be amateurs and the obstacles consist of fixed wooden rails. In 1965 Jay Trump became the first horse to pull off the Maryland Hunt Cup/Grand National double.

Point-to-points

Professional riders are prohibited in point-to-pointing, the third element of the racing scene in Britain and Ireland, which is still based on the same hunting field from which National Hunt racing sprang. During the nineteenth century, the infant National Hunt Committee, which was occupied with regulating jumping meetings on established courses, was happy to leave individual hunts to run an annual fixture for their own enjoyment.

These early private matches, therefore, became end-of-season entertainments for members of the Hunt. Today, the usual point-to-point program comprises five or six races, each run over a minimum of 3 miles (4,800 m).

right: One of the highlights of the racing calendar in the United States—the Kentucky Derby.

ENDURANCE RIDING

WHEN THE Tom Quilty Gold Cup 100 mile (161 km) endurance ride was first run in the mountains of New South Wales, Australia, in 1966, there was an outcry from animal-welfare supporters, protesting that this "cruel" horse race must be stopped. The Royal Society for the Prevention of Cruelty to Animals (RSPCA) was alerted but, when it heard how the organizers planned to safeguard the horses and saw the strict way in which veterinary rules were applied, the protests faded away. From the start, the fundamental principle of the sport has always been that the horses' welfare is paramount.

Endurance riding is the youngest equestrian sport, but today has a large international following. It began in its present form in the United States, with the inauguration in 1955 of the world's most famous 100 mile (161 km) endurance ride —the Tevis Cup. Named after the President of the Wells Fargo Company, the race follows the route of the company's Pony Express riders and stagecoaches (see also pages 22), passing over the Sierra Nevada range; the arduous route must be completed in one day, and only the very fittest horses will do so. After 1955, endurance riding continued to flourish in the United States for a decade before catching on in Australia. More recently, Britain, France, Germany, New Zealand, South Africa, and the Gulf States have become similarly involved.

A changing sport

Today, there is no doubt that the face of the sport is changing. The number of professional trainers—producing horses for others to ride—is on the increase, in a direct divergence from the original aim that one person should train one horse to complete 100 miles (160 km) in one day, with the precept that hands-on training of one's own horse was essential not only to success, but to the

right: Long-distance partners: Former U.S. champions R.O. Grand Sultan and Becky Hart.

horse's welfare and the satisfaction of taking part. Many purists find it extremely disturbing that this principle may no longer hold true in the future.

It remains to be seen whether horse-and-rider combinations that have not trained together can succeed over more traditional partnerships, but one way in which they might do so—giving another cause for concern—is by putting better and, inevitably, more expensive horses into their professional training programs. By contrast, past endurance riders have often excelled with the horses they simply happened to own, bringing partnerships such as triple world champions Becky Hart and the great R. O. Grand Sultan, or former European Champion Jill Thomas and Egyptian Khalifa, to mind. The graph of horse potential coming into endurance has curved

sharply upward in recent years, and the sport will be looking to its rule book to ensure that the amateur horse-and-rider partnership is not squeezed out as a result.

The advent of prize money (in major competitions at least) is another big change, and endurance has only to look at its effect in other equestrian sports to see how it might alter the historic scenario of friendly rivalry, with competitors helping one another. However, despite the metamorphosis at the top level, the lower levels of

right: A long day ahead— competitors in the 100 mile Golden Horseshoe Ride, Exmoor, England.

teams. Endurance championships have been run under the jurisdiction of the Fédération Equestre Internationale (FEI) since 1984. However, the Endurance Long Distance Rides Conference (ELDRIC) has existed since 1979 to act as an international forum for riders, and to establish international rules. Membership is open both to national organizations and to individuals.

ELDRIC runs its own annual Championship—the ELDRIC Trophy—which is hotly contested and based on points gained from rides in more than one country. Trophies are awarded for the over-all top horse/rider combination, the top rider and the top Arab horse.

endurance riding remain fundamentally unchanged and, for the rider whose horse is a hobby, still provide the fun of a challenge in a thoroughly friendly environment and without the element of competition.

Rules and levels of competition

The rules of endurance riding vary from country to country. The United States, for example, has its limited-distance program, while Britain has both the British Endurance Riding Association qualifying system and Endurance Horse and Pony Society competitive trail rides. At these, the aim is for entrants to complete the distance inside a maximum allowed time, and to pass the veterinary inspections held before, during, and after the ride. The reward is usually a rosette, as well as points which can accrue toward annual trophies.

Riders can progress from these basic rides of 20–60 miles (32–96 km) into the endurance "race" riding division. The term race is used advisedly: placings are introduced here, and the winner is the first horse past the post which also passes the veterinary inspections. However, the rides are run over distances from 50–100 miles (80–161 km) in one day (or in combinations of distances over a series of days), so horses have to be well paced; the competition is mostly run at trot or a hand canter—not at a gallop as in a flat race.

Only the top riders progress from national rides of this type into international

right: *Rides cover a variety of natural terrain. Here, horse and rider take a break during the Golden Horseshoe Ride on Exmoor, England.*

The endurance horse

Most people, when asked to imagine an endurance horse, will probably think of an Arabian, and this breed (and its crosses) have undoubtedly enjoyed more success in the sport than any other, combining the qualities of soundness and stamina with intelligence and the ability to take care of itself over difficult terrain. The Arab is also renowned for its weight-carrying ability in relation to size, while its high ratio of skin surface area to body volume means that it dissipates heat easily.

However, success in endurance riding depends on more than the breed of horse. Good conformation, and the capability of being trained to carry the rider with the minimum stress and energy output, are vital. Indeed, it is one of the sport's main attractions that no specific type of horse is needed for success. For instance, in the United States native breeds such as the Appaloosa, Morgan, and Standardbred are all in evidence, as well as the Arabian, Thoroughbred, and Connemara. In Britain the range is less extensive, but the Arabian and Thoroughbred (and their crosses) are popular, as are hunters and larger native breeds; while in Germany national breeds such as the Hanoverian, Trakehner, and Holstein are seen, as well as non-German breeds such as the Norwegian Fjord and Welsh Cob. From just these three countries it can be seen that the scope for horses is extremely wide, although higher-level riders generally prefer lean, athletic types. There is no maximum or minimum age limit for riders, but horses must be at least five years old to compete.

Training and fitness

For competition at riding-club level, a horse of good overall fitness will be able to tackle the basic endurance distances of 20–30 miles (32–48 km) in one day without a lot of extra work. From then on training is progressive, and taking part in competitions—perhaps every three or four weeks during the season—helps the process tremendously.

Most endurance training is carried out at the aerobic level, and some riders use heart-rate monitors to assess their horses' progress. The aim is to increase the distance and speed at which a horse can work aerobically, i.e., using oxygen and without calling on the anaerobic method of energy production, which can only be maintained for a few minutes before the horse tires. Training is, therefore, mainly undertaken at sub-maximal level, i.e., at a good working trot, with rest breaks at walk and occasional canters. When a horse starts to compete at faster speed and over the longer distances, training at home can be reduced to two or three days a week. Some fast work, in the form of interval training (see page 184) is usually introduced in the run-up to a competition. After a major ride, most horses are rested for two to three weeks to allow for full recovery.

Competition and veterinary inspections

The rides cover a variety of natural terrain, with the most challenging taking place in hill or mountain areas. The route—over tracks, fields, and woodland—is marked with biodegradable paint, lime, or colored tape, with a map usually provided as well.

Veterinary inspections take place before the ride to check that each horse is fit to start, as well as during and after it. The vet takes its pulse with a stethoscope. It must have recovered below a set parameter (usually 64 beats per minute); the horse is checked for signs of injury (which may be penalized); and finally trotted to check for soundness. Lameness incurs immediate elimination.

Veterinary knowledge has increased tremendously over the past decade, and it is rare today for a horse to need treatment for exhaustion. In particular, the Ridgway test (cardiac recovery index), where the horse's pulse is checked before and after trotting, is very successful in revealing which horses are tiring, and these will be pulled out of the race.

Riders usually have a support crew of family or friends to meet them on the route, provide drinks, electrolytes (to assist rehydration), washing water, and other essentials, and to help them to prepare their horses for veterinary inspections. At endurance "race" riding level, the clock runs until the horse is presented, so time is of the essence in passing the inspections, and an efficient crew is vital. At the lower levels, the crews have time to get to know one another, to exchange help and information, and generally to join the riders in the friendly endurance scene.

POLO

POLO IS A STICK-AND-BALL GAME played on horseback by opposing teams of four a side, and originated in the Orient over 2,000 years ago. In Persia the game was known as *chaugan* (a mallet), but its present name is derived from the Tibetan word *pulu*, meaning a root, from which the polo ball is made. The earliest references to polo are linked with Alexander the Great and Darius, King of Persia; the game is believed to have originated here, although it was certainly played in some form throughout the east.

Muslim invaders from the northwest and the Chinese from the northeast took the game into India where, in the mid-nineteenth century, it was discovered by English planters in Assam. Silchar, capital of the Cachar district, soon became the birthplace of modern polo, and the Silchar Club—founded in 1859—is the oldest in the world. Teams originally had nine riders, but were later reduced to seven and eventually to four, as the ponies became bigger and faster. In 1876 the height limit in India was set at 13.2 h.h., and in England at 14 h.h.; today the average height is about 15.1 h.h.

The spread of the game
In 1869, the game was introduced into England by army officers who played, eight a side, on Hounslow Heath, near London. It immediately caught on, and the Hurlingham Club in London became the headquarters of English polo, issuing the first English rules in 1875 (the Indian Polo Association was also formed at about this time, and framed its own rules until the Second World War). 1878 saw the first Inter-Regimental Tournament in England, and the National Pony Society was founded in 1893 to promote the breeding of polo ponies.

The game soon spread to other parts of the world. In Argentina it was an immediate success, and the Argentinians became the biggest breeders and exporters of polo ponies in the world. Polo was introduced into the United States in 1876 by James Gordon Bennett, and international matches began in 1886 with teams from Britain and the United States competing for the Westchester Cup. It was from the United States that the most successful players came—that is, until Argentina overtook them. After 1945 the Argentinians reigned supreme and were unbeaten in the Cup of the Americas, the only international championship still in existence. By then the country had some 3,000 active players, to 1,000 Americans and about 500 British players.

Polo skills
For a pony to be suitable for polo, it must be able to gallop flat out, stop in its own length, swing around 180 degrees, and start at top speed from a standstill in any direction. Courage is essential, as are a long neck, good shoulders, a short, strong back, strong quarters, and well-let-down hocks. The pony must also be taught to neck-rein, as it will be ridden with one hand.

For the player, basic horsemanship, good balance, and a secure seat are all necessary requirements. More important still are a good eye for the ball, courage, and accurate timing. Players are taught how to strike the ball on a dummy horse and, having mastered the strokes—offside and nearside forward and backhand, nearside under the neck, back shots under the tail, and so on—progress to mounted work and then to slow practice games.

Rules and safety
A polo ground may not exceed 300 yds. (274 m) in length. The goals, which are 8 yds. (7.3 m) wide and at least 10 ft. (3 m) high, must be no less than 250 yds. (227 m) apart. The ball is made of willow or bamboo root and is no more than 3 in. (8 cm) in diameter; the stick is made of sycamore, ash, or bamboo cane and is some 48–54 in. (120–37 cm) long with a right-angled head.

The aim of polo is to score goals against the opposing side. It is played in seven-minute chukkas, with games usually consisting of four or six chukkas. Every time a goal is scored, the teams change ends. Most games are played on a handicap basis, with all players given a handicap rating of –2 to +10 (the latter being the best).

The rules of polo are mainly for safety, and concentrate on clarifying right of possession of the ball. Players are penalized for infringing on this and causing danger—for example, by crossing the line of the ball in front of a player who has right of way. The game is stopped if a pony falls or becomes lame, or its gear is damaged, if a player is injured or loses his or her helmet, or if the ball goes out of play.

Polo is an expensive sport which has not prevented it from becoming increasingly popular, and the wish of participants to play all year round has led to the introduction of arena polo, where teams play on an all-weather surface rather than on grass.

above: Basic horsemanship, good balance, and a secure seat are all necessary in a polo player.

right: The Prince of Wales is a keen participant on the English polo circuit.

left: St. Moritz, Switzerland, is a popular and glamorous location for the world's top polo players.

SHOWING

SHOWING BEGAN some 200 years ago, and sprang from the desire of breeders to prove that they had used their skill to produce horses that were better made for the job they had to do and possessed greater strength, stamina, and a more classical conformation than those of their rivals. Successful breeders could also command top prices for their young stock.

A horse's movement, quality, proportions, and beauty of outline have always been the yardsticks by which it is assessed in the show ring, but the most essential quality of all is presence—that almost indefinable ability to command the viewer's attention. A horse may be better made and move better than others, but if it lacks presence it will not go far in the championship world.

Probably the purest form of showing is that of showing the young horse in hand. However, today there are in-hand and ridden classes for virtually every type of horse and rider, of which some of the major showing categories are described below. A number of other classes have also become popular in recent years, including those for colored horses, Quarter Horses, western riding, and miniature horses.

above: A horse's movement, quality, proportions, and beauty of outline are yardsticks in the show ring.

Hunter classes

In-hand and ridden hunter classes are among the most prestigious of all in the show ring. Ridden hunter classes are divided into eight categories, in each of which the horses are galloped, shown stripped (without tack), and—in Britain and Ireland, though not in the United States or Canada—ridden by the judge.

Weight classes are divided into light-, middle-, and heavyweight. These refer to the weight that the horse is capable of carrying, which is linked to the amount of bone that it possesses (measured around the cannon bone).

There are also classes for small hunters (of 15.2 h.h. or under); ladies' hunters,

ridden sidesaddle; novice, for horses that have not yet won a certain level of prize money; four-year-old classes; and classes for working hunters, which are expected to jump a course of 8–12 natural fences.

Classes for riding horses, hacks, and cobs

Riding horses suitable for showing should be good movers and animals that anyone could ride. Hacks, which are more lightly built than hunters, are the epitome of elegance and manners, and should exhibit an exemplary action at walk, trot, and canter. Their classes are divided into small

(14.2–15 h.h.) and large (15–15.3 h.h.).

Cobs are versatile and relatively inexpensive to keep, and their classes are among the most popular on the circuit. The ideal cob should not exceed 15.1 h.h., but should have the bone and substance of a heavyweight hunter. Classes are divided into lightweight (capable of carrying up to 196 lbs. [89 kg] with 8½ in. [21 cm] of bone), and heavyweight (carrying over 196 lbs. [89 kg] with at least 9 in. [23 cm] of bone).

Arabian horses

The Arab Horse Society runs classes for pure-bred Arabs, Anglo-Arabs (Arab-

Thoroughbred crosses), and part-bred Arabs (those with at least 25 percent Arab blood). These attract competitors around the world, with classes run in mainstream shows as well as specific AHS shows and championships.

Pony classes

These classes are very popular in Britain, but the show pony is a phenomenon rarely found outside Britain. Classes include those for lead-rein and first-ridden show ponies (divided into height categories); as well as for working hunter and show hunter (also divided by height). The working-pony classes are popular with those who believe that these more natural ponies make better mounts for children than the often highly strung individuals kept solely for showing.

right: Competitors survey the arena at West Palm Beach, Florida, United States.

Turnout for horse and rider

This depends on the class, but suitable turnout for a rider in mainstream classes is a well-cut tweed coat (women also may wear a blue or black coat); canary, fawn, or buff breeches; long boots, leather or string gloves; and a collar and tie.

Hunters—except novices, which wear a snaffle—are shown in a double bridle with plain noseband and browband; martingales are only permitted in working-hunter classes. The showing saddle is straight-cut to show off the shoulders and must suit the size of the horse, as a small saddle on a heavyweight horse (or vice versa) will not create a good overall picture.

right: After exhibiting excellence at walk, trot, and canter, horses are ridden by the show judge.

Show judging

The judging at shows is bound to be subjective, but a knowledgeable judge of any horse or pony will look for good limbs, a well-sloped shoulder going obliquely back into the body, depth in the girth and the loin, a nice front with generous outlook, and strong quarters and second thighs. Bad limbs, shortage of bone, straight shoulders, a shallow body, and weak hind legs are all obvious physical faults.

The show ring may not be to everyone's taste, but it is of very real value to all types of horse and pony. While there are still people who care about a breed, there will be shows at which breeders and owners can exhibit their horses, having done their best to achieve and perpetuate the best qualities of that breed.

right: Long hours go into preparing horses and prices for the show ring here, at West Palm Beach, Florida, United States.

HUNTING

left: Hunting in open country increased during the eighteenth century.

right: Hunting in France is still a way of life—there is little jumping and horses used are generally bred for the speed of a long, fast chase.

T HERE IS NO RECORD OF the first use of the horse as a means of transport in following hounds. The ancient Chinese, Egyptian, and Greek civilizations did much of their hunting on foot, although they used horses extensively on the battlefield. In Britain and Ireland, organized hunting—providing the pattern for that practiced in Australia, India, New Zealand, South Africa, the United States, and elsewhere—has been a major equestrian activity for some 300 years and, before the comparatively recent growth of competitive riding to its present level, was the principal horse sport. It was from the hunting field that show jumping and steeplechasing (see page 106) evolved, while show hunter classes (see page 130) display much of the best in modern hunter breeding.

The great horse master Xenophon (see page 16) made it clear in the fifth century B.C. that the same priorities of stamina, fitness, and obedience were required in the hunting horse then as are still sought by today's hunting fraternity. In the third century A.D., the Roman writer Oppian described the points he would look for in buying a hunter-charger as follows: "He must have size and substance and well knit limbs; a small head carried high, with a neck arching like the plume on a helmet; forehead broad, thick curly forelock; eye clear and fiery, broad chest; and back with a double chine [sic]; a good full tail; muscular thighs; fine, clean legs, pastern sloping, hoof rising high, close grained and strong." Oppian also referred to the necessity for "an active horse accustomed to leap over stone fences and dykes," but for many centuries—certainly throughout Medieval times—the hunting horse was not required to possess the jumping ability expected from the modern quality hunter.

Developments in hunting

Stag, boar, and fallow buck were the main quarry for hounds in Europe for centuries, and continued to be so long after William the Conqueror brought discipline to the chase in England. To pursue this quarry, the horse needed stamina for long days in the great royal hunting grounds, but there was little requirement for a horse capable of jumping obstacles at speed in the field until the latter half of the seventeenth century, which saw the fox becoming a more popular quarry.

The clearance of the great forests—coupled with field enclosures in the eighteenth century—increased the emphasis on hunting the fox fast in open country, rather than pursuing deer in woodland. Now the hunting horse was required to gallop while jumping fences and taking ditches in its stride. For instance, it had to clear without hesitation the new "oxer fence"—a hedge with a wooden rail in front, designed to prevent damage from cattle. A double oxer—a hedge with rails on both sides—was a formidable obstacle, and is still sometimes encountered in the hunting field, as well as in a more sophisticated form on show jumping courses.

These changes meant that riders required far more quality in their horses, and it became essential to use Thoroughbred sires to produce hunters. Clean-bred (full Thoroughbred) horses are still in a minority on the British hunting field, with the three-quarter-bred and half-bred hunter more widely used with input from hardy native breeds such as the Welsh pony and cob, while the Irish draft horse crossed with a Thoroughbred produces the renowned Irish hunter.

Foxhunting worldwide

After originating in Britain, foxhunting spread with remarkably little change to other parts of the world. However, in France—where deer, hare, and wild boar are still hunted—there are, in general, far fewer obstacles to be jumped, and a blood horse (or nearly clean-bred horse) would be appropriate to follow staghounds when the speed of the quarry and the stronger scent associated with deer decree many long, fast runs throughout the day.

Foxhunting is a popular sport in the United States, where the Thoroughbred is widely used for following hounds. In Virginia and Maryland—both of which are particularly favored for the sport—there is still plenty of grass and the horses are mainly faced with wooden fences, some of which are imposing in height and solidity.

Australian and New Zealand riders often use Thoroughbreds in the hunting field, but again the nature of the terrain is a major factor. In New Zealand there are no foxes, and it is the harrier packs that are well supported. Visitors are often impressed by the ease with which New Zealand hunters habitually jump formidable barbed-wire fences, five or six strands high.

right: The hunting horse shows ability over hedges and ditches at speed.

CARRIAGE DRIVING

CARRIAGE DRIVING, although primarily the main form of transport overland through the centuries, was from early times in many civilizations also regarded as a form of recreation and a popular sporting pastime. From the chariot racing of ancient Rome to the sporting wagers of reckless bucks in Regency England, the driving of horses and carriages for pleasure has culminated in the flourishing modern sport of competitive carriage driving.

The origins of driving

The roots of the carriage-driving tradition lie in Britain. In the early nineteenth century, when the advent of the railways brought an end to the golden age of travel by coach and horses, several driving clubs sprang up to preserve the traditions and skills of four-in-hand coaching. The Coaching Club of Great Britain, formed in 1871, still continues this tradition today, and its members meet with their coaches and four-in-hand teams twice a year, as well as competing in coaching classes at all the major horse shows around the country.

Similarly, in the twentieth century, with the emergence of the motor vehicle and the subsequent demise of horse-drawn transport on the roads, the art of driving horses was perpetuated and many original carriages were preserved by a handful of enthusiasts.

There was a resurgence of interest in coaching and carriage driving in Britain during the post-war years, led by enthusiasts such as Sir John Miller, George Mossman, and Sanders Watney, who founded the British Driving Society in 1957 to promote and encourage the driving of horses and carriages for pleasure. Through its area commissioners, the Society today organizes activities and events—such as rallies, picnic drives, instruction and training days—for its members all year round. Private driving is also on the increase, and

the showing of elegant horse-drawn carriages is a feature at many shows. The British Driving Society also holds an annual show in the summer, which continues to attract a growing number of entrants.

Carriage-driving competitions

In the 1960s horse-driving competitions became increasingly popular throughout Europe and, in 1969, HRH Prince Philip, the Duke of Edinburgh, in his capacity as President of the *Fédération Equestre Internationale* (FEI), was instrumental in

drawing up the first rules for horse-driving trials, based closely on the format used for ridden three-day eventing. The Duke has continued to act as one of the leading exponents of the sport.

A full horse-driving trials event consists of three separate competitions. Competition A is a driven dressage test; competition B is the rigorous cross-country marathon course of approximately 15½ miles (25 km), which culminates with the drivers negotiating their way around eight solidly constructed obstacles against the clock; and competition C,

left: The rigorous cross-country marathon covers around 15¹/₂ miles.

right: The driven dressage test commences a full horse-driving trials event.

above: Cone driving requires accuracy and is the "show jumping" phase of the horse driving trial.

left: In Britain, the Duke of Edinburgh has done much to popularize the sport with his team of Fell ponies.

the final phase of cone-driving, is, with its demands for accuracy from driver and horses after the previous phase, the equivalent of the show jumping phase in a ridden three-day event. The eventual winner is the driver with the fewest number of penalties incurred from all three phases.

The very first European Driving Championship for teams of four horses was held in Budapest, Hungary, in 1971. This was quickly followed by the first World Four-in-Hand Driving Championship, which was held in Munster, Germany, in 1972.

These initial carriage-driving competitions were restricted to four-in-hand teams of horses but, as horse-driving trials became increasingly popular, classes were added for teams of four ponies, and then for pairs, tandems (where one horse or pony is driven in front of another), and for single horses and ponies.

Carriage driving today

Horse-driving trials today enjoy a worldwide following. As a result, there are many international driving events organized in Europe, the United States, South Africa, South America, and Australia.

In addition to a biannual World Championship for four-in-hand horse teams, there are also now World horse pair-driving championships, World single-horse driving championships, and European pony team-driving championships. These are all held biannually at leading venues around the world and are run according to the international rules of the FEI Driving Committee.

HARNESS RACING

above: *The Red Mile held in Lexington, Kentucky, United States.*

THIS EXCITING SPORT is a form of racing in which horses maintain a non-galloping gait—either pacing or trotting—while being driven from a fragile, lightweight cart. Known as a sulky, the cart is little more than a lightweight framework—often constructed from aluminum or wood—and is perfectly balanced so that the weight of the driver makes little difference to the speed at which it travels, except perhaps in heavy-going terrain.

In many countries pacers and trotters are also raced *à monté*—under saddle—although the style employed by the riders is quite different to that of jockeys in Thoroughbred racing because balancing the horses requires longer stirrups and a much more upright stance. Despite many races being contested by pacers, trotting is often used as a loose term to describe the sport of harness racing at either gait.

Pacing

This is a lateral gait in which both of the horse's legs on the same side—i.e., the near fore and near hind—advance simultaneously. Also termed ambling, it is as natural a gait to some breeds of horse as it is to animals such as camels and giraffe. Pacers usu-ally wear hopples, which are light straps connecting the legs on the same side; these are painstakingly set for each individual horse to find its optimum stride at speed and help to balance the gait. Pacing is approximately three seconds faster per mile than trotting, and pacers are less likely to deviate from their gait (such a deviation is known as a break) than trotters. For this reason they are more popular with the betting public, and pacing is the dominant gait in Australia, Britain, Canada, Ireland and the United States.

Today, there are many "classic" pacing races with spectacular prize money offered; these include the Australasian Inter-Dominion and, in the United States, the Little Brown Jug and the Meadowlands Pace, to name but three. The fastest harness racehorse in the world is currently an American pacer called Cambest, who paced one racing mile in 1993 in one minute, 46.1 seconds.

Trotting

This is a diagonal gait—often termed as square—where the horse's near foreleg and off hind leg move forward at the same time, followed by the off fore and near hind, and

left: *Trotting is a diagonal gait—the only one permitted on harness racing circuits in mainland Europe.*

so on. Trotting is the only gait permitted on the harness-racing circuits of mainland Europe, where the sport outranks flat and jump racing combined, accounting for 90 percent of racing prize money in Scandinavia, 62 percent in Italy, 57 percent in Germany, and 51 percent in France.

The most prestigious trotting races in the world—which carry huge purses for the winners—are the Prix d'Amérique in France, the Elitlop in Sweden, and the Hambletonian in the United States. The American trotter Pine Chip currently holds the world record over 1 mile (1,500 m) for his gait, recording one minute, 51.1 seconds as a four-year-old in 1994.

Racing circuits and distances

Racing circuits in the English-speaking world are often ½ mile (800 m) in circumference, although there are circuits of ⅝ or 1 mile (1,000 or 1,500 m). In much of Europe, the circuit length is frequently 5 furlongs (1,000 m) or 1 mile (1,500 m), with the famous Grande Piste at Vincennes Hippodrome, Paris at 1¼ miles (2,000 m). Although, races of over 1 mile (1,500 m) are favored in Europe and the United States, in Australasia events over longer distances are preferred.

Breeds used for harness racing

The majority of harness racehorses in Australasia, Britain, and the United States are Standardbreds, so called because the initial standard for inclusion in the American Trotting Register—which was begun in the 1800s—was that a horse should pace or trot the mile in a time of two minutes 30 seconds or less.

The origins of the fastest harness racehorses in the world can be traced back to the English Thoroughbred, Messenger, who was imported into the American colonies in the late eighteenth century. The "great father" of harness racehorses in the United States was the mighty Hambletonian (born in 1849), whose influence on the bloodlines of the sport have been awe inspiring.

In Europe the French Trotter, the Scandinavian "Coldblood," and the Russian Orlov are also regular competitors on the circuits. However, the speed of the Standardbred has proved too attractive to ignore and, with the exception of France, Standardbred and Standardbred crosses predominate in all the harness-racing countries of the world.

above: The majority of harness racehorses are standardbreds.

left: Harness racing is popular in eastern Europe—seen here at the Hippodrome, Moscow.

WESTERN SPORTS

THE RODEO IS, to many people, synonymous with Western sports, and its roots lie in the work and leisure activities of nineteenth-century cowboys in the American West. In the decades preceding the Civil War of 1860–65, great numbers of Americans went to the southwestern region of the United States to work on ranches. Later, post-war industrialization—such as railroading—opened up lands west of the Mississippi River, and huge ranches were carved out from Texas to Montana and beyond.

Ranch life was demanding and hard. Herds of cattle needed to be brought in each spring from their winter pastures so that the calves could be branded and castrated; the herds then had to be tended until the autumn trail drives to the railroad depots (see page 21). Each cowboy required a string of horses for this work, and none could afford the time for niceties and refinements of training. Instead, unbroken horses were simply roped, saddles thrown on their backs, cowboys would climb aboard, and the education process continued until the animals—or their riders' bones—were eventually broken.

One of the few respites from this existence came at the end of annual trail drives, when all those involved got together in the local saloons and gambling halls. Conversations soon turned to prowess with lariat (rope) or horse, and proof of alleged expertise would be demanded. The town's main street or stockyard became the scene of these impromptu riding and roping contests, with part or even all of the year's wages gambled on the outcome. Competitions of this nature quickly caught on. Called a rodeo (from the Spanish for "round-up"), a more formal event was staged in Wyoming and another in Kansas during the 1870s. In 1883, the town of Pecos in Texas offered prize money for a steer-roping contest and, five years later,

when a rodeo in Denver, Colorado, charged admission to spectators, the rodeo became a fully fledged business.

Calf-roping
Two of the five classic, or standard, events staged at western rodeos today have their origins in actual ranch work. Calf-roping is one such event and is a basic test of a cowboy's skill, demanding a well-trained horse and great dexterity with a lasso. The idea is to rope, then tie a calf, as if to prepare it for branding. The calf is given a start of several seconds down the arena, before horse and rider gallop in headlong pursuit. When the cowboy is in the right position he tosses his lasso over the calf's head and—almost in one motion—secures the other end of the

rope around his saddle horn, throws himself from the saddle, and runs toward the calf. His horse, meanwhile, has been trained to step back to keep the rope taut.

The calf is thus restrained and becomes fair game for the approaching cowboy, who flips it onto its side and ties three of its legs together with a short length of rope that he has been holding in his teeth. Time is the deciding factor for the winner of the contest, although a cowboy will be automatically disqualified if the calf slips out of the tie within five seconds.

Saddle-bronc riding
The second classic rodeo event is saddle-bronc riding, which evokes memories of the method used by cowboys to break their

right: Barrel racing—negotiating an obstacle course at speed—is popular with cowgirls.

right: Calf-roping, one of the five rodeo events with its origins in ranch work.

mounts for riding. The saddle in this instance is a modified stock saddle (it is smaller in size and without a horn), while the rein is merely a rope attached to the horse's halter. A bucking strap is tightened around the animal's flanks to encourage its action. Horses and the order of going are selected by lottery.

Before the ride begins, the cowboy lowers himself into the starting chute and onto the horse. When he has wrapped the rope around one hand he signals for the gate to be opened, at which point the horse bucks wildly out into the ring. The rider is required to place his spurs on the horse's shoulders at the start, and to use them on the first jump out of the chute. The actual ride—which must last for 10 seconds—calls for extraordinary balance and timing to achieve maximum scores.

Two judges each award from 0–25 points for the rider's performance; the same range of points is also given for the horse's performance, so cowboys hope to draw difficult mounts. The aggregate makes up the rider's score for that round. Disqualification results from a rider changing hands on the rein, touching the horse with his free hand, or being thrown before the 10-second buzzer sounds.

Bareback bronc riding, bull riding, and steer wrestling

The three remaining classic events that form part of every rodeo arose from westerners bragging that they were tough enough ride a bronc bareback, stay aboard a brahma bull, or wrestle a steer to the ground. Naturally enough, from these taunts sprang the contests of bareback bronc riding, bull riding and steer wrestling.

Although bareback bronc riding certainly requires brute strength, the rider can use only one hand to hold the grip, which is attached to a strap around the horse's girth. The rules and scoring are similar to the sad-

dle-bronc competition, except that there is a time limit of eight seconds.

Bull riding is particularly perilous, because a bull will chase and attempt to gore an unseated cowboy. In this event, the rider can use both hands on the girth grip, and again must last until the eight-second buzzer sounds.

Steer wrestling (also known as bulldogging) begins when a steer is released from a pen and made to run the length of the arena. The cowboy gallops after it, with another rider (called a hazer) racing on the other side to keep the animal straight. When the cowboy draws level with the steer's head, he flings himself from the saddle and grabs its horns, planting his boots in the dirt to achieve a firm grip. With his arms tightly wrapped in a deadlock on the animal, the cowboy then wrestles the steer onto its side. The time taken for all this is the deciding factor of the competition.

Other rodeo events

Larger rodeos will feature other events in addition to the five classic competitions. These include an event for the cutting horse, which is trained to separate a calf or steer from a herd, and then to interpose itself in order to prevent the animal from returning to the group. Increasingly popular is team penning, in which teams of three riders separate three steers from a herd, and then send them into a pen.

Another event is team roping, which involves two cowboys, one of whom lassoes a calf around the head while his partner ropes the animal's hind legs. Colorful and wild affairs are the chuck-wagon races—reminiscent of a scene from the film Ben Hur—where teams of either four or six horses pull Connestoga wagons around a track at maximum speed.

Barrel racing is, in most instances, an event for cowgirls. Three large oil drums

above and left: The "suicide tour," as the rodeo is wryly known, goes on all year round.
below left: Chuck wagon racing at the Calgary Stampede.

right: Western riding classes are held at horse shows around the United States.

are placed to form a triangular course, around which horse and rider gallop in a cloverleaf pattern. The fastest time wins.

The rodeo tour

The "suicide circuit," as the rodeo tour is wryly known, goes on all year round. Rodeo riders have to pay their own way, including entry fees, room and board, and stabling. Not surprisingly, injuries are common as cowboys chase the title of All-Around Champion. Based on the amount of prize money won over the year, which can be considerable, the Championship also opens the door to additional sponsorship income from clothing manufacturers, as well as free beer and other equestrian-related products.

Western-style riding

Less dangerous and perhaps less spectacular than the rodeo—but equally enjoyable—are the four sections of western-style riding found at horse shows around the United States. These include stock-seat equitation classes, where contestants are judged on their riding skills and on their horse's performance at the walk, jog, and lope (the western term for canter), sometimes also performing movements such as figure eights and the impressive sliding stops; reining (formerly known as stock-horse) classes, where the western equivalent of a dressage test—including figure eights, turns on the forehand and haunches, and halts—tests the qualities needed for ranch work; trail-horse classes, where horses negotiate obstacles that might be found on a cross-country ride; and pleasure-horse classes, where horses are shown at the walk, jog, and lope to demonstrate their suitability as western hacks.

In addition, certain breeds, including the Appaloosa, Arabian, Morgan, Palomino, Pinto, and Quarter Horse are eligible to be shown in western sections of their divisions.

Riders wear the traditional and colorful gear of broad-brimmed hats and high-heeled boots, together with chaps or western pants. Horses are shown in stock saddles and bridles, with curb bits and split reins. Western riders are required to hold the reins in only one hand, and to sit with their legs hanging straight and slightly forward to the stirrups; they must not rise to the jog trot.

Part Four:
Physiology, Behavior,
and Care

LEARNING TO RIDE

L EARNING TO RIDE MEANS different things to different people, but whether you dream of competing internationally or simply wish to ride through beautiful countryside, the basics for success are the same: safe surroundings, a good teacher, and a suitable horse or pony. It does not matter what age you are, provided that you want to learn. Nor need a disability prevent you from riding—consult your doctor first, and then find a teacher and school with special qualifications and equipment.

If a friend offers you his or her horse or pony, you should take some lessons first to give you a solid foundation. The best place to learn the basics is at a good riding school, and finding a suitable one should be quite straightforward. In Britain, membership of the Association of British Riding Schools guarantees high standards, and British Horse Society approval and teaching qualifications are recognized worldwide. The United States has the American Riding Instructor Certificate Program (although the National Equestrian Federation of the United States points out that there are many excellent instructors who do not complete this). Other good options, wherever you live, are to seek the advice of friends who ride, and to look in equestrian magazines for suitable schools.

Choosing a riding school

Once you have a list of possibilities, make an appointment to look around and, if you can, arrange to watch lessons for novice riders. You will not need to be an expert to spot a good school.

right: *A young rider samples the taste of freedom that riding can bring.*

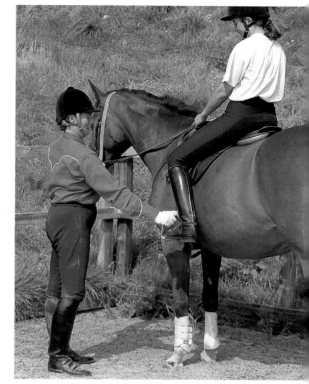

right: *Before a lesson begins, the instructor will check the novice rider's stirrups and equipment.*

The basic points to watch for are:
● *A tidy stable yard and friendly staff.*
● *Horses and ponies that seem friendly and look in good condition.*
● *Tack and equipment that are both clean and in good repair.*
● *Well-maintained stables, fields, and fencing.*
● *Pupils who seem to be enjoying their lessons and teachers who enjoy teaching.*

However, think again if you see:
● *A dangerously untidy yard with tools and equipment lying around.*
● *Horses that threaten to bite or kick, or look in poor condition.*
● *Dirty or broken tack.*
● *Broken-down fences or buildings, and poor-quality grazing.*
● *Unfriendly staff, or teachers who are rude or sarcastic.*

Basic riding equipment

You do not need to buy all your riding gear at once, but you must be both safe and comfortable. A riding hat or skull cap made to the highest current safety standard is essential (some schools will lend hats, but it is much better to buy your own from an experienced fitter). Safe footwear is another must, and jodhpur boots or long rubber boots are inexpensive. Sneakers or boots with ridged soles are dangerous, as your feet could slide through or become wedged in the stirrups.

If you do not wish to invest in jodhpurs right away, leggings without side seams will be more comfortable than jeans. Wear unrestrictive tops, and finish off with woolen or cotton riding gloves. Once you start jumping—especially across country—you may also wish to buy a body protector.

First lessons

Your first lessons should be one-to-one; later on, you may have more fun joining a group lesson. It is natural to be nervous about your first lessons, and questions that go through your mind may include:

● *Will I lose control?*
● *Will I fall off and hurt myself?*
● *Will I make a fool of myself?*
● *Will I be stiff afterward?*

The answer to all these questions should be a definite no! Your instructor will find you a quiet, experienced horse of the correct size, and at first you will be led from a leading rein or a lunge rein (a long rein used to control the horse while it moves on a circle) so that the instructor is always in charge. All you will have to concentrate on is adjusting your position as your instructor explains the basics and as you become used to the horse's movement.

Riding should not make you uncomfortable, but may make you use unaccustomed muscles. Bicycling, swimming, and jumping rope are all useful ways to increase suppleness and muscle tone between lessons. Ideally, as a beginner you will need at least one lesson per week, although riding twice a week will help you make better progress.

Communicating with horses

Learning to ride means learning to communicate with your horse. When the instructor shows you how to sit correctly, it is not just to make you look nice but to enable you to direct your horse by signals given with your legs, seat, hands, and voice.

The first lesson you will learn is to stay in balance at walk, trot, and canter. In walk, you will be able to count 1, 2, 3, 4, to the horse's hoofbeats; in trot, its legs will move in diagonal pairs in a 1, 2 rhythm; and in canter the rhythm is 1, 2, 3. A cantering horse takes longer strides with one foreleg (the leading leg). If you are cantering a circle, the horse should lead with its inside leg for balance, so, for example, when moving on the left rein (i.e., counterclockwise) the left (nearside) leg will be leading.

Becoming a good rider takes practice, and even top riders readily agree that they never stop learning. Aspects to think about include the following:

● *Look in the direction in which you wish to go—not down at the horse's ears.*
● *Remember to breathe! Many people hold their breath when concentrating, and this may make you tense. Conversely, riding in a relaxed way never means flopping on the horse's back.*
● *When you hold the reins, imagine that you have a pair of birds in your hands. You need to hold them so that they do not escape, but not so tightly that you are squeezing them.*
● *If you find sitting to the trot or canter difficult, think about absorbing the movement through your lower back. A good rider may appear to be sitting still, but is, in fact, following the horse's movements.*

Understanding the equine mind

Learning to think as a horse does and how to handle it correctly will increase your confidence. Even the laziest riding-school pony acts on instinct—it likes the company of others, runs away if frightened, and dislikes sudden movements and loud noises. Take any available chances to handle, groom, and tack up your school horses, talking to them quietly. Never worry about looking silly— horses are very responsive to tone of voice.

Approach a horse from the side so that it can see you. The horse's eyes are set into the sides of the head, which gives it almost all-round vision but with a blind spot directly ahead. Try to tune your body language to that of the horse—for instance, if you look it straight in the eye it will tend to back off.

Moving on

You will soon progress with your riding but, as already mentioned, the most important lesson is that you will never stop learning. Don't worry if your progress seems erratic or if you hit problem areas, and tell your instructor if anything worries you.

Once you have learned the basics on the lunge, you are likely to start to ride in an enclosed school. This will usually have letters around it to act as markers for riding circles and other figures that will improve your control of the horse. These letters (also

above: A correctly fitting riding helmet or hat is a vital piece of equipment for the rider. This modern design is light and cool.

used in dressage arenas) are A, K, E, H, C, M, B, and F; their significance is unknown, but an easy way to remember them is with the sentence: "All King Edward's Horses Can Manage Big Fences."

As soon as you can walk, trot, and canter safely, you may join a group lesson and start riding out. Riding in the open will increase your confidence, and you may find that the school horses become brighter and more interested in their surroundings. You should also take any chance to watch experienced riders (whether taking lessons, at competitions, or on video), because keeping a mental picture of what an accomplished rider looks like will influence your own riding.

above: Lunge lessons are beneficial at any stage in a rider's training, enabling the novice to concentrate on position, rather than worrying about control of the horse.

left: For a lesson involving several riders to be successful, the instructor has to encourage teamwork and a sense of fun.

Jumping and flatwork

Many riders enjoy jumping but, even if you prefer to keep your horse's feet on the ground, you will benefit from working over poles and small fences. This helps to teach balance, coordination and rhythm, and encourages the horse to work from behind—something you will hear more about as you progress. Jumping and flatwork, or dressage, complement one another. Your horse's "engine" is in his hindquarters and hind legs: this is where energy (or impulsion) is created, while your hands control and direct that energy. As time goes on you will learn how to influence the way your horse goes, so that you are both in perfect balance and harmony.

Your early jumping lessons will be over poles on the ground and tiny fences. Your instructor will teach you to ride through grids—lines of fences set for the horse's stride—so that it arrives at each fence correctly. When you are ready, jumping a small course will combine all these skills. You may also enjoy riding across country, developing the skills to jump in rhythm at a faster pace.

By the time you finish your first year of lessons, you will doubtless be hooked on riding. With your instructor's help, you can then start to develop the areas that interest you most, and perhaps even look forward to owning or sharing your first horse.

above and right: As the rider progresses, the instructor will judge when to introduce new challenges. Early jumping lessons will greatly increase confidence, as will improving balance, coordination, and rhythm.

TRAINING THE YOUNG HORSE

TRAINING A YOUNG HORSE IS a rewarding and fascinating process. A good trainer needs to be calm, patient, and firm, and to understand the equine mind, which means working with horses of different types and temperaments to gain experience before attempting to train a horse or pony from scratch (see pages 174–175).

You will not have to be a top-class rider to educate a horse successfully, but you do need to be competent, quiet, and effective; you must have a balanced seat and understand which questions to ask and when to ask them. If you are only accustomed to riding and handling schooled horses, it will be much better to work under the guidance of someone experienced with young horses, who will achieve good results. Before taking on a young horse, you must also think about the following:

● Are proper facilities available to you for training? A safe, secure area with good footing will be absolutely essential.
● Do you have the right temperament for training a young horse? Patience and perseverance are both vital qualities.
● A horse can be backed (taught to accept a rider) at three years old, but will not be ready to start proper work for another year. Will you be prepared to wait for this?

Changes in training methods

Accustoming a horse to accept a rider on its back was always traditionally described as breaking in. At one time, it was sometimes accomplished by force rather than persuasion—although thankfully those days have now gone and good trainers work by gaining their horses' confidence. Well-known trainers such as Monty Roberts in the United States and Britain's Richard Maxwell have had a great influence on the way in which we educate horses; they both work by making use of the horse's natural instincts and body language, and describe the process as "starting" a horse rather than breaking it in.

The join-up procedure is an important part of their technique. This is where the trainer works with the horse in a confined space—ideally a 164 ft. (50 m) circular arena or pen. Here, the trainer mimics the behavior of the dominant mare in a herd by repeatedly chasing the young horse away until it submits, accepting that the safest, most pleasant place to be is with him or her and waiting for leadership. We can all learn a great deal from the approach of these

trainers, but it is important to remember that they are highly skilful and experienced, and can stay out of danger. If you want to try their techniques, practice with a safe, older animal at first, and never take risks. Whatever stage of training you have reached, it is always better to go slowly and play safe.

Appreciating and paying attention to a horse's body language will help you to understand when it is worried and when it is confident in what you are asking it to do. For instance, a horse that lays its ears flat

right: Work on the lunge forms the basis of a young horse's schooling. Here a lunge cavesson and rein are fitted.

back is frightened or aggressive, but if a horse flicks its ear back to listen to its rider, it is paying attention.

Early lessons

The training process begins when a foal is just a few days old. Most foals are curious creatures and, when they see their dams (mothers) accepting and enjoying human attention, they will adopt the same attitude. Many breeders teach their foals to wear lightweight headcollars and to be led behind their dams from the day they are born. Foals and young horses need to spend most of their time in the paddock, but their education should be a continual process. If you leave a horse untouched until it is ready to back, you will have more problems because it will by this time be physically stronger and able to push you around.

Be kind but consistent, and insist on good manners from the start—bearing in mind that what you consider cute behavior in a foal may be less appealing when it is a strapping three-year-old! Simple techniques will prepare a foal for its later education. When it accepts you running your hands over its body, including vulnerable or sensitive areas such as the legs and belly, it is showing that it trusts you; massaging the

top of the gums will prepare it for having its teeth rasped, and for accepting a bit. Always try to make things easy: for instance, before asking the foal to let you pick up a foot, make sure that it is balanced on the other three legs. Teaching the foal to accept a rug introduces the idea of something on its back, while holding and then tying a stretchy bandage around its belly suggests the pressure of a girth. Stand on a safe box or crate to groom the foal so that it gets the idea of someone over its back, and lean over it to brush the other side.

Many breeders like to show their young, unbacked horses to give them experience of different sights and sounds. This can be useful, but remember that young horses quickly become tired and bored, so it will not be fair to take a yearling to a show every weekend.

Further training

Some trainers only introduce a bit when a horse is ready to be backed, while others prefer to do this earlier. Whatever approach you take, you must ask your veterinary surgeon or equine dentist to check your horse's teeth and mouth beforehand to ensure that there is no soreness or other problem. Some trainers like to begin with a mouthing bit,

which has dangling keys that sit on the tongue and encourage the horse to chew; others prefer a jointed or unjointed snaffle. The most important factor is that the bit you choose is the right size and is correctly adjusted (see page 165). Introducing the horse to the saddle is a process involving the use of a surcingle or roller initially, and then a saddle (loosely girthed at first), without and finally with stirrups.

Long-reining can be introduced as early as the age of two years. Using this technique, a skilled trainer can teach a horse to stop, start, and turn without the hindrance of a rider's weight, and to make it responsive to voice commands. Many trainers also long-rein on quiet roads and tracks to accustom the horse to sights and sounds that it will encounter when ridden out. Lunging in a circle puts greater stress on the joints, and should not be started until the horse is at least three years old. Whatever training you are doing, work only in short sessions—young horses, like children, cannot concentrate for long periods.

Horses that have been handled correctly from the start are rarely worried when the time comes for backing. The usual method here is to use three people: one to stand at the horse's head to reassure it; an agile, lightweight rider; and an experienced handler to leg up the rider. At first, the rider is simply legged up to put a little weight across the saddle, and the horse is turned in small circles to become used to the feel. Gradually, the rider puts more weight on the horse until he or she can quietly put a leg over and sit on its back—leaning forward initially so that the horse is not startled by someone suddenly looming above it.

Riding a young horse

When you ride a young horse, your commands must be particularly clear and consistent, but never rough. Use your voice, ride with a light seat, and always give the

above: Lunging in a circle puts stress on the joints and is only introduced when the horse is at least three years old.

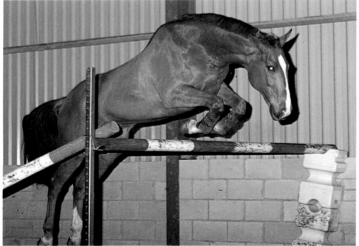

left: Free movement is encouraged through loose jumping exercise, enabling the horse to move unimpeded by a rider.

horse plenty of time and room to change direction; opening a rein to the inside (without pulling back) will help to steer it.

Once the horse can walk, trot, and canter in the school in a calm, basic way and has been ridden out first with a quiet companion and then alone, it is a good idea to let it enjoy a rest. It will have had a good deal to cope with both physically and mentally, and will need a break. Many trainers turn away their three-year-olds until their fourth spring, when they repeat the previous year's lessons before starting to teach new ones.

The four-year-old horse can be introduced to poles on the ground, leading on to small grids and courses. As its muscles develop, correct riding will teach it to work from behind and eventually to come on to the bit (see page 182). Lessons should be varied in order to maintain interest, and the four-year-old should gradually be given more to think about and introduced to small competitions.

When training a young horse you are bound to hit occasional problems, but keep calm and, if necessary, go back a stage. It is vital to have a trainer or someone experienced who can watch you both and help you to work out why things are not going quite right. It is also important that you ride well-schooled horses as well as your youngster, so that what you are aiming for remains fresh in your mind.

GENERAL MANAGEMENT

LOOKING AFTER a horse or pony is a rewarding task as well as a highly responsible one, and it is important to make sure that your horse has the right home. For many owners the combined management system, where the horse lives partly outdoors and partly stabled, works very well: the horse lives a comparatively natural life and keeps fit without the absolute necessity of exercise, needs less care and attention, and, having worked off surplus energy outdoors, is likely to be an easier ride than a horse that is kept permanently indoors. Ideally, it should be brought in each morning, given a feed, quickly groomed and checked for injuries and then, if it is not needed, turned out again. In winter, it is best to reverse the summer plan if the horse is to be worked: that is, to bring it in at night and turn it out for whatever part of the day it is not needed (wearing a rug if necessary).

The other management choices are to keep a horse either entirely at grass or

left: For many owners a combined system whereby horses are partly stabled and partly live outdoors is most suitable. Variety also prevents the horse from becoming bored.

permanently stabled. For the grass-kept horse, the basic requirements are safe and good grazing, a constant source of clean water, shelter from the elements in winter and from insects in summer, company, and a daily routine. The term grass-kept is, however, slightly misleading, since—unless the climate is exceptionally kind and the grass always sufficient and nutritious—a horse that has to work must have more than a plain grass diet if it is to have energy and maintain condition. For the stabled horse,

left: An ideally designed stable yard—airy and yet sheltered and with a view for each horse, allowing for sociability and interest.

priorities are to prevent boredom in what is essentially an artificial environment, cut off from the free-roaming, gregarious lifestyle that it would naturally have. In this case, not only physical care but also an understanding of the character requirements of horses in general will be needed.

Keeping a horse at livery

Many owners cannot keep their horses at home, and so have to make some sort of livery (boarding) arrangement. If this is your position and you are planning to keep your first horse, you will need to find a setup run by experienced people who will be able to help you if necessary.

There are five basic livery systems: full, DIY (do it yourself), grass, part, and working. Full livery means that you pay the stable to do all the work and even exercise the horse when necessary. This is an expensive option and, for many owners, less rewarding than being involved in their horse's care. At the other extreme, DIY livery—as the name suggests—means that everything will be up to you, so you will need plenty of time (or to link up with another owner). Grass livery suits horses that can live out all year round, but they must still have a shelter. Part livery means that you do part of the work and the yard does the rest, and can be a good way of being involved while making sure that your horse has a routine. Working livery usually involves the horse being used by the stable for lessons; disadvantages of this system are that the horse may be needed when you wish to ride, and you may prefer other people not to ride it.

Outdoor requirements

In general, each horse needs a minimum of ½–1 acre (0.2–0.4 hectare) of grazing, depending on the length of time in which it is turned out. Fields must be safe and free from poisonous plants such as nightshades and ragwort—check your field every day to make sure that there are no dangers such as rabbit holes, broken fencing, or trash. Not all types of fencing are safe for horses, so look for post and rails, hedging, electric, high-tech plastic, or wire fencing designed especially for them. Barbed wire should never be used and can cause horrific injuries, and plain wire and wire designed for other stock should also be avoided.

A field shelter will give protection from

bad weather. The front should be open and large enough to allow horses in and out without arguments, and the back should face the prevailing wind. If possible, the shelter should be sited on the highest ground to achieve the best drainage.

Horses are herd animals and need company—preferably that of other horses. If this is impossible, try keeping your horse with other companions such as llamas, donkeys, or goats. However, consult your

below: Good quality fencing and grassland management are the hallmarks of a well-run stable.
bottom: Horses correctly turned out in New Zealand rugs in the depths of winter.

veterinarian before putting your horse in with other animals (especially a donkey), as you may need to take special worming precautions.

You should check on your horse twice a day, even if it lives out all the time. This is the only way in which you can deal quickly with any injuries, and can make sure that there are no problems with fencing and water supplies.

Stabling and bedding

A horse's stable should be light and airy, and as large as possible. The American barn system—with rows of stalls inside a large building with a central walkway—makes life easier for the people looking after the horses, but it must be well ventilated. The same applies to individual stables: rather than closing the top stable door in bad weather, give your horse an extra rug. The other basic prerequisite is a constant supply of fresh, clean water.

Bedding will help to keep your horse warm and comfortable, and will lessen the risk of scrapes to the hocks or elbows when it lies down. Many types of bedding are now commercially available, from straw to rubber matting, and your horse's health must be the most important factor in deciding which to use. When you stable your horse, you will be exposing it to dust, mold spores, and ammonia fumes from bedding and perhaps also from its hay. All horses should have an environment that is as dust-free as possible (some horses suffer from allergies, and their management should be worked out with a vet).

All types of bedding have pros and cons. Wheat straw is the traditional material but can be dusty—and horses love to eat it. Dust-extracted chopped straw gives a good bed but, again, some horses like its taste. White wood shavings are suitable if the dust has been extracted (shavings collected from your local lumber mill may be cheap, but

below: Stable yards must be kept as clean and hygienic as possible.

Left: A collection of stable yard tools for mucking out includes a shovel, pitch forks, shavings rake, and yard broom.

left: To keep a horse healthy it must be mucked out every day. Straw bedding is the traditional method, with hemp shavings, paper and rubber matting the modern alternatives.

will contain a lot of dust). Hemp bedding has recently become popular: this makes a springy, hard-wearing bed, but not all samples are free from dust and some horses will eat it. Shredded paper is dust-free but not always easy to remove, and tends to blow about. Rubber matting is generally used with a small amount of bedding on top, and works well in stables with good drainage although, if the drainage is poor, a layer of liquid sludge may become trapped under the matting.

Cleaning the stable

To keep your horse healthy, you must muck out its stable every day. If you are using straw, this means a full clean every time; with shavings, hemp, and paper the best system is to take out all the droppings but avoid disturbing the bottom layer of the bed, and to do a full "lift and clean" once or twice a week—the frequency depending on how clean your horse's living habits are! If the stable starts to smell of ammonia, this is a sure sign that you are not doing a full clean often enough.

The right tools make mucking out easier. You will need a wheelbarrow, a straw or shavings fork, a shovel, and a broom. The easiest way to take out droppings is to wear strong rubber gloves and to pick them up, but if you prefer not to do this you can use a fork. Each time you do a full clean you will need to take out all the wet, dirty bedding (remembering to dig it out from the corners), sweep the floor, and wash it with stable disinfectant, leaving this to dry. When you put down the new bed, place the clean but already used bedding in the areas that usually become dirty, then add enough new material to give a deep bed. Banking up the bedding around the sides of the stable will help to prevent the horse from becoming cast (trapped on its side against the wall) if it lies down or rolls.

Grooming

Grooming must be an important part of your horse's daily routine, and not only to keep the horse looking smart. Much more importantly, it will enable you to check a grass-kept horse for signs of injury or prob-

lems: for instance, carefully feeling your horse's legs every day will allow you to detect heat or swelling, or early indications of problems such as mud fever (see page 176); while a stabled horse—unable to roll or rub as it would do outdoors—needs daily grooming to keep its coat and skin healthy. Simply spending time with your horse will also make you more aware of changes in its mood or general well-being.

The grooming routine that you use and the kit you will need depend on the type of horse and on its lifestyle. For instance, a pony living out full-time needs the grease in its coat for maximum water-resistance, whereas a hardworking horse or pony that is stabled for part of the time, and clipped and blanketed in winter (see page 166), can be groomed more thoroughly. Most horses enjoy being groomed as long as they are always treated considerately. Brushes with stiff bristles are too harsh for thin-skinned animals (such as Arabs or Thoroughbreds, for instance), and all horses are very sensitive around the face and belly.

left: The basic grooming kit comprises, clockwise from top left: a body brush, sponge, hoof pick, water brush, finishing brush, plastic curry comb, stable pads, mane combs, rubber curry comb, and curry comb.

right: The feet must be picked out and checked every day.

The grooming kit

To prevent the spread of infections, your horse should have its own grooming kit. A basic kit consists of: a hoof pick for cleaning the hooves; a brush with stiff or soft long bristles—called a finishing brush—for general coat cleaning; a body brush with short, **soft** bristles to remove dirt and grease from the coat of the stabled horse (see below); a curry comb for cleaning grease and dust from brushes (a rubber curry comb can be helpful for gently removing dried mud from the coat, but the metal variety must only be used to clean brushes); a plastic mane comb; fly repellent in the summer; and cotton pads, which can be dampened with clean water for cleaning around the eyes, the nostrils, and under the tail (these should only be used once on a particular area and discarded).

You may want to add extra items such as hoof oil or polish, round-ended scissors for trimming, shampoo, and pulling combs for thinning and shaping the mane and tail. A cactus cloth removes stains, and a damp-ened stable rubber (soft cloth) or sheepskin mitt adds a final polish to the coat.

The grooming routine

If you have a grass-kept horse or pony, you must pick out its feet every day and check that its feet and shoes are always in good condition. Any dried mud should also be brushed from the coat, especially from areas on which tack or rugs will rest, as infections can start when dried mud is rubbed into the skin. Also, clean the eyes, nose, and under-tail area, and brush out its mane and tail. If you have a gelding, you will need to clean the sheath area regularly and gently, using lukewarm water (special products are avail-able for this). The stabled horse should have a similar routine although, because it does not need the grease in its coat for protection, you can use a body brush to remove this and to massage the skin at the same time.

Everyone develops his or her own way of doing things, but the following tips should help you to achieve a really professional appearance:

● *If possible, take a stabled horse outside for grooming so that you are not releasing dust into its living space.*
● *Start at the top of the body and work down, holding your brush in the hand nearest the horse.*
● *Use a dandy brush in light, short strokes, flicking up at the end to whisk dust out of the coat.*
● *Use a body brush in short strokes, but put more weight behind them. Clean your brush on a curry comb every three or four strokes, and tap the comb sideways on the ground every now and then to remove the grease.*
● *If your horse has a pulled tail (i.e., shaped at the top by pulling out hairs—ask an expert to show you this), put on a tail bandage for an hour or two several times a week to train the hairs to lie flat. Never apply the bandage too tightly or leave it on for long periods, or you may restrict the blood circulation in your horse's tail.*

above: A sponge is used to
keep the nostrils clean.
Separate sponges are used
for the eyes and dock.

FEEDING AND NUTRITION

FEEDING HORSES IS BOTH an art and a science: the artistry comes from feeding to suit the individual character of the horse, and the science from knowledge of how the horse has evolved and its nutritional requirements. In the wild, horses used to roam freely, grazing and drinking constantly and covering large distances daily, and they could select from all the grasses and plants they encountered. Their digestive system, therefore, adapted to that of the trickle feeder, digesting mainly forages on a little-and-often basis.

However, as humans progressively domesticated the horse over hundreds of years, it had to cope with greater physical effort and a more controlled diet. Today the horse is used mainly for pleasure activities, from children's riding on ponies to hacking and hunting, as well as the sports of racing, show jumping, eventing, polo, and the disciplines of dressage and carriage driving. Feeding has altered markedly as a result of these changing requirements, and a wide range of commercially available feeds has sprung up to fulfill them.

The horse's digestive system

Despite dietary changes, the horse's digestive system is still fundamentally the same as that of its ancestors. The front teeth and lips select and pick up food while the rear teeth grind it, and this chewing and grinding action begins the digestive process. As the horse swallows, the food enters the gullet. From there it passes to the stomach and then to the small intestine, large and small colon, and rectum. With a capacity of only 1¼ gallons (8 liters), the horse's stomach is relatively small. It works well when two-thirds full and should not be over-filled—hence the rule of feeding little and often. The small intestine is a narrow tube about 70 ft. (21 m) long where starch, sugar, protein and oil—together with some minerals and vitamins—are broken down and absorbed.

However, the largest part of the horse's digestive tract is the large intestine. It is here that fiber is broken down, and this provides the horse with most of its energy. The horse cannot break down fiber by itself—it has evolved a system by which it allows bacteria and other microbes living in its lower gut to do so by fermenting the fiber. The microbial population will adapt to match the diet, so any sudden changes to a horse's food will cause upsets because the wrong microbes will be present.

left: In the wild, horses will roam freely, grazing and drinking constantly and covering large distances.

Essential nutrients

A good, balanced equine diet is one that includes the correct proportions of all the following elements.

Water

Water is vital for life, and is present in every cell in the body. A young horse's body is actually made up of 80 percent water; in the adult horse this drops to 50–60 percent. Water loss can cause illness and, in a severe case, death. The water requirements of any horse will depend on its age, the type of feed it is eating, the amount of exercise it is taking, and the external temperature.

Carbohydrates

These are sugar, starch, and certain compounds within fiber. Sugar is found, to some extent, in all foods. Molasses also contains good levels of sugar, as does fresh grass. Starch is mainly found in cereals.

above: Fresh water must always be available. A horse's body is made up of up to 80 percent water.

above: The main constituent of a horse's diet will always be forage—grass, hay, or a hay substitute. Hay is often soaked to eliminate dust and spores.

Fats and oils

These are concentrated sources of energy, containing two-and-a-half times as much energy as carbohydrates. Oil is found in small quantities in most commercial foods, and is also commonly added (as vegetable oil) to horses' diets.

Fiber

This important dietary component is found in all feeds, and in greater levels in grass, hay, and straw.

Protein

When broken down, proteins provide the body with essential amino acids; these are mainly used for growth, milk production, pregnancy, and repair of body tissues.

Minerals

The major minerals are calcium, phosphorus, magnesium, potassium, sodium, and chloride; the main trace elements are copper, zinc, manganese, selenium, and iron. The most important mineral balance is that of calcium to phosphorus: there needs to be more calcium than phosphorus in the diet, with the ratio at approximately one-and-a-half parts calcium to one part phosphorus.

Vitamins

These are required in minute quantities to maintain health, helping to control chemical reactions and processes. The main vitamins are A, D, E, K, and the B group. Green feeds and grass are good sources, while hay and many straight feeds have a poor vitamin content.

Rules of good feeding

The following rules are all founded on the principle of imitating the horse's natural feeding habits to suit its digestive system.

● Allow the horse free access to fresh, clean water at all times.

● Feed compounds (see below) and hard feeds on a little-and-often basis. In practice, you should give at least two feeds a day to a horse in light to medium work, and three to four feeds a day to one on a full work program.

● Feed by weight, not by volume. Weigh a scoop of each feed, and know the weight of each portion that you give.

● Feed according to the horse's weight (consult your veterinary surgeon or an experienced horse owner if you are unsure about this). A horse can be weighed on a weighbridge, or by using a measuring tape from which a simple calculation is made. Monitor any changes, and consult your vet if you are at any time concerned about your horse's diet.

● Increase the feed quantity and type according to the level of work required from the horse.

● Use high-quality feeds and never use dusty or moldy feed.

● Make any changes to the diet gradually to avoid digestive problems.

● Do not exercise the horse right after feeding, or feed immediately following exercise. After feeding, be sure to allow two to three hours before working the horse, and do not feed for at least one hour after working.

● Feed at the same time each day—horses are creatures of habit.

● Feed your horse plenty of good long fiber. Horses have evolved to live on a high-fiber diet, and at least 50 percent of the diet should therefore consist of roughage.

What to feed

In order to maintain the energy and physical well-being necessary to carry out the work expected of it, a horse's diet should supply a correct balance of the following components.

Forage

The main constituent of a horse's diet will always be forage, and this falls into the categories of grass and preserved forages. The latter include hay, hay replacers (fed as a replacement to hay or grass, and are usually chopped into short lengths), and haylage (a preserved forage which is sold sealed in plastic to inhibit mold development). Haylage is particularly popular in the U.K. and northern Europe.

Cereals

The cereals that are most commonly fed to horses are oats, barley, and maize (corn). These are either fed rolled or, to break open the cereal, flaked or micronized (cooked) to improve digestibility.

Bran

This is the fibrous outer husk of wheat, and has been a traditional feed for horses over many generations. It is still commonly used today in bran mashes, as well as to bulk out a ration.

Sugarbeet pulp

This is a by-product of sugar extraction and is a good, palatable feed. It must always be soaked beforehand because, once water is added, the pulp will absorb the water and swell a great deal. This must happen before the horse eats it or digestive problems are likely to result.

Compounds

Compounds are balanced blends of ingredients formulated to produce a ration to complement the forage. They are available in cube form or as coarse mixtures (also known as sweet feeds). Compounds are fully balanced and offer a consistent nutrition that requires no extra feed apart from forage and water. They are formulated to provide differing amounts of protein, energy, fiber, vitamins, and minerals to suit individual horses.

Succulents

Adding something succulent—such as pieces of raw carrot or apple—will make the feed more appetizing. This is also another way of adding bulk.

above: Succulents such as carrots are a good way of providing bulk as well as adding interest to a feed.

Feed-related disorders

Changes in feeding patterns, or incorrect feeding, can lead to a number of disorders. In a severe case of colic, or in a suspected case of laminitis or azoturia, always seek your vet's advice. (See also pages 176-181.)

Colic

Colic covers a set of symptoms indicating abdominal pain in the horse. The causes may include:

- *A sudden change in the diet.*
- *Moldy feeds.*
- *Giving free access to water when a horse is overheated.*
- *Cribbing/windsucking.*
- *Ingestion of sand.*
- *A parasite infestation.*
- *A twisted gut.*
- *Greed/bolting the food.*

Prolonged rolling is a typical symptom, but an affected horse should be kept walking until veterinary help arrives as rolling could result in a potentially fatal twisted gut.

Laminitis

A condition often affecting ponies over-eating lush grass, laminitis involves a painful inflammation of the sensitive laminae of the feet and is caused by any of the following:

- *Over-feeding of starch.*
- *Concussion.*
- *Foaling (linked to inflammation of the womb).*
- *Any great stress.*

Azoturia

Symptoms involve muscular stiffness at exercise. The causes can be many, including:

- *Over-feeding of grain to resting horses.*
- *A mineral imbalance.*
- *Hormonal changes. Fillies and mares are substantially more susceptible than males.*

SADDLERY AND EQUIPMENT

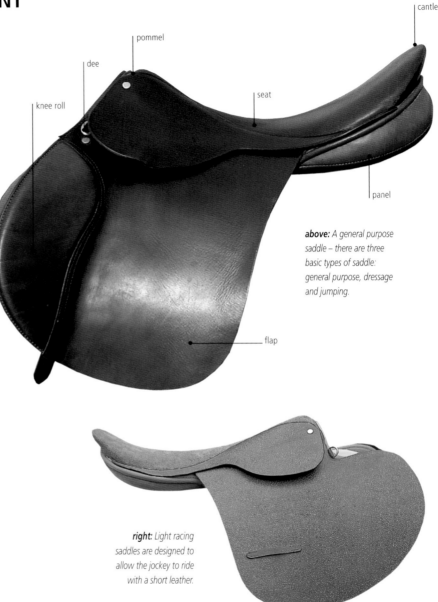

pommel

dee

cantle

knee roll

seat

panel

above: A general purpose saddle – there are three basic types of saddle: general purpose, dressage and jumping.

flap

USING THE CORRECT TACK will be vital to the way your horse goes—and to its well-being. An unsuitable or wrongly adjusted bit will cause discomfort and set up resistances such as head tossing and pulling, while a badly fitting saddle can cause permanent damage. A trip to the saddler may leave you feeling overwhelmed by all the designs available, but you must get the basics right so you may want to take along a knowledgeable helper, as well as seeking the advice of trained staff.

Always buy the best-quality tack you can afford, as it will be safer and last longer. If you are buying a horse its owner may offer to sell you the tack and, provided that it fits well and is in good condition, this could save you money. Again, if you are unsure, ask a good professional to check all the tack for you first.

SADDLES

Saddles are made to suit different riding positions and specialities: dressage, endurance, jumping, general-purpose, racing, and sidesaddles are all available. The general-purpose saddle combines elements of both the dressage and jumping saddles, and will allow you to hack, school, and jump reasonable fences in comfort.

Any saddle must fit well: if it pinches, rubs, or bangs on the horse's back it will cause pain and possibly permanent damage. The basis of a good fit depends on the tree (the saddle's frame) being the correct width. An expert fitter will advise you, and may be able to adjust the saddle's stuffing to give the best weight distribution. Basic points are that the saddle sits centrally, has a clear channel so that it does not press on the withers or spine, and does not interfere with the shoulders. It is not possible to judge saddle fit on a standing horse—the fitter will need to see you ride.

When you put the saddle on the horse, place it forward before gently sliding it back

right: Light racing saddles are designed to allow the jockey to ride with a short leather.

so that the hair lies flat. The saddle must be sufficiently far back not to pinch the horse's moving shoulder, but not so far back as to put pressure on the loins. When the girth is fastened, you should be able to fit your hand beneath it.

Saddle accessories

Many people like to use a numnah or pad under the saddle. Some are designed to try

to give better weight distribution, but nothing can turn a badly fitting saddle into one that fits well.

For general use the main priorities of the girth are strength, and comfort for the horse. Traditional leather girths are popular but do not allow air circulation and have little "give"; other materials include the German cordstring girth, which has thick cotton cords held by panels (the familiar

below: The dressage saddle , with its straight cut flap and slight kneeroll, encourages the rider to sit deep into the saddle and brings the legs close to the horse's body.

below: The highly specialized sidesaddle viewed from the near side.

below: Numnahs or pads under the saddle keep the saddle clean and some are designed to ensure an even weight distribution. None will make up for an ill-fitting saddle.

right: The jumping saddle has a forward cut saddle flap and is designed for riding with shorter stirrup leathers.

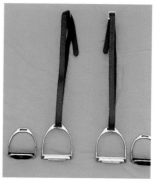

above: Stirrup leathers with dressage irons and, at the side, jumping irons.

above: Tack should be cleaned thoroughly and often.

left: Four types of girth: dressage, Atherstone, balding, and padded.

nylon-string girth used on ponies is not a good choice, as it can pinch), lampwick, and foam-padded cotton.

Stirrup irons must be made of stainless steel for safety; the most popular type is the basic pattern. Any stirrup must be large enough to fit your boot easily, and the heavier the better. Stirrup leathers should be strong, and narrow enough to fit easily through the irons.

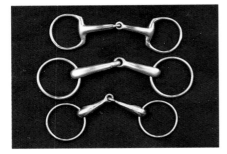

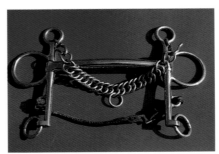

above top: A correctly fitted snaffle bridle with flash noseband.
above: Three types of snaffle bit: the loose snaffle ring, heavy German snaffle, and Eggbutt snaffle.

above top: A correctly fitted double bridle. Double bridles must be used in expert hands.
above: The Pelham bit reproduces the action of the double bridle in one mouthpiece.

There are many kinds of mouthpiece material, including stainless steel, rubber-covered metal, copper alloys, and special plastics; many trainers feel that copper and sweet-iron bits taste nicer to the horse and so encourage them to accept the bit.

The double bridle

This is the most sophisticated bitting system, and allows a good rider to use delicate aids on a schooled horse to produce fine adjustments to the way it carries itself. It should not be used by inexperienced riders or on unschooled horses.

The double bridle has two bits, each with separate reins: the bradoon resembles a thin snaffle and fits above a curb bit, which is used with a curb chain that fits into the curb groove under the horse's chin.

The pelham

This bit reproduces the action of the double bridle in one mouthpiece, which has two sets of rings for the reins. Although less subtle, many horses work well in pelhams and they can give greater control. The pelham should ideally be used with two pairs of reins (those on the bottom ring giving greater leverage), but some riders prefer to fit leather roundings to the bit and then to use a single rein.

Similar to the pelham is the kimblewick (sometimes called the kimberwick in the United States). This is fitted with a curb chain, but has a single ring at either end of the mouthpiece and is used with a single rein. It exerts little leverage, but some horses go well in it.

The gag snaffle

The gag is technically a snaffle, but also has a leverage action; it is a strong bit and requires sensitive handling. Any snaffle mouthpiece can be fitted with gag cheek-pieces: these are made of rolled leather and run through the bit-rings, terminating in a

BRIDLES

The bit and bridle provide the basic lines of communication between rider and horse. There are many types of bit, but for English-style riders they fall into four basic groups: snaffles, double bridles, pelhams, and gag snaffles, with bitless bridles offering further options.

The snaffle

This is the simplest, most universally popular bit. Snaffles are available in many designs, but the one you choose will depend mainly on whether you want the bit to remain still in the horse's mouth, or to make constant tiny movements (for instance, a horse that tends to lean is usually better with a bit that offers more movement).

The basic mouthpiece types are the straight-bar, mullen-mouth, single- and double-jointed snaffles. A straight-bar bit puts pressure on the tongue, and most horses go better in the slightly curved mullen-mouthed variety. The single-jointed bit has a mild nutcracker action and many horses go well in this, but others prefer a double-jointed bit such as the French link snaffle. This has a kidney-shaped central link that reduces the nutcracker effect but gives a less definite "feel" in the hands, so too strong a contact may unintentionally be taken. The French link snaffle, should not be confused with the Dr. Bristol, which is often used on strong horses and has a flat-sided central plate to increase pressure on the tongue.

Cheek pieces include the loose-ring, egg-butt, full-cheek and D-ring snaffle. The loose-ring gives mobility, while the eggbutt and D-ring mean that the bit has less natural movement. Full cheeks can help with steering on a young horse.

above: *A good strong headcollar, either in leather or webbing, as shown, is a basic necessity.*

Martingales: the standing **(above right)** *and running martingale* **(above)** *is used to stop a horse from raising its head too high.*

small ring to which the rein attaches. A second rein should be attached to the bit-ring and used as a snaffle.

When used correctly, the "gag" action is brought into play sparingly. It can be very confusing to the horse: the snaffle action asks it to raise its head, but then it faces a contradictory downward pressure from the gag rein. This will make a horse stop and listen, but only if used occasionally—otherwise the horse will become stiff with a forced head-carriage. There are occasions when a gag is appropriate—for instance, to teach a horse that it can actually jump fences in a controlled way, without running on blindly—but these are rare.

The American gag is even more severe, with considerable leverage. It can be useful where a back-up braking system may become necessary, such as when galloping cross-country.

The bitless bridle

Generally called the hackamore, the bitless bridle is useful on some horses. It works on nose pressure, and must be used with just as much care as the conventional bitted bridle.

Western riders often train their young horses in bitless bridles before graduating to special curb bits. These may look severe, but Western riders rely on balance and neck-reining (see page 138), using a loose rein or the lightest possible contact with their horses' mouths.

Fitting a bit

Your chosen bit must be the correct size and at the correct height in the horse's mouth. If the mouthpiece is jointed, straighten it gently in the horse's mouth by putting a thumb in each ring before judging the size. If correct, there will be a gap of no more than ½ in. (1 cm) on either side between the junction of cheek piece and mouthpiece, and the horse's face. A loose ring-bit may need to be very slightly wider to avoid pinching; rubber bit-guards (discs) will help to prevent this.

With a curb bit, the curb chain must lie flat under the horse's chin. Hook it first on the off (right-hand) side, then twist it clockwise and hook it to the near (left) side. Fasten the chain on the last links, again in a clockwise motion, with your thumbnail upward. If it needs to be shorter, take the link and hook it over the first one, using an counterclockwise movement. The chain should be tight enough to act when the curb cheeks are drawn back at no more than 45 degrees.

Nosebands

The noseband can affect the action of the bit. The cavesson noseband—simply a strap around the center of the nose—makes the horse's head look smarter and can be used to attach a standing martingale (see below). The Flash noseband resembles a cavesson but has a second, narrow strap that fastens below the bit, which helps to keep the bit central and prevents the horse from opening its mouth too wide.

The drop noseband also fastens below the bit, and should be fitted with at least 3 in. (8 cm) above the nostrils; you must also be able to fit two fingers beneath it. The Grakle or crossover noseband looks like a figure eight, and gives extra control by preventing the horse from opening its mouth and crossing its jaw. When using any noseband that fastens below the bit, remember that you are not trying to strap the horse's mouth shut.

The cavesson noseband is the only type to use with a double bridle. Otherwise, it should ideally be used with a pelham or kimblewick, although some riders prefer to use a Flash or Grakle noseband with these bits.

A badly fitting bridle will make your horse uncomfortable. Make sure that the noseband does not rub its facial bones, and also that the browband is long enough not to pinch its ears. There should be a hand's width between the fastened throatlash and the horse's face.

Martingales

Martingales provide an important control factor. The basic types are the standing and running martingale, both designed to keep the horse from raising its head too high—never to strap it down.

The standing martingale fastens to the cavesson, passing between the forelegs and attaching to the girth. It should not be used on a noseband fastening below the bit, as this would affect the horse's air supply. The running martingale splits into two straps, each ending in a ring through which the reins pass, and fastens to the girth.

A standing martingale fits when it can be pushed into the horse's gullet; the rings on a running martingale should stretch into the horse's gullet when the straps are laid along the underside of its neck.

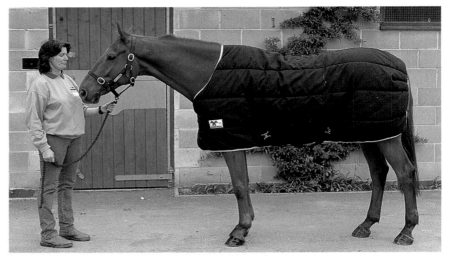

right: The stable rug keeps the stabled horse warm in winter. During cold weather, several rugs will be used. All should be light and washable.

below: Western riders rely on balance and neck reining—using a loose rein and the lightest possible contact with the horse's mouth.

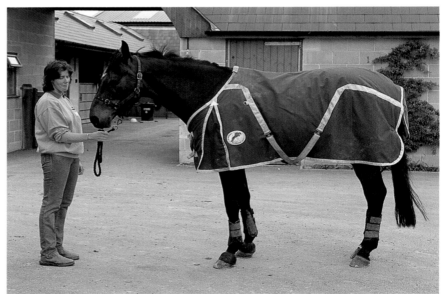

above: New Zealand rugs should be tough and durable to keep horses dry and warm when grazing.

CARING FOR TACK

Tack can be made from leather or synthetic materials. Synthetics are cheaper and easy to look after, but leather usually looks nicer. Check your tack every time you ride, as broken stitching or cracked leather could lead to an accident. If you drop your saddle or your horse rolls on it in a fall, you must have the tree checked before using it again, as a damaged tree could hurt your horse's back.

If you keep your tack clean and in good condition, it will last longer as well as being more comfortable for your horse. It is good practice to wash the bit, wipe off any dirt or mud, and make sure that the girth and numnah (if used) are clean every time you ride, and to take your tack apart for a thorough cleaning once a week.

ADDITIONAL EQUIPMENT

Other basic horse equipment includes a good headcollar and lead rope, a first-aid kit (ask your vet's advice on this if necessary), and a grooming kit (see page 156).

Any further equipment you may need will depend on how you keep your horse. For instance, a stabled horse in work must be clipped in winter or its heavier coat will make it sweat excessively and lose condition; this means that (depending on the type of clip) it will need to wear rugs for part or all of the time. Even a grass-kept horse is likely to need a rug in wet or cold weather.

Traditional rugs are the waterproofed canvas New Zealand rug for outdoor use, the woolen day rug, and the wool-lined jute rug for use in the stable at night. Numerous

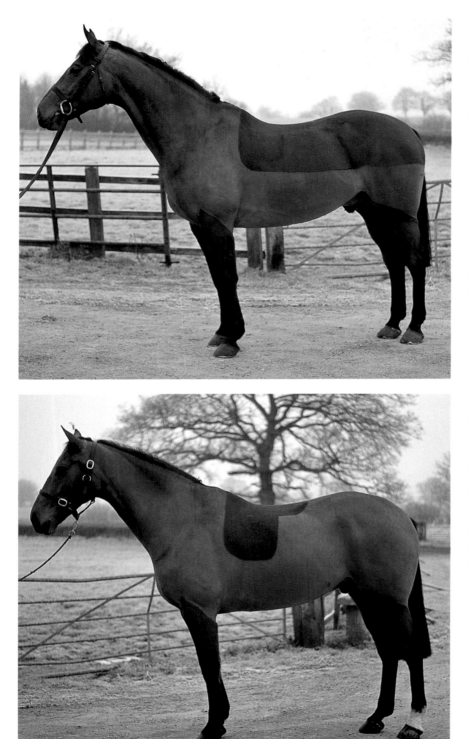

*Two types of clip: the blanket (**left**) and the more efficient hunter clip. (**below left**). Stabled horses in work through the winter will be clipped to keep them from sweating excessively.*

variations are available today, and are light, warm, and easy to wash. Rugs are secured with a webbing or leather surcingle or roller.

You may also need bandages, including tail bandages (see page 177), stable, and exercise bandages. Stable bandages—which should run from the knee down over the fetlock joint—are used to provide warmth, to dry the legs after exercise, on top of soaked cotton or gamgee (commercially produced padding) to reduce heat and swelling, and for protection while traveling (many types of leg protector are also available for traveling and are easier to put on).

Exercise bandages support the tendons and protect against thorns, and are put on over cotton or gamgee; alternatively, special tendon boots can be used. Young horses should wear one or the other during early schooling to prevent bumps; some older horses may also need them. Young horses should wear knee boots as a precaution when first ridden on hard surfaces. Over-reach boots are rubber or leather cones that sit over the coronets, and will be required by a horse that over-reaches (knocks into the heels of the forefeet with its hind feet).

SHOEING

Good foot care and shoeing are vital if a horse is to stay sound, and are a routine part of management. Foot care should start with the foal, as an experienced farrier will be able to correct many problems as long as they are caught early enough; becoming familiar with the experience of being shod from an early age should also mean that a horse is relaxed and easy for the farrier to handle. All horses and ponies should be checked by the farrier and have their feet rasped (shaped) every five to six weeks, even if they are not working or wearing shoes. However, most horses need to wear shoes in order to work comfortably and to keep their feet in good condition, and these should not be left on for more than six weeks at a time—even if they are not worn down—as the feet will have grown and will need reshaping.

Before starting work, a good farrier will examine the horse's whole conformation, especially that of its limbs, as this will allow him to help the horse to move in the most efficient way. Your job is to make regular shoeing appointments, to pick out your horse's feet at least once a day—even if it is not being ridden—and to check their condition and that of its shoes in case you need an emergency appointment.

You should also know how to remove a loose shoe if necessary to reduce the risk of the horse hurting itself before the farrier arrives. You will need to do the following:

- *Pick up the foot and cut off the clenches with a buffer or similar tool (clenches are the turned-over nail ends that hold the shoe to the foot).*
- *Use pincers gently to ease the shoe loose from the foot, starting at the heels and then moving along the branches (sides) of the shoe.*
- *Grip the toe of the shoe with the pincers, and pull the shoe off backward.*

Shoeing methods

A farrier will use one of two methods of shoeing, known as hot and cold shoeing. With the former, a pre-heated shoe is held on the foot; the resulting charred area reveals any unevenness that needs to be filed or cut before the cooled shoe is nailed on. This part of the foot has no nerve endings, so burning and nailing cause no pain. In cold shoeing, ready-shaped shoes are nailed to the feet. The farrier can still make small alterations to the shape of the shoes, although the fit will be less accurate than with hot shoeing. However, a horse that has been well shod by the cold method will still be better off than one that has been badly hot shod.

Types of shoe

Horseshoes are usually made of steel. The exceptions to this are the special lightweight aluminum shoes worn by racehorses, which are called racing plates. Special glue-on plastic shoes are also available for horses with problems such as brittle feet that cannot take clenches. There are also many types of surgical shoe available to help in

relieving other problems, including special designs for conditions such as laminitis and navicular syndrome (see page 179). In such cases, it is important that the farrier and veterinary surgeon work together to deal with the condition.

Metal shoes have triangular clips which hold them in place while the clenches are put in. Shoes for the forefeet usually have a single toe clip at the front, while hind shoes usually have two quarter clips—one on either side of the foot. Quarter clips prevent the shoe from moving sideways and mean that the farrier can bevel the toe—in other words, to slant it slightly so that the horse is less likely to over-reach (strike the heel of its front foot with the toe of its hind shoe), which can cause wounds that are difficult and slow to heal. Over-reach boots can also be worn to prevent this (see page 167).

Studs

Many riders fit studs into their horses' shoes to give them better grip, especially when galloping or jumping. These screw into specially made holes in the heels of the shoes, and come in different shapes: pointed studs are used for hard going, and squarer ones for soft ground. The studs are removed when the horse is not being worked, and the holes in the shoes must be plugged with special keepers or cotton to prevent them from filling with impacted dirt.

above & right: A general purpose steel shoe, two surgical shoes, a "T" shoe (center) and a bar shoe (right), which can help relieve conditions such as navicular syndrome and laminitis.

right: A farrier at work. Building a good relationship with your horse's farrier is important—a good farrier will look at the horse's overall conformation.

THE HORSE'S BODY

THE BODY OF THE HORSE is a fine example of nature's ability to relate structure to function—expressed elsewhere in the sharp carnassial teeth of the dog accustomed to tearing at flesh and using its bite for defense, or in the fins of a fish developed for propulsion through water. The horse's body is adapted for speed and size.

Other animals are as fast as the horse but not as big, and it is this combination that gives the clue to much of the equine body structure. It accounts for highly specialized limbs in which the number of bones has been reduced to a minimum, accompanied by a loss of muscle (it is these muscles and extra bones that give humans or animals the ability to grasp objects). During its evolution the horse has lost this ability and can move its limbs only forward or backward. This provides the optimum means of propulsion, while the necessary

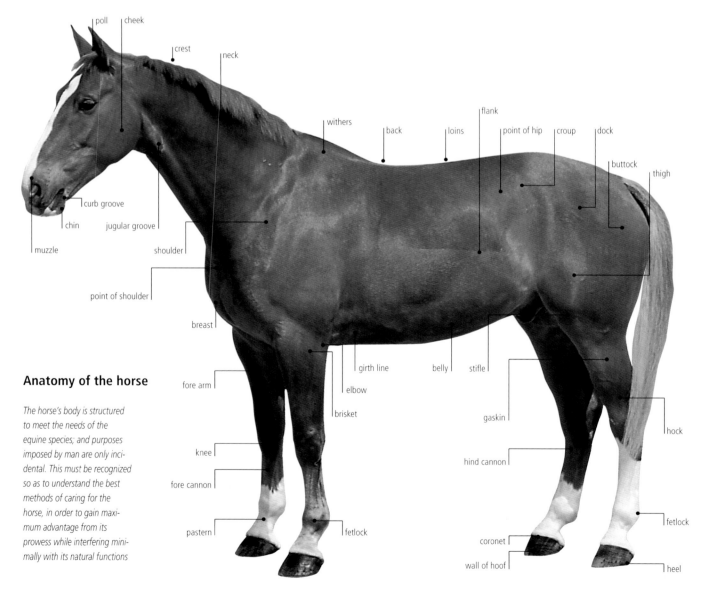

Anatomy of the horse

The horse's body is structured to meet the needs of the equine species; and purposes imposed by man are only incidental. This must be recognized so as to understand the best methods of caring for the horse, in order to gain maximum advantage from its prowess while interfering minimally with its natural functions

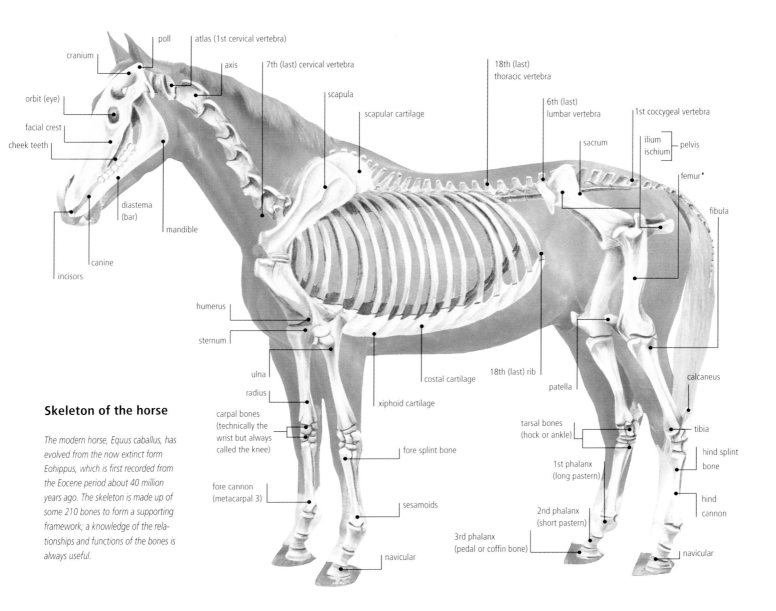

poll

atlas (1st cervical vertebra)

cranium

axis

7th (last) cervical vertebra

18th (last)
thoracic vertebra

scapula

6th (last)
lumbar vertebra

1st coccygeal vertebra

orbit (eye)

scapular cartilage

facial crest

sacrum

ilium
ischium

pelvis

cheek teeth

femur

diastema
(bar)

fibula

mandible

canine

humerus

incisors

sternum

ulna

radius

calcaneus

18th (last) rib

costal cartilage

patella

tibia

Skeleton of the horse

carpal bones
(technically the
wrist but always
called the knee)

tarsal bones
(hock or ankle)

hind splint
bone

*The modern horse, Equus caballus, has
evolved from the now extinct form
Eohippus, which is first recorded from
the Eocene period about 40 million
years ago. The skeleton is made up of
some 210 bones to form a supporting
framework; a knowledge of the rela-
tionships and functions of the bones is
always useful.*

fore splint bone

1st phalanx
(long pastern)

hind
cannon

fore cannon
(metacarpal 3)

sesamoids

2nd phalanx
(short pastern)

3rd phalanx
(pedal or coffin bone)

navicular

xiphoid cartilage

navicular

force is provided by highly developed muscles attached to the bones of the forearms,
thighs, and body.

The skeleton

The horse's skeleton consists of approximately 210 bones (excluding those of the
tail). The skeleton provides support for the
muscles and protection for the internal
organs, and its parts have sufficient mobility to allow the horse to move at different
speeds, to lie down, or to graze.

Varying degrees of mobility are provided by different joints—for example, the

joint between the femur and the tibia, forming the stifle, gives great mobility, while
those between vertebrae in the backbone
allow only restricted movement. The bones
forming all joints are capped with cartilage,
which is softer than bone and can repair the
effects of wear and tear. The joints are completed by a capsule that produces lubricating synovia (joint oil), and are strengthened
by ligaments (fibrous bands) connecting the
bones on either side.

The horse's skeleton gives several examples of nature's way of adapting structure to
meet requirements. For instance, the broad,

flat surface of the shoulder blade and trans-
verse processes of the lumbar vertebrae provide ample space for the attachment of the
powerful muscles needed to move the fore-
and hind legs. The elongated skull allows
space for the teeth, while the eye orbits are
positioned well above ground level during
grazing, giving the horse greater vision to
watch out for danger.

The muscles

The muscles that enable the horse to move
consist of muscle masses attached to bone
at one end and to their respective tendons at

the other. For example, the superficial digital flexor of the forelimb is attached to the humerus bone and the posterior aspect of the radius bone. At its lower end it forms the tendon, which runs behind the knee and fetlock joints. Its action is to flex the toe and knee, and to extend the elbow joint.

The tendon is encased in a synovial sheath as it runs behind the knee and fetlock joints. The thin, fibrous sheet that composes this sheath produces lubricating synovia. As in the joints, sheaths enclose

tendons wherever there is likely to be friction between tendon and bone, or with other structures. A bursa is a similar structure, except that it does not surround a tendon but acts more as a cushion between parts that would otherwise suffer friction.

Like the tendons, the ligaments vary in length. Most are relatively short, such as the joint-strengthening ligaments already mentioned. The check and suspensory ligaments of the forelimb both deserve a special mention. The check ligament is attached to the

ligament at the back of the knee joint and, at its lower end, joins the deep digital flexor tendon at the back of the cannon bone, and forms part of the apparatus that prevents over-extension of the toe. The suspensory ligament is also concerned in this and is attached above to the back of the cannon bone and lower row of knee bones, and below to the sesamoid bones behind the fetlock joint. From here it sends branches around the front of the first pastern bone on each side to join the common digital exten-

The walk is a four-time pace in which the horse takes four separate steps, which when on a hard surface, can be heard as four distinct, evenly timed beats. The sequence is generally; hind foot, fore foot on the same side, opposite hind foot and lastly, opposite fore foot (for example, offside hind, offside fore, nearside hind, nearside fore). In a well balanced horse, the hind feet should "track up," i.e., follow the track left by the fore feet.

The trot is a two-time pace in which the two diagonal pairs of legs (i.e., offside hind and nearside fore; nearside hind and offside fore) move alternately, followed by a split second in which all four feet are in the air. The rider can either rise or sit to the trot.

sor tendon, through which they are inserted into the second phalangeal and pedal bones. There is a similar arrangement to this in the hind leg.

The skin

The horse's skin consists of three layers: an outer cellular or epithelial layer, which is capable of replacing itself as its outer surface is eroded; a sub-epithelial layer which nourishes the outer layer and in which pain endings and other sensitive structures are found; and the sub-dermal layer which binds the skin to the underlying bone or muscle. The hair follicles occur in the sub-dermal layer. The skin contains the sweat glands, and other glands which secrete an oil substance known as sebum; this provides a waterproofing layer to protect the horse from wet and cold weather.

A knowledge of the anatomy and physiology of the horse is vital in order to enable him to perform to his maximum potential. For the rider, gaining an understanding of the horse's movement through the four paces; walk, trot, canter, and gallop, is important, particularly in the early stages of learning to ride. Watching the sequence of footfall from the ground and then from the saddle by following the movements of the shoulders and hindquarters will help develop the rider's sense of balance as well as correct position in the saddle and ultimately foster an understanding of the way in which a horse performs the transitions between each pace.

The canter is a three-time pace in which there are three distinct beats. As in the trot, the diagonal pairs work together. The sequence is as follows; offside hind, followed by the right diagonal (nearside hind and offside fore), and then nearside fore followed by a moment of suspension in which all four legs are off the ground. Canter is probably the most comfortable pace for the rider, who should be trying to sit as deeply as possible into the saddle.

The gallop is the horse's fastest pace. This is a four-time pace in the sequence; near-hind, off-hind, near-side fore, off-fore, followed by a split second of suspension. Here the rider sits forward and slightly out of the saddle.

THE HORSE'S MIND

THE HORSE HAS EVOLVED through the centuries as a herd animal reliant on speed to escape its natural predators. Horses in the wild will form herd groups, usually consisting of one stallion and about five or six mares with their offspring, thus increasing their chances of survival in terms of avoiding predators and finding food. The behavior of all horses and ponies—whether used for riding, driving, or other activities, or whether living wild—has remained inextricably linked to natural instincts that have been a key factor in the survival of the fittest.

The horse's defense mechanisms—that is, the possession of highly developed senses and the ability to move swiftly away from the threat of attack—are in the main directed toward flight as a means of preservation, and any study of the equine personality must take this into account. The instincts for flight in the face of danger can be clearly seen in the reaction of a startled horse: even an experienced, well-trained individual may quickly accelerate away from an unexpected noise or movement. Some horses may remain suspicious of passing a particular object, but few will still refuse to do so if others have already passed it safely and are walking into the distance. The horse, therefore, remains very much a herd animal.

Horse psychology and training

An understanding of the horse's mind is important for training and handling, particularly when dealing with youngsters. For example, a young horse's first encounter with heavy traffic, its first journey in a trailer, or its first experience of cross-country schooling through water will be much more nerve wracking if it is takes it by itself. However, if it is accompanied by an older, sensible horse, the youngster will be much more confident in tackling the new tasks.

In recent years the psychology of the horse has been accepted as being of greater significance in training, and methods of teaching the horse to accept a saddle and rider—based on aspects of equine behavior—have been developed by many trainers. For instance, when working in an enclosed area, a trainer may mimic the behavior of the dominant mare in a herd by chasing away the young horse until it submits and stands quietly awaiting further signals—in other words, looks to the trainer for leadership. Having gained the horse's trust, the trainer can proceed with training in the conventional manner of working slowly and quietly when introducing tack and, subsequently, a rider.

Artificial living conditions

The mental state and some aspects of behavior of any horse in captivity will be determined partly by its environment. Ideally, given suitable weather, shelter, and feed availability, horses would be kept together in groups for 24 hours a day, 365 days a year. However, because of the value of many horses (and the risk of injury from being kicked by another horse), or because of the need for convenience, it is often impractical for horses to live as they would do in the wild.

Stereotypical behavior problems such as windsucking (swallowing air, causing indigestion), weaving (rocking persistently from side to side on the forelegs) and box-walking (walking endlessly around the stable) may develop in some horses, and are generally exhibited more frequently by individuals that are stabled for much of the day. These types of behavior can, therefore, be considered to be man-made, as they tend to be seen exclusively in domesticated horses, possibly due to boredom. Modern stabling can address this problem of removing the horse from a herd environment—some designs, for instance, have bars or grilles on adjoining walls to allow the horses to see one another. In the American barn system horses are turned out together in a large barn, and this option is also favored by some owners in other countries.

The stallion in captivity

The stabling of stallions is perhaps furthest removed from their situation in the wild, as they are often isolated from direct contact with other horses except for the purposes of covering mares. However, some studs—particularly those containing native breeds—will turn out a stallion with a group of mares. Although this carries a greater risk of injury, the horse will often have a higher conception rate, linked to its more natural living conditions, and this provides another example of the way in which harmony between human and horse is best achieved by those who understand the equine mind.

left: Survival of the fittest: in the wild, natural instincts are key to survival.

right: The psychology of the horse is a subject of growing interest in relation to training.

DISEASES OF THE HORSE

EQUINE AILMENTS MAY BE classified in the following three ways: as infectious or non-infectious; by cause (for example, bacterial or parasitic); and by the part of the horse involved (for example, heart disease). Rhoddococus pneumonia in a foal, for instance, would within these classifications be described as an infectious disease, a bacterial disease, and a lung problem.

Infectious v. non-infectious disease
An infectious disease is one that spreads from one horse to another. If direct physical contact is necessary between the horses for the spread of infection to occur, the disease or condition is also said to be contagious (for instance, lice are contagious because they cannot survive away from the horse, and they can only pass from one horse to another by contact). However, even contagious diseases can often be spread by indirect contact: for example, brushing a lice-infested horse and then a non-infested one may transfer some of the lice on the brush.

All contagious diseases are infectious, but not all infectious diseases are contagious. Equine influenza is a good example of an infection that is not necessarily contagious (in other words, requires direct contact to spread). Every time a horse suffering from influenza coughs, it will send out microscopic droplets of water into the air, carrying virus particles with them, and a horse which is up to 200 yards (150 m) away could breathe in one of these droplets and become infected.

Non-infectious causes of disease include trauma, which in many cases involves not the dramatic trauma of an injury such as a broken leg, but the wear and tear that result in degenerative joint disease.

Causes of disease
The causes of disease may be grouped under the following major headings.

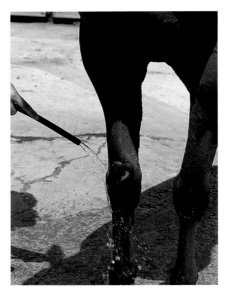
below: First aid: a wound is hosed down to cleanse and reduce swelling.

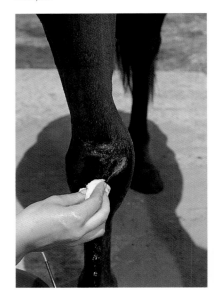
below: The wound is cleaned and dried with a sterile pad.

Viruses
Viruses are minute packages of genetic material. They are sometimes capable of invading one of the host's normal cells and multiplying inside the cell until they destroy it. There are no worthwhile antiviral drugs available, so we have to rely on the horse's natural defenses, perhaps stimulated by the use of vaccines.

Bacteria
Bacteria are single-celled organisms, and usually multiply by division. They have an outer cell membrane, and so are more resistant than viruses to environmental factors. Drugs called antibiotics are also available to kill bacteria, although the sensitivity of the different species of bacterium to antibiotics varies tremendously. In time a bacterium may become resistant to a particular antibiotic, and in some cases this resistance may be passed on to another bacterium that had previously been susceptible to the drug. It is,

therefore inaccurate to say that one antibiotic is "stronger" than another when a bacterial infection is being treated: it is, in fact, a question of whether that infection is sensitive to the drug being used.

Fungi
Fungi are single-celled organisms linked together in strands or filaments. They can often produce spores that are extremely resistant to environmental conditions, ensuring the long-term survival of the fungus: for example, ringworm spores can survive for many months in the wood of a stable, or on fencing rails. Spore production can also sometimes make it difficult to kill fungal infections with drugs.

Parasites
Parasites are complex organisms. Internal parasites include the worms that live in a horse's intestine, while lice are common external parasites. The distinguishing fea-

right: Bandaging is an art which requires some practice. Here, padding is first wrapped around the foreleg.

below: Stable bandages are applied to both front legs to help the good leg carry the extra weight it will take off the bad leg.

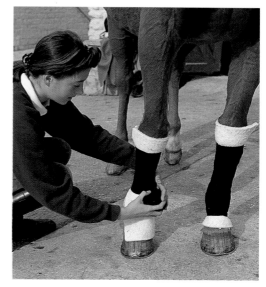

below: A horse is walked in front of the vet, who is checking for lameness. The test is conducted in a straight line, on a flat, hard surface.

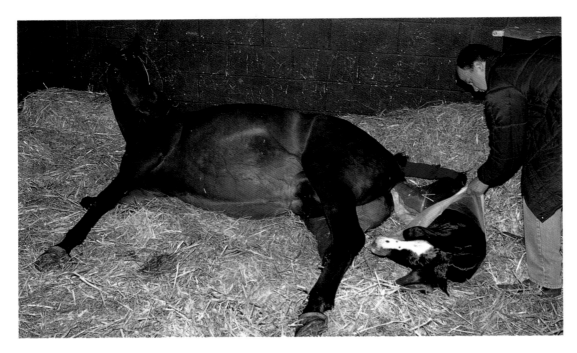

left: The birth of a foal is always something to celebrate.

ture of a parasite is that it lives by using food material provided by the host animal. It is, therefore, not in the parasite's interests to kill its host, because without this source of food it would die. Worms may be controlled by regular treatments and prompt removal of feces from the horse's environment. Effective treatments are also available for conditions such as lice infestations.

Immunity against disease

The horse's tissues have an in-built ability to recognize foreign materials which gain entry to the body. Foreign proteins (the building blocks from which viruses, bacteria, and so on are made) are referred to as antigens, and when an antigen is recognized the horse will produce other proteins called antibodies which will attempt to block its activity. If the levels of antibody in a horse's blood are measured against a particular antigen, it is possible to tell whether or not the horse has been exposed to that antigen.

It takes about 10 to 14 days for maximum antibody production to be reached so, if antibody levels are measured twice at 10 to 14 day intervals, a rising level will indicate that an active infection is present.

When a foal is born, it has no antibodies and is, therefore, unable to deal with any diseases. However, provided that it receives some of its dam's first milk (known as colostrum) during the first 12 to 18 hours of life, it will obtain temporary protection against all the diseases to which the mother is herself immune, having been protected through vaccination. This protection is only temporary and decreases from 12 weeks of age, making vaccination for a foal of that age essential.

When fighting some diseases, the horse relies not on the production of antibodies but on the development of killer cells which can destroy the antigen involved. This process is known as cell-mediated immunity (CMI). It is not possible to measure cellular

immunity, so in the case of some diseases it may be mistakenly assumed that the affected horse has made no attempt to deal with the antigen.

Vaccines are an artificial attempt to prevent a horse from acquiring particular infections. Live vaccines contain living viruses which have been modified so that they can no longer cause disease, but can still stimulate immunity. The latter function is achieved by stimulating the horse's immune system to produce antibodies, so that it will be able to fight the disease if it actually encounters it. Live vaccines usually only require one dose, whereas dead vaccines (made from all or part of the killed organism) require two doses, usually four to six weeks apart. Live vaccines can allow the organism to spread to non-vaccinated horses, and are likely to cause mild symptoms. Dead vaccines do not carry these risks and are, therefore, usually preferred to live vaccines. Increasingly, active components of

left: Checking for a lower limb disorder. The vet is looking for swellings and heat that may be the result of sprains such as spavin or jarring.

below: Tooth rasping and checking is carried out on an annual basis. Over-rasping can cause the surface of the teeth to become too smooth and reduce grinding.

below: Taking the temperature is the first step to establishing the condition of a horse.

above: Worms are controlled by regular treatment and the removal of feces from fields and stables.

a vaccine are combined with chemical carriers called adjuvants, which increase stimulation of the immune system.

Diseases of locomotion

A horse is said to be lame when it experiences pain in bearing weight on one or more legs; lameness may be recognized because the horse compensates by taking extra weight on the other leg, nodding its head (for a foreleg) or sinking its hindquarters (for a hind leg) in the process. The most common site of lameness is the foot. The presence of the rigid hoof causes pressure if an internal structure becomes swollen, so, if a stone or nail penetrates the foot and sets up an infection, the pressure resulting from the formation of pus can be very painful. The horse may be unwilling to put the foot to the ground but, if the pus is located by a vet and a hole is made to release the pressure, there will be an immediate improvement.

Regular trimming of a horse's hooves is essential, to keep each foot balanced so that undue weight is not placed on the various structures. Navicular disease—the most common cause of chronic front foot lameness—is associated with extra weight or percussion on the heel region where the navicular bone is situated. This interferes with blood supply to the area. Treatment consists of using a special shoe to provide extra protection over the heels. A drug called isoxuprine may be used to improve the blood supply.

Lameness may involve more than one leg at the same time; in laminitis, all four legs may be involved. In this condition, a temporary shut-down of the blood supply to the foot—often due to the effect of chemicals released as a result of eating rich grass or grain—causes the delicate tissue between the hoof wall and pedal bone to die from lack of oxygen. The resulting instability inside the hoof is very painful, and occasionally results in the pedal bone rotating and penetrating the sole. In the past horses with laminitis were often forced to exercise. We know that this makes the instability worse. Complete box rest, the use of a shoe that supports the frog area, and drugs to lower the blood pressure in the foot are now the recommended treatments.

Diagnosing and treating lameness

Diagnosis of the cause of lameness means pinpointing the origin of the pain. The only way in which a vet can do this is to use local anesthetic to block off the nerve supply to an area, and then to see whether that temporarily removes the lameness. X rays taken of the area will reveal the structure of the

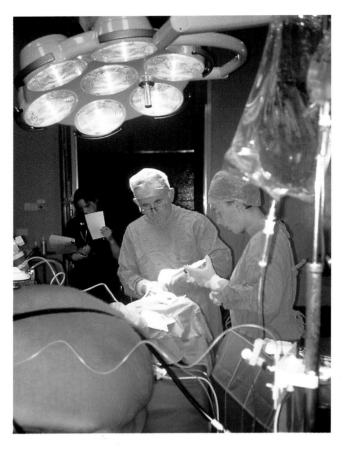

right: The operating theater at work. In recent years there have been great strides in surgery. Lower limb fractures, for example, are often successfully repaired.

below: Ringworm is a highly contagious fungal condition in which the hair comes off in small, round patches.

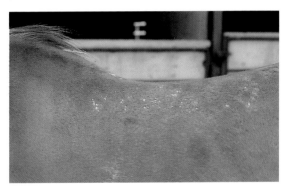

bone, and ultrasound scans will show the internal structure of soft tissues such as tendons.

Degenerative Joint Disease (DJD), or arthritis, can develop in one or more of a horse's joints without causing any clinical symptoms, but X rays of a sound horse may reveal such changes. The factors that cause the joint to become painful and cause lameness are unclear, but frequently involve alterations in the horse's exercise routine—periods of rest are as likely to trigger off lameness as periods of excessive activity. DJD is a progressive disease and no treatment will reverse the physical changes, although it may reduce the lameness.

In recent years there have been great advances in orthopedic surgery, but it is still not possible to repair a complete fracture of one of the major long bones in the horse. However, fractures of the knee, or hock, and fractures lower down the leg are often successfully repaired.

Diseases of the respiratory system

Many respiratory infections spread rapidly within horses that are kept together for training or competition. Compulsory vaccination programs have reduced the incidence of epidemics caused by equine influenza virus, but respiratory infections are still responsible for major economic losses in the racing industry and in other areas of equine sport. Equine herpes virus may not cause such severe clinical disease as equine influenza, but it is much more widespread. Recent research has also re-emphasized the importance of bacteria in equine respiratory disease.

Chronic obstructive pulmonary disease (COPD) results in constriction of the small airway in a horse's lungs, and is caused by an allergic reaction to the fungal spores found on hay and straw. The incidence of COPD has increased in recent years, especially in the aftermath of infectious respiratory disease.

Physical defects affecting the flow of air into the lungs can have a major effect on performance. Laryngeal paralysis—often recognized from the "roaring" noise heard when the horse breathes in, through the partially collapsed larynx—is perhaps the most feared of these defects. The debate about the efficacy or otherwise of the Hobday operation to increase airflow continues. The operation reduces the noise by obliterating the cavities behind the vocal cords where the turbulence occurs, but many horses still require additional surgery to "tie back" the collapsed vocal cord and cartilage away from the airflow.

Diseases of the heart and circulation

Most people are familiar with the concept of listening to the sounds of a heart beating through a stethoscope. Extra noises, or murmurs, are often the result of abnormal blood flow through the heart valves;

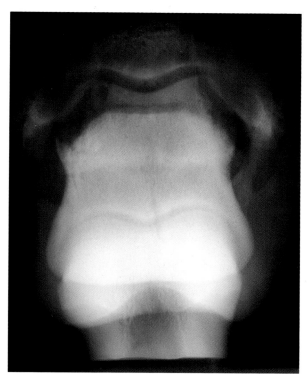

left: An X ray of a patient with navicular disease— the most common cause of chronic front foot lameness.

below: Testing bacterial cultures against antibiotics. A clear area around the antibiotic impregnated disc means the bacteria is sensitive to the antibiotic.

below: A horse suffering the painful condition, laminitis. Box rest and remedial shoeing are the recommended treatments.

abnormal rhythms (arrhythmias) reflect changes in the electrical impulses which control the contraction of the heart muscle. An electrocardiograph can be used to measure these electrical impulses and shows them visually, while ultrasound scanning enables a vet to see the internal structures of a horse's heart as it beats; it is even possible to measure blood flow at precise points in the heart. The general rule has been that abnormal rhythms are more significant than heart murmurs, and that abnormalities which worsen with strenuous exercise are more likely to cause problems than those which are unaffected by exercise. In the horse, heart problems rarely cause sudden death.

There are a number of infections which result in damage to the lining of blood vessels. In the case of infectious arteritis, fluid leaks out into the surrounding tissues, causing swelling (edema). In another condition, worm larvae of Strongylus Vulgaris migrate along the blood vessels supplying the small intestine, and may block the flow completely; the result is death of the portion of bowel supplied by that blood vessel. Regular worming with drugs that can kill the migrating larvae, such as vermectin, will prevent the condition occurring.

Diseases of the alimentary tract

Humans have imposed many alterations on the horse's natural diet, some of which are too inflexible for its digestive system. Feeding hay rather than grass, for example, means that dental problems, which result in the horse chewing its food less efficiently, are more significant in the domesticated horse. Regular filing, or rasping, of the teeth should be carried out to prevent this.

The horse relies on thousands of bacteria living in its large bowel to digest fibrous plant material. Disturbances in the numbers of these bacteria can mean lack of digestion and the formation of an impaction. Colic is a group of symptoms rather than a disease in itself, and refers to abdominal pain, the external signs of which include rolling, kicking at the abdomen, repeatedly looking around at the flanks, and patchy sweating. Very acute colic tends to be caused by a physical displacement of the bowel—such as a twisted gut—and generally requires surgery. Acute intermittent, or spasmodic, colic tends to be due to abnormal nerve control of contraction/relaxation of the bowels, and often responds well to bowel-muscle relaxants and pain killers. Chronic low-grade colic tends to be associated with physical impactions: this may respond to purgatives such as liquid paraffin, although surgery is sometimes necessary.

GLOSSARY

Above the bit *Evasion of the bit, where the horse pushes its nose in front of the vertical.*

Action *The movement of the horse.*

Against the clock *In show jumping, a competition or jump-off decided by time, the winner being the competitor with the least number of faults in a round completed in the fastest time.*

Aids *Signals used by a rider to give instructions to his or her horse (see also Artificial aids; Natural aids).*

Air above the ground *A High School movement performed with the forelegs, or with both fore- and hind legs, off the ground (see also Ballotade, Capriole, Courbette, Croupade, Levade).*

Albino *A color type (rather than a breed) comprising pure white hair, pale skin, and pale, translucent eyes.*

Amble *A slow gait in two-time, in which the horse's fore- and hind legs on the same side are moved forward at the same time.*

Anvil *(a) A heavy iron block with a smooth flat face, usually of steel, on which horseshoes are shaped; (b) (Western United States) A horse, particularly one that is shod, which strikes the forefeet with the hind feet.*

Apprentice *A trainee jockey.*

Artificial aids *Items such as whips, spurs, and martingales, which are used by a rider to help convey instructions to his or her horse.*

Back (at the knee) *Where the lower leg (below the knee) is exaggeratedly concave.*

Back (cold) *When a horse reacts badly to a "cold" saddle being placed on its back.*

Back (dipped) *Common in older horses, where the dip between the withers and croup is noticeably sunken.*

Back (hollow) *Exaggeration of the horse's naturally concave back line.*

Balance *When the horse is moving correctly and efficiently, and is able to carry itself well with a rider on its back.*

Ballotade *An air above the ground in which the horse half-rears, then jumps forward—drawing the hind legs up below the quarters—before landing on all four legs.*

Bandages *Available in three types: exercise bandages (to protect the legs and support the tendons during exercise); stable bandages (for warmth and protection, especially when traveling; and tail bandages (to prevent rubbing and to help the hairs to lie flat).*

Barrage *A jump-off.*

Barrel *The part of the horse's body between the forearms and the loins.*

Barrel racing *Racing around barrels, popular in Australia and the United States.*

Barren *Term used to describe an infertile mare.*

Bay *(a) A dark-skinned horse with a dark brown to bright reddish- or yellowish-brown coat, with a black mane and tail and (normally) black markings on the legs; (b) The noise made by a hound.*

Bed down *To put down bedding for a horse in a stable.*

Bedding *Straw, wood shavings, peat, or shredded paper used to line the floor of a horse's stable for warmth, as well as to prevent the horse from injuring itself as it lies down or rolls.*

Behind the bit *An evasion of the bit where the horse brings its nose behind the vertical.*

Bit *A device, normally made of metal or rubber, attached to the bridle and placed in the horse's mouth (on the tongue) so as to regulate the position of its head and to help control its pace and direction. The bit is manipulated by use of the reins.*

Bitless bridle *Any of a variety of bridles used without a bit, with which control is grained by exerting pressure on the horse's nose and curb groove rather than on the mouth.*

Black *A horse with a black coat, mane, and tail with no other color present (except possibly white markings on the face and/or legs).*

Blemish *A scar left by an injury or wound.*

Blinkers *A pair of leather eye-shields fixed to the bridle or on a head-covering, often used on driving harness and in racing, to prevent a horse from looking anywhere other than straight ahead.*

Blood *The blood in a horse's body constitutes approximately 1/18 of its total body weight.*

Blood horse *The English Thoroughbred.*

Bloodstock *Thoroughbred horses—particularly race and stud animals.*

Body brush *A tightly packed, short-bristled brush used to remove dust and scurf from a horse's coat, and to condition the skin.*

Boots *Protective items of equipment for a horse's legs, including: brushing boots (to prevent damage caused by a hoof "brushing" the inside of the opposite lower leg), knee boots (often put on young horses for protection in case of a fall), over-reach boots (to protect the heels of the forefeet from being struck into by the hind feet) and tendon boots (for support and protection).*

Breaking in *The initial training of a horse for whatever purpose it may be required (see also Starting).*

Breastplate *A piece of tack used to prevent the saddle from slipping back; it attaches to the front D-rings of the saddle and passes around the horse's neck and between the forelegs to the girth.*

Bridle *The part of a horse's saddlery or harness that is placed on the head; numerous types are available for different purposes (see Bitless bridle, Double bridle, Snaffle bridle).*

Bronco *An unbroken or imperfectly broken wild horse.*

Bronc riding *One of the standard rodeo events. The only piece of tack worn by the horse is a wide leather band around its middle, from which there protrudes a leather handhold.*

Brood mare *A mare used for breeding.*

Browband *The part of the bridle which lies across the horse's forehead, below the ears.*

Brumby *An Australian wild horse.*

Buck *A leap into the air by a horse—usually in an attempt to dislodge its rider—in which it arches its back and comes down with the forelegs stiff and the head held low.*

Bulldogging *Steer wrestling on horseback—one of the standard events at a rodeo.*

Bull riding *A standard rodeo event in which the contestant has to ride a bull equipped only with a rope around its middle; the rider may hold this with only one hand.*

Bumper *(a) An amateur race rider; (b) an amateur race.*

By *Used to describe a horse's breeding, i.e., Sired by.*

Cadence *The rhythm of the horse's movement.*

Camp drafting *A uniquely Australian rodeo contest, in which a rider separates a large bullock from a group of cattle and drives it at a gallop around a course marked with upright poles.*

Canter *A three-time pace in which the horse's hoofs strike the ground in the following order: near hind, near fore and off hind together, off fore (leading leg); or off hind, off fore and near hind together, near fore (leading leg).*

Cantle *The raised back of the saddle.*

Capriole *An air above the ground in which the horse half-rears with the hocks drawn under its body, then jumps forward and high into the air—at the same time kicking out the hind legs with the soles of the feet turned upward—before landing collectedly on all four legs.*

Cast *Description of a horse that rolls in its stable and is unable to stand up again.*

Cavalletti *A series of small wooden jumps used in the basic training of a riding horse to encourage it to lengthen its stride, improve its balance, and loosen up and strengthen its muscles.*

Cavesson *A plain type of noseband (see also Lunging cavesson).*

Check *A halt in hunting when hounds lose the scent.*

Cheek piece *(a) The leather part of the bridle to which the bit is attached at one end and the headpiece at the other; (b) The side pieces of a bit, to which the reins are attached.*

Chef d'équipe *The manager of an equestrian team, responsible for making all the arrangements—both on and off the field—for a national team competing abroad.*

Chestnut *(a) A horse with a gold to dark reddish-brown coat, usually with a matching or slightly lighter or darker mane and tail, or sometimes with a flaxen-colored mane and tail; (b) A small, hard, hairless area on the inside of each of a horse's upper legs.*

Chukka *One of four periods of play in a game of polo (see also Polo).*

Claiming race *A race immediately after which any runner, if it loses, may be claimed for a previously stated price; or, if it is the winner, must be offered for sale at auction.*

Classic *Any one of the five main English flat races for three-year-old horses: the Derby, the Oaks, the St. Leger, the 1,000 Guineas, and the 2,000 Guineas.*

Clear round *A show jumping or cross-country round completed with neither jumping nor time faults.*

Clipping *Using electric clippers to remove part or all of a horse's coat in cold weather, to prevent excessive sweating and loss of condition during work. The different types of clip are: the full clip (where the whole coat is removed), the hunter clip (the legs to the elbows/thighs and saddle patch are left unclipped for warmth and protection from injury), the blanket clip (the underside of the belly and neck are clipped) and the trace clip (the underside of the neck and belly, down to the forearms and thighs, are clipped).*

Cob *A type rather than a breed; a short-legged animal with a maximum height of 15.1 h.h. (153 cm), with the bone and substance of a heavyweight hunter and the capability of carrying a substantial rider weight.*

Colic *Sharp abdominal pains, usually requiring veterinary attention; often the symptom of flatulence, an obstruction created by a mass of hard food, or feces in the bowel. The condition can lead to a potentially fatal twisted gut.*

Collection *Shortening of the horse's pace by means of a light contact from the rider's hands and a steady pressure with the legs to make the horse flex its neck, relax its jaw, and bring its hocks well underneath the body so that it is properly balanced.*

Colt *An ungelded male horse of less than four years.*

Combination fence *In show jumping, an obstacle consisting of two or more separate jumps which are numbered and judged as one obstacle.*

Combined-training competition *(See Eventing.)*

Contact *The link between the rider's hands and the horse's mouth, made through the reins.*

Corn *Bruising of the sole in the angle between the wall of the hoof and the heel.*

Cribbing *A harmful habit in which a horse bites a fence or some other object, simultaneously swallowing air. Also called crib biting, windsucking.*

Courbette *An air above the ground in which the horse rears to an almost upright position, then leaps forward several times on its hind legs.*

Croupade *An air above the ground in which the horse rears, then jumps vertically with its hind legs drawn up toward the belly.*

Crupper *A piece of tack attached to the back of the saddle and fitted beneath the top of the tail to prevent the saddle from slipping forward; generally used on small, fat ponies and as part of driving harness.*

Curb bit *Type of bit used in conjunction with a snaffle bit in a double bridle, consisting of two metal cheek pieces and a mouthpiece with a central indented section (known as the port).*

Curb chain *A metal chain fitted to the eyes of a curb or pelham bit, which gives the rider greater control; the chain lies in the curb groove of the horse's jaw.*

Curry comb *A grooming tool made of metal or rubber, with a flat back and a front consisting of several rows of small metal teeth. It is used to remove dirt and scurf from a body brush; the rubber type may also be used gently to remove mud from a horse's coat.*

Cutting horse *A horse specially trained for separating selected cattle from a herd.*

Dam *The mother of a foal.*

Double bridle *A bridle consisting of two bits—a curb and a snaffle—which are attached via two cheek pieces and may be operated independently using separate pairs of reins.*

Dressage *(a) The art of training a horse to perform all movements in a balanced, supple, obedient, and keen manner; (b) A competition in its own right, or the first phase of an eventing competition.*

Dressage test *A test consisting of a specified sequence of movements to be performed in an arena and assessed by a judge or panel of judges.*

Event horse *A horse which competes or is capable of competing in a combined-training competition.*

Eventing *A comprehensive test of both horse and rider, consisting of three phases—dressage, cross-country, and show jumping—held over a period of one, two, or three days.*

Farrier *A person who makes and fits horseshoes.*

Fault *In show jumping or cross-country, a scoring unit used to record any knockdown, refusal, run-out, or fall by a competitor during his or her round.*

FEI *The Fédération Equestre Internationale (International Equestrian Federation), which is the governing body of international equestrian sport and was founded in 1921 by Commandant G. Hector of France; its headquarters are in Brussels. The FEI makes the rules and regulations for the conduct of the three equestrian sports of the Olympic Games—show jumping, the three-day event, and dressage—as well as international driving competitions. All national federations are required to comply with these regulations in any international competition.*

Fence *(a) An obstacle to be jumped in steeplechasing, cross-country, show jumping, or hunting; (b) In racing, to jump over an obstacle.*

Filly *A female horse of less than four years old.*

Finishing brush *A long-bristled brush for removing the surface dirt or mud from a horse's coat.*

Flapper *A horse that runs at an unauthorized race meeting.*

Flat racing *Racing in which there are no obstacles for the horses to jump.*

Foal *A young horse of up to 12 months old.*

Forehand *The part of the horse which is in front of the rider: that is, the head, neck, shoulders, withers, and forelegs.*

Frog *The soft, sensitive, triangular-shaped area in the base of a horse's foot.*

Full-mouthed *Description of the mouth of a horse at six years old, when it has grown all its permanent teeth.*

Gall *A skin sore, usually occurring under an ill-fitting or dirty saddle or girth.*

Gelding *A castrated male horse .*

Gestation *The period between conception and foaling (normally about 11 months).*

Girth *(a) The circumference of a horse. This is measured behind the withers around the deepest part of the body; (b) A band, usually made of leather, webbing, or nylon, which is passed under the belly of the horse and is used to hold the saddle in place.*

Going *The condition of a racetrack, cross-country course, or other ground over which a horse travels; variously classified as soft, good, etc.*

Good mouth *Description of a horse with a soft, sensitive mouth.*

Gray *A dark-skinned horse with a coat of mixed black and white hairs, the whiter hairs becoming more predominant with each change of coat.*

Green *(a) A horse that is broken in (or "started") but not fully trained; (b) A trotter or pacer which has not been raced against the clock.*

Groom *(a) A person responsible for looking after a horse; (b) To clean the coat and feet of a horse.*

Grooming kit *Collectively, the brushes and other items of equipment used to groom a horse.*

Gymkhana *Mounted games, most frequently for children under 16 years old, many of which are adaptations of children's party games.*

Habit *The clothing worn by a woman riding side-saddle.*

Halter *A hemp-rope headpiece with lead rope attached, used for leading a horse when a bridle is not worn, or for tying up a horse in the stable.*

Hand *Abbreviated to h.h., a linear measurement equaling 4 in. (10 cm), taken at the highest part of the withers and used to denote the height of a horse.*

Handicap *(a) The weight allocated to a horse in a race; (b) A race in which the weights to be carried by the horses are estimated so as to give each an equal chance of winning.*

Haunches *The hips and buttocks of a horse.*

Haute Ecole *(See High School.)*

Hay *Grass cut and dried at a particular time of the year for use as fodder.*

Headcollar *A bitless headpiece and noseband, usually made of leather or webbing, for leading a horse that is not wearing a bridle, or for tying up a horse in the stable.*

Heavy horse *Any horse belonging to one of the breeds of large draft horses: for example, Clydesdale, Percheron, Shire, or Suffolk Punch.*

Height *The height of a horse is measured in a perpendicular line from the highest part of the withers to the ground.*

Hoof wall *The part of the hoof that is visible when the foot is placed flat on the ground; it is divided into the toe, the quarters (sides), and the heel.*

High School *The classical art of equitation.*

Holloa *The cry given by a person when hunting to indicate to the huntsman that he or she has seen the fox.*

Hood *(a) A fabric covering for the horse's head, ears and part of its neck, used when traveling or for warmth indoors or out in cold weather; (b) Blinkers.*

Hoof *The insensitive horny covering that protects the sensitive parts of a horse's foot.*

Hoof pick *A hooked metal instrument used for removing stones and dirt from a horse's feet.*

Horseshoe *A shaped band—usually made of metal—nailed to the hooves of working horses to protect the hoofs and prevent them from splitting (see also "Racing plates").*

Hunter *A type of horse bred and trained to be ridden for hunting.*

Hurdle *One of a series of wattle fences over which a horse must jump in hurdle racing (in the United States these fences are made of brush).*

Inbreeding *The mating of related individuals, such as brother and sister, sire and daughter, or son and dam.*

Independent seat *The ability of a rider to maintain a firm, balanced position on a horse's back without relying on the reins or stirrups.*

In foal *Term used to describe a pregnant mare.*

In-hand class *Any of various show classes in which the horses are led—usually in a show bridle or headcollar, but otherwise without saddlery (with the exception of heavy horses, which are often shown in their harness)—and in which they are judged chiefly on their conformation and/or condition.*

Interval training *A program of work—often used by eventers and endurance riders—to build up a horse's fitness by giving it a timed period of work followed by a brief interval of semi-rest (walk), during which it is allowed to recover partially before being asked to work again; the lengths and speed of the "fast" periods are built up as fitness increases.*

Jockey *(a) A person engaged to ride a horse in a race; (b) Formerly, a dealer in horses—especially a disreputable one.*

Jog *A short-paced trot.*

Jump-off *In show jumping, a round held to decide the winner of a competition among riders who have achieved a clear round; this may go on to one or more further jump-offs, the last of which may be against the clock.*

Keep *A grass field used for grazing.*

Laminitis *A very painful inflammation of the sensitive laminae (membranes) that lie between the horny wall of the horse's hoof and the pedal bone.*

Levade *A High School movement in which the horse rears, drawing in its forefeet, while the hindquarters are deeply bent at the haunches and carry its full weight.*

Linseed *The seed of flax—generally used in the form of linseed jelly, oil, or tea—as a laxative or to improve the condition and gloss of a horse's coat.*

Livery stable *An establishment at which privately owned horses are kept, exercised, and cared for, for an agreed fee.*

Long-reining *Method of training a young horse and introducing it to new sights and sounds, in which the trainer follows the horse and controls it by means of long reins running along either side of its body; long-reining is also used in High School training to achieve advanced movements.*

Loriner *A person who makes the metal parts of saddlery and harness such as bits, curb chains, and stirrup irons.*

Lunging *A means of exercising a horse from the ground, working in a circle.*

Lunging cavesson *Similar to a headcollar, but with three rings in varying positions at the front of the noseband to which the lunge rein is attached.*

Maiden *A horse of either sex which to date has not won a race.*

Mane *The long hair growing at the horse's forehead and along its neck (crest).*

Mane-and-tail comb *A small, long-toothed metal comb used for cleaning or pulling the mane and tail (removing hairs to create a trimmed, even length).*

Mare *A female horse of four or more years old.*

Martingale *A device used to help in keeping a horse's head in the correct position. It generally consists of a strap, or arrangement of straps, fastened to the girth at one end, passing between the forelegs and, depending on the type, attaching at the other end to the reins, noseband, or directly to the bit.*

Muck out *To clean out a stable, removing the droppings and soiled bedding.*

Mud fever *An inflammation of the upper layer of a horse's skin, caused by prolonged subjection to muddy and wet conditions.*

Nap *(a) A horse is said to nap if it fails to obey properly applied aids: for example, refusing to go forward or to pass a certain point or object; (b) In racing, a good tip.*

National Federation *The governing body of equestrian affairs in any country affiliated to the FEI.*

Natural aids *Instructions given by a rider to the horse using his or her body, hands, legs, and/or voice.*

Navicular A bone in the heel region of a horse, the restriction of blood supply to which causes lameness.
Near side The left-hand side of a horse.
Neck (a) One of the measurements of distance by which a horse may be said to win a race; (b) The length of a horse's head and neck.
Nose The shortest measurement of distance by which it is possible for a horse to win a race.
Noseband The part of a bridle which lies across the horse's nose, consisting of a leather band on an independent headpiece which is worn below the cheeks and above the bit.
Numnah A pad placed under the saddle to prevent undue pressure on the horse's back, cut to the shape of the saddle and a little larger. Commonly used materials include sheepskin, cloth-covered foam rubber, or felt.

Objection In racing, an objection may be made against any of the placed horses, and must be heard by the stewards at the meeting where it is raised.
Off side The right-hand side of a horse.
One-day event An eventing competition consisting of dressage, show jumping, and cross-country phases; it is generally completed in one day, but may be spread over two days if there are numerous competitors.
On the bit Said of a horse that is working with impulsion while maintaining the correct head position, and with a light rein contact from its mouth up to the rider's hands.

Pace A lateral gait in two-time, in which the horse's fore- and hind leg on the same side are moved forward together.
Paint A horse of Pinto coloring whose sire and dam are registered with the American Paint Horse Association, making it also eligible for registration.
Parabola The arc made by a horse as it jumps an obstacle, from the point of take-off to the point of landing.
Parallel bars A type of spread fence used in show jumping and cross-country courses, consisting of two sets of posts and rails.
Passage One of the classical High School airs, comprising a spectacular elevated trot in slow motion; there is a definite period of suspension as one pair of legs remains on the ground with the diagonally opposite legs raised in the air.
Pelham A bit designed to produce the combined effects of the snaffle and curb bits of a double bridle in one mouthpiece. It is made of metal, vulcanite, or rubber, and may be used with two pairs or one pair of reins; if the latter, a leather rounding is used to link the upper and lower ring on each side of the bit.

Piaffe A classical High School air, comprising a spectacular trot—performed on the spot with great elevation and cadence.
Piebald A black-and-white Pinto.
Pinto A horse whose coat consists of very large, irregular, and clearly defined patches of white and another color (see also Paint, Piebald, Skewbald).
Pirouette In dressage, a turn within the horse's length (that is, the shortest turn it is possible to make). There are three different kinds of pirouette: the turn on the center, the turn on the forehand, and the turn on the haunches.
Place A horse is described as being placed if it finishes second in a race.
Planks A show jumping obstacle comprising painted planks, each about 1 ft. (30 cm) wide.
Polo A mounted game bearing a resemblance to hockey, played between two teams of four a side. Popular in many parts of the world, it is recorded as having been played as long ago as the reign of Darius I of Persia (521–486 B.C.).
Polocross An Australian mounted game rather like a horseback version of lacrosse: the ball is scooped up in a small net at the end of a long stick and is then either carried or thrown.
Pony A horse not exceeding 14.2 h.h. (148 cm) in height at maturity.
Post and rails A type of obstacle in show jumping and cross-country courses, consisting of upright posts with a number of horizontal posts laid between them. In show jumping the rails are simply supported by the posts; on a cross-country course they are fixed to the posts.

Quarter-in A dressage movement in which the horse's hindquarters work on a different track from that of the forehand; often used as a suppling exercise.
Quarters The hindquarters, or the area of a horse's body extending from the rear of the flank to the root of the tail and downward on either side to the top of the leg.

Racing plates Thin, very lightweight horseshoes used on racehorses.
Racing saddle A saddle designed for use on racehorses, which may range from the very light type weighing less than 2 lbs. (1 kg), used for flat racing, to the heavier, more solid type used for hurdling and steeplechasing.
Rack The most spectacular movement of the five-gaited American Saddle Horse, this is a very fast, even gait in which each foot strikes the ground separately in quick succession.

Rear A movement in which a horse rises up on its hind legs in fright, obstinacy, or in an attempt to dislodge its rider.
Red flag A marker used in equestrian sports to denote the right-hand extremity of an obstacle; it is also used to mark a set track (for example, in the roads-and-tracks phase of a three-day event) and must always be passed on the left-hand side.
Red ribbon A piece of red ribbon tied around the tail of a horse, especially when hunting, to indicate that it is a known kicker and to warn other riders to keep their distance.
Refusal (a) In racing, the failure of a horse to attempt to jump a hurdle or steeplechase fence; (b) In show jumping or cross-country, a horse stopping in front of an obstacle to be jumped.
Rein back To make a horse step backward while being ridden or driven.
Reins A pair of long, narrow straps attached to the bit or bridle and used by the rider or driver to guide and control the horse.
Renvers A dressage movement on two tracks in which the horse moves at an angle of not more than 30 degrees along the long side of the arena with the hind legs on the outer and the forelegs on the inner track. The horse looks in the direction in which it is going and bends slightly around the rider's inside leg.
Resistance Refusal by a horse to go forward, stopping, running back, or rearing.
Ride off In polo, to push one's pony against that of another player in order to prevent him or her from playing the ball.
Roan Description of a horse whose coat is black, bay, or chestnut with an admixture of white hairs (especially on the body and neck) that modifies the color.
Roller A broad strap that circles the horse's body and is used to hold a rug in position; integral pads sit on either side of the spine to alleviate pressure.
Runner A horse taking part in a race.
Run out (a) In racing, to avoid an obstacle that is to be jumped, or to pass on the wrong side of a marker flag; (b) In show jumping or cross-country, a horse's avoidance of an obstacle that is to be jumped by running to one side.

Saddle A seat for a rider on horseback, made in various designs—dressage, general-purpose, jumping, racing, and sidesaddle—according to the purpose for which it is required.
Saddler A person who makes or deals in and fits saddlery and/or harness.
Saddlery The bridle, saddle, and other items of tack used on a horse that is to be ridden as opposed to driven.

over grass courses as opposed to dirt tracks; (c) the world of horseracing in general.
Turn on the forehand A movement in which the horse pivots on the forehand while describing concentric circles with the hind legs.
Turn on the quarters A movement in which the horse pivots on the hind legs while describing concentric circles with the forelegs.

Unentered Said of a hound that has not completed a cub-hunting season.
Unraced Said of a horse that has not yet taken part in a race.
Unseated A rider who has in some way been put out of the saddle.
Unsound Said of a horse suffering from any defect that makes it unable to function properly.
Unwind To start to buck.

Walk A four-time pace in which the hooves strike the ground in the following sequence: near hind, near fore, off hind, off fore.
Walking Horse Class Any of various competitions held for the Tennessee Walking Horse at shows in the United States.
Water To provide a horse with water to drink.
Water brush (a) A brush used to wash the feet and to dampen the mane and tail; (b) In show jumping, a small sloping brush fence placed in front of a water jump to help a horse to see the point from which it should take off.
Water jump (a) In show jumping, a spread obstacle consisting of a sunken trough of water with a minimum width of 14 ft. (4.2 m) and a length of up to 16 ft. (4.8 m); (b) A fence including a water element on a cross-country course.
Weaving A horse's habit of rocking persistently from side to side on the forelegs—often the result of boredom while stabled.

similar fittings used to support the poles or other suspended parts of a show jumping obstacle.
Winter out Said of a horse that is left out in the field during the winter rather than being brought into the stable.
Wisp A grooming tool usually made from braided or twisted straw and used with a firm action to bring a shine to a horse's coat.
Withers The area at the base of a horse's neck between the shoulder blades; this is the highest part of the back, and the place at which a horse's height is measured.
Worms Horses will suffer from worm infestations unless they are regularly dosed with an appropriate wormer; the advice of a veterinary surgeon should be sought on which treatments to use and when to administer them.
Wrangle To round up, herd, and care for horses.

School *(a) To train a horse for whatever purpose it may be required; (b) An enclosed area—either covered or open—in which horses are trained and/or exercised.*

Selling race *(see Claiming race).*

Servicing *The mating of a mare by a stallion.*

Shoeing *Putting shoes on a horse. A horse normally needs its shoes renewed approximately every six weeks depending on the type of work it is doing, on whether it is worked on soft or hard ground, and on how fast its feet grow.*

Shoulder-in *A dressage movement in which the horse's shoulders work on a different track from that of the hindquarters; often used as a suppling exercise.*

Show *(a) To compete in a horse show; (b) In the United States, to finish third in a race.*

Show class *Any of various competitions held at a horse show in which entrants are judged for their conformation, condition, action and/or suitability for whatever purpose they are used (or intended to be used).*

Shy *A sudden balk or swerve away by a horse in fear—or occasionally from mere high spirits—from an obstacle or sound.*

Sidesaddle *A saddle designed for a woman, on which the rider sits with both feet on the same side of the horse (normally the near side), with the upper leg supported by a raised pommel and the lower foot resting in a stirrup.*

Silks *The peaked cap and silk or woolen blouse worn by a jockey in racing, and designed with colors of the horse's owner.*

Sire *The father of a foal.*

Skewbald *A Pinto whose coat is white and any color except black—see Piebald.*

Slow gait *One of the gaits of the five-gaited American Saddle Horse; this is also known as the single foot, and is similar to the rack. It is a true prancing action in which each foot in turn is raised and then held momentarily in mid air before being brought down.*

Snaffle *The oldest and simplest form of bit, which is available in a variety of types but consists chiefly of a*

Sprinter *A racehorse that is able to move at great speed over a short distance, but is seldom able to maintain the pace over a long distance.*

Spur *A blunt-ended, protruding metal device strapped on to the heels of a rider's boots and used to urge the horse onward.*

Stable *(a) A building in which one or more horses is kept; (b) A collection of horses belonging to one person—such as a racehorse owner or riding-school proprietor—or kept at one establishment.*

Stallion *An ungelded male horse of four or more years old.*

Standard event *Any of the five rodeo events—bareback riding, bull riding, calf-roping, saddle bronc riding and steer wrestling—recognized by the governing body, the Rodeo Cowboys Association.*

Starting *A term often used instead of the traditional expression "breaking in," which is felt by many trainers to describe more accurately the process of introducing a horse to tack and to accepting a rider.*

Stayer *A term applied to a horse that has great strength and power of endurance, and is, therefore, likely to be successful in a race over a long distance.*

Steeplechase *A race over a course of a specified distance, on which there are a number of obstacles to be jumped.*

Steer wrestling *One of the standard events at a rodeo. The contestant rides alongside a running steer, and jumps from the saddle onto the head of the steer, the object being to stop it, twist it to the ground, and hold it there with the head and all four feet facing in the same direction. The contestant completing the event in the shortest time is the winner.*

Steward *An official at a race meeting, who is appointed to ensure that the meeting is conducted according to the rules.*

Stirrup iron *A loop, ring, or similar device made of metal, wood, leather, etc., suspended from the saddle to support the rider's foot.*

Stirrup leather *The adjustable leather strap by*

Stud *(a) An establishment at which horses are kept for breeding purposes; (b) Any large establishment of racehorses, hunters, etc., belonging to one owner; (c) In the United States, a stud horse or stallion; (d) A metallic head screwed into a horseshoe to give the horse a better grip on a slippery surface.*

Surcingle *A webbing belt, usually about 2½– 3 in. (6–8 cm) in width, which passes over a racing or jumping saddle and girth and is used to keep the saddle in position.*

Sweat scraper *A curved metal blade with a wooden handle, which is used to scrape sweat from a horse's coat.*

Sweet itch *A dermatitis usually found in horses that are allergic to a particular pasture plant, and therefore most likely to occur in the spring and summer months. It particularly affects the crest, croup, and withers, causing intense irritation and producing patches of thick, scaly, and sometimes ulcerated skin, which the horse often rubs bare in its attempts to find relief.*

Tack *Saddlery.*

Tail *The horse's tail includes the dock together with all the hair, which is usually allowed to grow about 4 in. (10 cm) below the point of the hock.*

Teeth *When fully mouthed, the horse has 40 teeth: 12 incisors (six in each jaw), four canines (one in each side of the upper and lower jaw), and 24 molars (six above and six below on each side). Mares lack the canine teeth.*

Temperature *The normal temperature of a healthy horse is 100.5°F (38°C).*

Tetanus *An infectious, often fatal, disease caused by the microorganism Tetanus bacillus, which lives in the soil and enters a horse's body through wounds, especially of the foot.*

Three-day event *A combined-training competition completed over three consecutive days. It consists of a dressage test; a speed-and-endurance section, which includes a steeplechase course and two circuits of roads*

INDEX

Page numbers in *italics* refer to picture captions; **bold** numbers refer to main entry for each breed.

ACKNOWLEDGMENTS

Foreword: **David Broome** CBE
Introduction: **Elizabeth Peplow**
The Pre-Domestic Horse: **Juliet Clutton-Brock**
Domestication and the Early Horse Peoples: **Marsha Levine** *(adapted from The Oxford Companion to Archaeology edited by Brian M. Fagan, Oxford, 1996. Copyright © by Oxford University Press, Inc. Used by permission of Oxford University Press, Inc.)*
The Development of Classical Equitation: **Leslie Grossmith & Jennifer Baker**
The History of Western Riding: **Nancy Jaffer & Charles Chevenix Trench**
The Horse at War: **Allan Mallinson**
The Working Horse: **Allan Mallinson**
The Influence of the Arabian: **Marcy Pavord & Margaret Greely**
The Thoroughbred: **Jane Kidd**
The Spanish Horse: **Leslie Grossmith**
The Genetic Jigsaw: **Sue Montgomery & Elizabeth Peplow**
Principal Horse Breeds: **Deborah Frowen & Judith Draper**
Principal Pony Breeds: **Deborah Frowen & Jennifer Baker**
Dressage: **Leslie Grossmith & A.P.C. Crossley**
Show jumping: **Annabel Kendal & Alan Smith**
Eventing: **Annabel Kendal & Jane Pontifex**
Racing: **Diana Butler & Hugh Condry**
Endurance Riding: **Marcy Pavord & Ann Hyland**
Polo: **Diana Butler & Pamela MacGregor-Morris**
Showing: **Deborah Frowen & Pamela MacGregor-Morris**
Hunting: **Elizabeth Peplow & Michael Clayton**
Carriage Driving: **Andrew Cowdery**
Harness Racing: **Stella Havard**
Western Sports: **Nancy Jaffer & Steven D. Price**
Learning to Ride: **Carolyn Henderson**
Training the Young Horse: **Carolyn Henderson**
General Management: **Carolyn Henderson**
Feeding and Nutrition: **Ruth Bishop**
Saddlery and Equipment: **Carolyn Henderson**
Shoeing: **Carolyn Henderson**
The Horse's Body: **Elizabeth Peplow & Peter D. Rossdale**
The Horse's Mind: **Jane Barron**
Diseases of the Horse: **Colin J. Vogel** B. VET. MED., M.R.C.V.S. & **Peter D. Rossdale**
Glossary: **Elizabeth Peplow**
The publisher would also like to thank **Cheryl Lutring** *of the American Saddlebred Association for her advice on American saddlery and equipment.*

Cover: **Gabrielle Boiselle**
All pictures inside by **Bob Langrish** *with the exception of the following:*

*Animal Photography/***Sally Anne Thompson** *61 Bottom, 76 Center, 78 Center /***R. Wilbie** *87 Bottom.* **Bridgeman Art Library/***Caves of Lascaux, Dordogne 8–9/***Christie's, London** *34/***City Art Gallery, Leeds** *26 Bottom/***Galleria degli Uffizi, Florence** *24–25/***Jockey Club, Newmarket, Suffolk** *118/***Library of Congress, Washington D.C.** *21 Center/***Roy Miles Gallery** *38/***Schloss Schonbrunn, Vienna** *17 Bottom/***Victoria & Albert Museum, London** *128.* **Corbis UK Ltd/Kevin Morris** *122 Top/***Bettmann/UPI** *123.* **Mary Evans Picture Library** *16 Top, 17 Top.***Werner Forman Archive/Schimmel Collection, New York** *13 Center/***The Egyptian Museum, Cairo** *12.* **Elizabeth Furth** *102 Top Left.* **Reed Consumer Books Ltd.** *13 Bottom Right, 13 Bottom Left, 24 Top, 25 Bottom, 27 Top, 27 Bottom, 28 Bottom, 28 Top, 32–33, 41, 132/***Palazzo Publico, Siena** *24 Center.* **Robert Harding Picture Library/Robert McLeod** *29 Bottom.* **Horse and Hound/Trevor Meeks** *18, 19 Bottom, 104, 105.* **Houghton's Horses** *40, 50 Bottom, 56 Top, 57 Bottom, 58 Top, 62 Center, 63 Center, 65 Center, 86 Bottom, 89 Top, 100, 119.* **Dr D. C. Knottenbelt** *180 Top Right, 181 Top, 181 Top Left.* **Peter Newark's American Pictures** *20 Top, 20 Center, 21 Top Right, 21 Top Left, 26 Top/***Edward S. Curtis** *20 Bottom.* **Lizzie Orcott** *161.* **Dr J F Pycock** *47 Center, 47 Center Right, 47 Center Left.* **George Selwyn** *46–47.*